ADAM A. J. DeVILLE

ORTHODOXY

and the

ROMAN PAPACY

Ut Unum Sint and the Prospects of East-West Unity

University of Notre Dame Press
Notre Dame, Indiana

Library of Congress Cataloging-in-Publication Data

DeVille, Adam A. J., 1972–
Orthodoxy and the Roman papacy : Ut Unum Sint and the prospects of
East-West unity / Adam A. J. DeVille.
    p.   cm.
Includes bibliographical references and index.
ISBN-13: 978-0-268-02607-3 (pbk. : alk. paper)
ISBN-10: 0-268-02607-6 (pbk. : alk. paper)
1. Christian union—Orthodox Eastern Church. 2. Christian union—Catholic
Church. 3. Orthodox Eastern Church—Relations—Catholic Church.
4. Catholic Church—Relations—Orthodox Eastern Church. 5. Papacy and
Christian union. 6. Orthodox Eastern Church—Doctrines. 7. Catholic Church—
Doctrines. 8. Papacy.   I. Title.
BX324.3.D44   2011
280'.042—dc22
                                                                2010049947

CONTENTS

ACKNOWLEDGMENTS

I am indebted to the Metropolitan Andrey Sheptytsky Institute of Eastern Christian Studies at Saint Paul University, Ottawa, for providing the only doctoral program in Eastern Christian theology in all of North America. The Institute has been an enormously welcoming and gracious place, and the professors and staff there whom I have known have been a joy and gift to me. I am in an especial way grateful for several doctoral bursaries and other assistance granted to me by the Institute as well as other scholarships granted by Saint Paul University.

Among the people at the Institute, I am primarily indebted to her founding director and my *Doktorvater,* the mitred protopresbyter Andriy Chirovsky. His enormous wisdom, graciously and patiently imparted to me at every turn, has been a splendid gift. He is a living embodiment of the Evagrian dictum that the theologian is the one who truly prays, and only one who prays is a theologian properly so called.

I am grateful also to the Institute's Peter Galadza, not only for serving on my doctoral committee and jury, but for other kindnesses along the way, including our editorial collaboration on *Logos: A Journal of Eastern Christian Studies* and our work on *Unité en division: Les lettres de Lev Gillet ("Un moine de l'Eglise d'Orient") à Andrei Cheptytsky 1921–1929* (Paris: Parole et Silence, 2009). He is a wonderful exemplar of someone who demands rigor and fidelity and refuses mediocrity in matters both academic and ecclesial.

Others to whom I am indebted include Professor Catherine Clifford and the archpriest and Professor John Jillions, who along with Professor Thomas Fitzgerald made up my jury, whose examination of my work so helpfully provided an Eastern Catholic, Roman Catholic, Greek Orthodox, and Russian (OCA) Orthodox evaluation of my work.

I am grateful to the Province of Ontario for an Ontario Graduate Scholarship and to the Social Sciences and Humanities Research Council of Canada for a Doctoral Scholarship. In highly competitive and financially straitened circumstances, both agencies provided very substantial funding for which I am grateful.

Others whose counsel along the way has been invaluable include the Archpriest Robert Anderson, whom I first met in Ukraine in 2001 and who has since been a wonderful adviser and friend from whom I continue to learn much. The two anonymous reviewers for the University of Notre Dame Press wrote very helpful reports which strengthened this work, and I thank them for their insights.

I am, finally and most importantly, grateful to my family: to my wife Annemarie, and to my children Ephraim, Aidan, and Anastasia: *sine qua non.*

Introduction

*The issue of ecclesiology, and not minor liturgical and
administrative adjustments, or even ecumenical statements,
will finally solve the problem of Christian unity.*

JOHN MEYENDORFF

Meyendorff's words, now nearly a half-century old,[1] are seen to be
more and more correct with each passing decade. Spoken in the middle
of the Second Vatican Council, the landmark ecclesiological and ecumenical event of the twentieth century, the truth of these words has
been recognized by Orthodox and Catholic theologians in a variety of
ways. Both sides have increasingly come to wrestle with questions of
what constitutes the Church as such as well as other important questions of synodality, canonical territory, episcopacy, and especially primacy at the regional and international levels. At the end of the first
decade of the twenty-first century, much progress on ecclesiological
issues may be noted, but much work remains to be done.

Nowhere is that dynamic of successful work-in-progress more
clear than in the continuing efforts of both Catholics and Orthodox
to grapple with the question of the Roman papacy. Among those issues that continue to divide the Catholic Church from the Orthodox

Church—the two largest Christian bodies in the world—the question of the papacy is widely acknowledged by both Catholics and Orthodox to be the most significant stumbling block that remains to unity between these two Churches.

On the Catholic side, no less a figure than Pope Paul VI himself frankly acknowledged in 1967 that the papacy is "undoubtedly the gravest obstacle to the path of ecumenism."[2] In 1971, the theologian Emmanuel Lanne argued that "there is no doubt that the primacy of Rome is the principal obstacle standing in the way of a reconstituted unity with the Orthodox Churches. Other differences are not negligible . . . but the Orthodox regard these as essentially 'papist innovations' which stem from the pretensions of the See of Rome."[3] The Eastern Jesuit George Maloney would write in 1979 that "no greater obstacle toward reunion exists than the question of papal primacy. . . . No one can doubt that this remains the key issue."[4] The 1980s evidently saw little progress since the 1988 Valamo Statement of the Joint International Commission for Theological Dialogue (JIC) between the Roman Catholic Church and the Orthodox Church declared that "the question . . . [of] the primacy of the bishop of Rome . . . constitutes a serious divergence among us . . . which will be discussed in the future."[5] Finally and perhaps most authoritatively, Walter Cardinal Kasper, head of the Pontifical Council for Promoting Christian Unity (PCPCU) in Rome, confirmed that "the only seriously debated theological issue between us and the Orthodox Church . . . is the question of Roman primacy."[6]

On the Orthodox side, the French Orthodox layman Olivier Clément argued that "the problem of the papacy is certainly the most difficult one today in the ecumenical dialogue, particularly between Catholicism and Orthodoxy."[7] This was seconded in 1997 by the prominent Orthodox theologian, Metropolitan John Zizioulas, who acknowledged that "the most important and at the same time the most difficult problem in the Roman Catholic–Orthodox relations is undoubtedly that of papal primacy."[8] Later that year, the prominent Ukrainian Orthodox hierarch, Bishop Vsevolod Majdansky wrote that "the most important difficulty between the Catholics and the Orthodox is the question of the basis, the significance, and the practical exercise of the 'universal primacy' of the Bishop of Rome.'"[9]

From the time of the Second Vatican Council, then, until the close of the twentieth century, there was an emerging consensus on the key issue about which Catholics and Orthodox disagree. This consensus is perhaps seen most clearly in the fact that the JIC, established officially in 1979, issued its first agreed statement in 1982 on eucharistic ecclesiology but quickly realized that primacy and especially papal primacy were the most significant issues.[10] These issues were placed at the top of its agenda for several years before the JIC was sidetracked by the "Uniate" problem (that is, by the re-emergence of the long-suppressed Eastern Catholic Churches, especially in Ukraine and Romania, where they had been forced into the underground by a collusion of Communist politicians and Orthodox hierarchs, each acting for different motives but both motivated by fear and animus) in the last decade of the twentieth century and first five years of the twenty-first.[11]

By 2005, however, the JIC would carefully begin its work again, with a full meeting in Belgrade in September 2006.[12] That meeting was a quiet success—though at the end of that meeting, there was a substantial if little noticed or understood conflict between Orthodox participants themselves.[13] That conflict again came to the surface at the most important meeting to date, that of Ravenna in October 2007, where Hilarion Alfeyev, then the Russian Orthodox bishop of Vienna and head of the Russian delegation to the dialogue,[14] objected to what he saw as an attempt in the dialogue to unjustifiably elevate the role and authority of the Ecumenical Patriarch of Constantinople, about whom there is no clear consensus on the part of Orthodox canonists and ecclesiologists.[15] Hilarion's objection led him to take the Russian delegation out of the Ravenna meeting as he protested that "the Orthodox participants are not authorized to 'invent' an ecclesiological model for the Orthodox Church similar to the one existing in the Roman Catholic Church in order that the Patriarch of Constantinople could occupy a place like the one the Pope occupies in the Church of Rome."[16] In another article, Hilarion was even more explicit in saying that some Orthodox "rather regard this primacy as purely honourable, while others give certain coordinating functions to the patriarch of Constantinople and see him as highest court."[17]

This 2007 "Ravenna Statement" has generated considerable discussion among ecumenists as well as raised several issues among the Orthodox participants themselves.[18] Alfeyev's question of the place and prerogatives of Constantinople's patriarch has not been resolved but, thankfully, has not kept the JIC from continuing to meet, as it did again in full session in October 2009 in Cyprus.[19] That Cyprus meeting, whose groundwork had been laid by a committee of the JIC meeting in Crete in 2008, resulted in a working statement, "The Role of the Bishop of Rome in the Communion of the Church in the First Millennium," which continues to be discussed by the JIC and will apparently be released during their next meeting in September 2010 in Vienna.[20] The role of the pope in the first millennium is, as Pope Benedict XVI himself said in a November 2009 letter to Ecumenical Patriarch Bartholomew, "certainly complex, and will require extensive study and patient dialogue if we are to aspire to a shared integration of the traditions of East and West."[21] Emerging scholarship on the papacy during the first millennium offers considerable hope that a way forward can be found.[22]

All this work on the papacy was prompted by a historic and unprecedented request in Pope John Paul II's 1995 encyclical letter *Ut Unum Sint* (*UUS*). While the papacy of John Paul II was revolutionary in many ways—as George Weigel has convincingly documented[23]—the zeal for Christian unity manifested by John Paul II was among his most singular hallmarks. In *UUS* he would note: "This is an immense task . . . which I cannot carry out by myself. Could not . . . Church leaders and their theologians . . . engage with me in a patient and fraternal dialogue on this subject. . . ?"[24]

While many Protestants have responded,[25] only a tiny handful of individual Orthodox theologians have done likewise. No single canonical Orthodox *Church* has responded, either through its synod, chief hierarch, or other official entity.[26]

I propose *an* answer to John Paul II which was developed by listening and then responding to numerous Orthodox voices on the question of the papacy. This proposal does not pretend to be *the* definitive answer to the problem of the papacy, nor the *only* such answer. It is offered in the hope that it will be of use in the long, complex, and difficult work of finding that unity which Christ wills for his Church. It is also offered in response to the request made of theologians in *Ut Unum Sint,* where the pope notes that the process of working for unity

> must be carried forward with prudence and in a spirit of faith, [and] will be assisted by the Holy Spirit. If it is to be successful, its results must be made known in appropriate ways by competent persons. Significant in this regard is the contribution which theologians and faculties of theology are called to make by exercising their charism in the Church. (§81)

This study is concerned with both Catholic *and* Orthodox "audiences." In attempting to hold together Orthodox and Catholic concerns about the papacy, I have sought to fulfill the "task" set forth in Michael Magee's recent and superb work on patriarchates:

> [T]he task that was left unfinished at the time of the great Schism between East and West, of effectively incorporating the notions of papal Primacy and the Patriarchal institution into a workable synthesis, by means of a mutual refinement of the underlying ecclesiological principles of each with the effective elimination of potential contradictions, is thus perhaps the single most important key to re-union between East and West.[27]

Such a synthesis and mutual refinement (what Thomas Norris has called "a comprehensive 'view,' a description of a dynamic continuity avoiding the Scylla of corruptive innovation and the Charybdis of a statuesque immobility"[28]) must, it seems to me, avoid two (at least) obviously deadly traps. The first I would call "radical conservatism," which, in essence, is a Catholic refusal to countenance any substantial or serious changes to the papacy to accommodate Orthodox concerns but is rather a demand that the papacy be accepted *tout court* as it is.[29] The second I would call "radical rejectionism," which, in essence, is an

Orthodox refusal to consider unity with Catholics until and unless all problems the Orthodox perceive in the Catholic Church, chief among which is, of course, the papacy, are rejected by Rome and swept away in one ironically grand—and presumably final—act of papal omnipotence. Neither is a serious response to the papacy; both seek to evade reality.

Though what is advanced here is indeed something new, I have sought to ensure that the resulting model of papal primacy will be recognizable to, and reconcilable with, Catholic *and* Orthodox Tradition: a creativity not *ex nihilo* but *ex traditione*. In this regard, I have in mind to follow the counsel of the eminent Catholic ecclesiologist and ecumenist, Yves Congar, who has said that "the great law of Catholic reform will begin with a return to the principles of Catholicism. It is necessary to interrogate the tradition and to dive back into it, understanding that 'tradition' does not mean 'routine' nor even, properly, 'the past'."[30] In mining Catholic tradition, as Congar counsels, I do so with the following goal in mind:

> It would seem that what is needed at the present time is an inquiry into how the patriarchal institution might be understood so as to be reconcilable with defined Catholic dogma, in a manner acceptable also to our separated Eastern brethren because of its rootedness in sources shared by them, supported by the facts of the first millennium, fully consistent with the significant developments in ecclesiology provided by the Second Vatican Council, and open to the new possibilities that the future affords.[31]

Orthodox problems with the papacy, then, will be given every possible consideration here, but Catholic problems with any proposed reform of the papacy to deal with Orthodox concerns must and will be given serious consideration also. Stated simply, it is unacceptable to the Catholic Church simply to disregard the more acutely difficult aspects of the papacy by flatly rejecting them out of hand or demanding that they simply be suppressed or abolished.[32] Such an approach fails to acknowledge seriously and responsibly the organic nature of Tradition which one can never summarily dismiss or disregard without doing violence to it and the ecclesiological rupture that would be brought about by destroying (or even disregarding) so central a part of the Catholic Church's very structure and self-understanding.[33] For these reasons, then, one simply cannot deal with difficult aspects of the papacy as so much historical detritus to be rubbished as outmoded, inconvenient, or ecumenically infelicitous. Rather, one must deal with the office as it has developed and is today received and understood by the Catholic Church and, only after having done so, propose reforms to it.

Moreover, because of the inherent institutional "conservatism" (in a non-ideological sense) of the Church of Rome, subjecting the papacy to such a treatment of radical rejectionism would almost inevitably render impossible any prospect of being taken seriously by those to whom it most directly and immediately pertains, namely the bishop of Rome and his Curia.[34] While Walter Cardinal Kasper, former president of the PCPCU, has noted that, in reforming the papacy, "far-reaching developments are possible," he is quick to note that reforms must not touch "that which is essential and indispensable to the Petrine office."[35] It is with the Roman Curia in mind, and, more important, with respect for the received Tradition of the Church of Rome, that I propose that we move forward, not backward, allowing the papacy to undergo several "developments" so that, in the end, it becomes more fully the instrument of unity it is supposed to be.

Before proposing such developments, I begin by situating *UUS* in its historical context and then briefly reviewing its contents. The second chapter provides a survey of the major Orthodox literature on papal primacy, particularly that of the postwar period, taking note of what work has been done and then carefully enumerating the problems with the papacy from an Orthodox perspective.

The third chapter advances a multi-part proposal for the renewal of patriarchal structures within the Latin Church as the necessarily first move for the reform of the papacy. After an initial "apologia" for continued use of the title "Patriarch of the West" against the rather unexpected Roman decision of February 2006 to de-list the title "Patriarch of the West" from the 2006 *Annuario Pontificio*,[36] the third chapter reviews Catholic theological writings on the importance of a Roman patriarchate—writings that owe their origins to the article of no less a figure than Pope Benedict XVI, writing as Joseph Ratzinger in the late 1960s.

This review of Catholic perspectives on patriarchates is then followed, in the fourth chapter, by a review of how Orthodox patriarchates are structured and function. I review ten such patriarchates—the four original eastern members of the "pentarchy" (Constantinople, Alexandria, Antioch, and Jerusalem), three "Oriental" Orthodox patriarchates (Coptic, Armenian, and Syrian), and three more "modern" patriarchates (Moscow, Sofia, Bucharest). This chapter is the first serious, recent study of patriarchal polities of which I am aware.

With this twofold survey of Catholic and Orthodox perspectives on patriarchates in mind, the fifth chapter then proposes the creation of six continental patriarchates within the Latin Church and the attendant institutions that go along with them, chiefly a permanent synod and a full synod. The extensive historical survey in this chapter illustrates that the Roman Church has, for much of its history, had such synodal bodies even if they have often functioned under different names.

Once the many aspects of the papacy currently thought of as "papal" but actually "patriarchal" in nature have been returned to the regional patriarchates and local Churches, the "papal" functions *qua* papal in the Church will be clearly visible. The sixth and final chapter returns to *UUS* for a renewed understanding of how the pope *qua* pope would function in a reunited Church where East and West are again in full communion. Here the proposal is made for the creation of a permanent "ecumenical synod" that, under papal presidency, would consist of all the patriarchal heads of Churches and would gather together to assist the pope in maintaining the unity of the one Church of God.

CHAPTER ONE

Ut Unum Sint in Context

Catholic Ecumenism in the Postconciliar Period

The Second Vatican Council effected dramatic, far-reaching, and even revolutionary change in the Catholic Church. Renewal in the Church began in 1959 with the announcement of the Second Vatican Council and the creation of the Secretariat for Promoting Christian Unity.[1] The Secretariat would guide the ecumenical debates and discussions of the council, whose greatest fruit was *Unitatis Redintegratio (UR)*.[2] *UR*, however, was not a "stand-alone" document: *Orientalium Ecclesiarum* and many of the other documents—above all *Lumen Gentium,* and its controverted eighth section ("this Church constituted and organized in the world as a society subsists in the Catholic Church")—were also of ecumenical significance. As Walter Cardinal Kasper has argued, "all the texts of the Council should be read in an ecumenical perspective."[3]

Of the various provisions of *UR*, none is more germane to this study than section 16 on ecclesial governance in the East:'"

> [T]his holy Council solemnly declares that the Churches of the East, while remembering the necessary unity of the whole Church, have the power to govern themselves according to the disciplines proper to them, since these are better suited to the character of their faithful, and more for the good of their souls. The perfect observance of this traditional principle, not always indeed carried out in practice, is one of the essential prerequisites for any restoration of unity. (§16)

In some respects *UR* is important not only for what it says, but *that* it said anything at all, and, especially, that it said so in a "binding" and irrevocable manner.[4] In addition, *UR* is significant especially for generating a wholesale entrance of the Catholic Church into the ecumenical movement in so many ways that cannot be recounted here.[5] Let us now turn briefly to what is arguably the greatest successor of this conciliar decree, *Ut Unum Sint*.

Ut Unum Sint: An Overview of Its Contents

In 1995, Pope John Paul II issued his landmark letter *Ut Unum Sint*, immediately and widely acclaimed by Protestants, Orthodox, and other commentators as being a major document of profound significance. It is in fact the very first papal encyclical devoted entirely to ecumenism and a positive assessment of it. Promulgated on the Feast of the Ascension in May of that year, the encyclical is divided into three chapters, preceded by an introduction and followed by a short "exhortation" at the end.

The first chapter, "The Catholic Church's Commitment to Ecumenism," made it clear that there would be no turning back on the decisions of the Second Vatican Council in *Unitatis Redintegratio* and elsewhere. The pope states that ecumenism is an obligatory part of being a Christian:

> [I]t is absolutely clear that ecumenism, the movement promoting Christian unity, is not just some sort of "appendix" which is added to the Church's traditional activity. Rather, ecumenism is an organic part of her life and work, and consequently must pervade all that she is and does; it must be like the fruit borne by a healthy and flourishing tree which grows to its full stature. (§20)

Such a search for unity can only be founded upon prayer (§§21–27), which is to have a "primacy" (§21), a "pride of place" (§22) as the "soul of the ecumenical movement" (§28).

Once rooted in prayer, and the work of conversion and renewal begun, we can begin to undertake the ecumenical dialogue, which is the subject of the second chapter, "The Fruits of Dialogue." Here various accomplishments of the last century are reviewed to show the progress toward Christian unity.

The third chapter notes five main areas requiring further study and agreement, especially between Catholics and Protestants: the relationship between Scripture and Tradition; the Eucharist; sacramental ordination to the traditional three orders of bishop, priest, and deacon; the Magisterium of the Church; and the role of the Mother of God (§79).

Next is what I regard as the central and most important part of the encyclical, sections 88–97, entitled "The Ministry of Unity of the Bishop of Rome." The pope begins by attempting to describe that office in the most ecumenical and ecumenically acceptable language possible, resorting to the ancient title of "*servus servorum Dei*" and arguing that "this designation is the best possible safeguard against the risk of separating power (and in particular the primacy) from ministry. Such a separation would contradict the very meaning of power according to the Gospel: 'I am among you as one who serves' (Luke 22:27)" (§88). This irenic and humble language, however, cannot hide how objectionable the papacy has become to many "Christians, whose memory is marked by certain painful recollections. To the extent that we are responsible for these, I join my Predecessor Paul VI in asking forgiveness" (§88).

Such a request is itself no small thing, though papal requests for forgiveness became a singular hallmark of John Paul II's papacy.[6] What is even more astounding than such an apology is the famous request that comes next.

[A]s Bishop of Rome I am . . . convinced that I have a particular responsibility in . . . acknowledging the ecumenical aspirations of the majority of the Christian Communities and in heeding the request made of me to find a way of exercising the primacy which, while in no way renouncing what is essential to its mission, is nonetheless open to a new situation. . . .

. . . This is an immense task, which we cannot refuse and which I cannot carry out by myself. Could not the real but imperfect communion existing between us persuade Church leaders and their theologians to engage with me in a patient and fraternal dialogue on this subject, a dialogue in which, leaving useless controversies behind, we could listen to one another, keeping before us only the will of Christ for his Church.[7]

These admissions and requests are nothing short of astounding in a papal encyclical. George Weigel has remarked that

> perhaps the boldest stroke in *Ut Unum Sint,* a singularly bold encyclical, was Pope John Paul II's proposal that Orthodox and Protestant Christians help him conceive an exercise of the Petrine primacy that was "open to a new situation" and that could be of service to them. . . . It was, and remains, a daring, even breathtaking suggestion, certainly one of the most potentially consequential in ecumenical affairs.[8]

As Weigel would go on to comment, "at the same time, it should be candidly admitted that the response from Peter's Orthodox and Protestant brothers and sisters has not been overwhelming." That so few responses should be forthcoming, especially from the Orthodox, is a question and problem of some magnitude.[9]

The Problematic of Orthodox Responses to *Ut Unum Sint*

A legitimate question to ask is why so few Orthodox responses have been forthcoming, and it is a question that certain Orthodox have themselves asked. Olivier Clément, calling *UUS* an "unprecedented and prophetic initiative," went on to admit that "I find it inadmissible that the proposal has gone almost unheard. I would hope that the Oriental Patriarchs would get to work and be in a position to present their reflections to Pope John Paul II . . . in 1999."[10]

Clément's exhortation produced little fruit: by 2002, the PCPCU, summing up responses received to date, noted that

> answers came from a broad spectrum of western Churches and ecclesial Communities (the Old Catholic Church, Churches of the Anglican Com-

munion, Lutheran Churches, Presbyterian Churches, Reformed Churches and Free Churches). In geographical terms, most answers came from North America and Europe, mainly from the British Isles, Germany and the USA. . . . *There were no official answers from the Orthodox Churches.*[11]

We are therefore left to ponder the paucity of *official* responses.[12] One theory immediately (if somewhat uneasily) suggests itself here, especially in view of the many Protestant responses, and that pertains to the differences between Western (especially Protestant) and Eastern Orthodox cultures. The former are "Western" not just geographically but also sociologically, and thus, having come through the so-called Enlightenment, tend to place greater weight on the role of reason, of dialogue, of discussion and shared agreements among perceived equals.[13] Most of the Orthodox, by contrast, place far less weight on "reason" theologically understood and have historically spent most of their recent existence under various forms of nationalistic slavery and ideological tyranny—the Greeks under Ottoman and then Turkish domination; the Armenian and Slavic Orthodox under Communist (and, previously, tsarist) tyranny; the Copts and Syrians under "Islamist" persecutors.[14] Such experiences have exacted a high cost on all the Orthodox Churches and left them struggling to survive, and thus not equipped to engage in "Western" methods of dialogue, in which they tend to have far less faith than theologians and hierarchs trained in the universities of Western Europe or North America. Such experiences have also inculcated a healthy suspicion of authority figures and the often capricious "requests" of powerful leaders, of which the pope is clearly one. Beyond this sociological theorizing, an exhaustive answer to why there are few responses is not possible, but it is not implausible to consider that, broadly speaking, there are at least four further reasons, in increasing order of seriousness and plausibility.

First, one must not discount basic ignorance of the encyclical. If the vast majority of *Catholics* themselves remain at best only vaguely aware of the existence of *UUS,* it does not seem reasonable to expect that many Orthodox will have read it.

Second, the spring of 1995 was overloaded with pronouncements from Rome: more than one wag spoke of belonging to an "encyclical of the month club" as, within the space of a few short weeks, the pope promulgated a major encyclical on the "culture of death" (*Evangelium Vitae,* issued 25 March 1995), a substantial apostolic letter on the Christian East (*Orientale Lumen,* issued 2 May 1995), and then of course *Ut Unum Sint,* issued 25 May 1995. These came on the heels of other major documents issued less than two years before, including the controversial *Veritatis Splendor* and, in some circles, the even more controversial *Ordinatio Sacerdotalis.* The sheer volume of documents produced by the late pope made keeping up with him a formidable task.

Third, there are no internal organizational mechanisms within Orthodoxy which would allow for a co-ordinated response. The Orthodox Churches are not centrally governed or administered in the way the Church of Rome is, and it is both rare and difficult (indeed, rare *because* difficult) for them to come together in co-ordinated action even if they desired to do so (evidence of which is not always clearly or easily found). There is, at least organizationally speaking, no such thing as *the* Orthodox Church understood as a uniform monolith and possessing one spokesman who could issue authoritative and binding utterances on behalf of all the faithful in the way the pope of Rome can.[15] There is, then, no organizational mechanism or forum by which all Orthodox Churches could speak with one voice.

Fourth and finally, and perhaps most substantially, in certain Orthodox circles there is a resurgent mistrust of ecumenism in general[16] and of Rome in particular, a mistrust which, in its more fantastical expressions, would regard John Paul's request as—in the memorable words of David Bentley Hart—"merely the advance embassy of an omnivorous ecclesial empire" set to devour the Orthodox Churches and their fiercely guarded "independence."[17]

Orthodox mistrust of Catholic ecumenism cannot be separated from its cultural context, which often reinforces it. In the late 1980s and early 1990s, as seventy years of history were crumbling along with the Berlin Wall, the Orthodox—above all the Russians—were confronted with socioeconomic collapse of their countries as well as the resurrection of such enemies as the "Uniates."[18] In the once communist lands of Eastern Europe, cultural chaos was only compounded by the re-emergence of the much-maligned Eastern Catholic Churches—particularly in Western Ukraine—whose existence was thought to have been dealt with shortly after the Second World War.[19] All these problems led to what one commentator has called an "ecumenical meltdown"[20] and what John Erickson called a "retreat" from ecumenical engagement. Revealingly, Erickson cites a student from Eastern Europe who said that "when the communists were in control, we had to be ecumenical. Now we can be Orthodox."[21] Such an attitude is part of what one scholar has called a movement "from ecumenism to confessionalism," a movement begun in the ideological vacuum left after the fall of communism and often led by poorly educated zealots who understand neither their own purported Orthodox tradition nor the Western culture and Churches against which they so defensively rail.[22]

In addition to the emergence of the Ukrainian and Romanian Greco-Catholic Churches in particular, the Russian Orthodox were also confronted in 1992 with renewed Catholic structures in Russia as the pope erected Roman Catholic "apostolic administrations" there.[23] Regardless of the merits or justice of this action, the Roman Curia handled it badly, which thereby inflamed Russian Orthodox sentiments even more, as the often overly apologetic papal biographer George Weigel admitted in print.[24] The result of this bungling was what Erickson would call a "new crisis in Catholic-Orthodox dialogue"[25] that led to a historic meeting of nearly all the chief hierarchs of the Orthodox Churches in March 1992 in Constantinople to condemn "Roman Catholic . . . activities absolutely contrary to the spirit of the dialogue of love and truth," namely "missionary networks . . . and proselytism."[26]

These charges, which one commentator has called an "ecumenical cattle prod"[27] to be brought out whenever needed against the Vatican, have been examined and repeatedly rejected by Rome. That is not to say, however, that Rome is without fault, as several commentators have realized. At the very least—as even George Weigel was forced to concede—Rome's *modus operandi* in this regard requires a greater degree of diplomatic sensitivity. As a retired American archbishop recognized, "if Rome creates parallel hierarchical structures in the territories in the East, the Orthodox fear that Roman Catholic imperialism is at work."[28] Indeed, the Orthodox Church did not hesitate to repeat that these administrative structures were a manifestation of aggressive Catholic "proselytism"[29] and a refusal to recognize Russian "canonical territory." These charges would be repeated a decade later when, in 2002, these administrations were raised to full-blown dioceses,[30] a move that further exacerbated the extant tension causing a German Lutheran commentator, Gerd Stricker, to diplomatically suggest that "perhaps the Catholic Church does sometimes lack the necessary gentle touch" when dealing with the Russian Orthodox Church.[31] If Rome lacks a diplomatic touch, it must also be said that Moscow sometimes takes leave of its senses, too, tendentiously indulging, for domestic consumption, in a long-standing and not always rationally justified suspicion of Rome.[32]

Given Moscow's pre-eminence in the Orthodox world (of which it does not cease to remind everyone), it follows that Moscow's hostility would influence the reaction of the other Orthodox Churches, who similarly viewed the emergence of the Eastern Catholics, together with the institution of Roman Catholic ecclesiastical structures, as *prima facie* evidence of Catholic expansionist-colonialist claims and thus as anti-ecumenical actions at cross-purposes with ecumenical rhetoric. The result has been a devastation of trust and goodwill on the part of the Russian Orthodox in particular and the Orthodox Churches in general, who thereafter retained a high level of suspicion of any and all gestures emanating from Rome, including, of course, *Ut Unum Sint*. This suspicion remained until the end of the pontificate of John Paul II, and only in late 2005 and 2006 did it begin to show signs of lessening when, among other things, it was announced by both Rome and Constantinople that the JIC was to resume meeting in the autumn of 2006 after a hiatus of more than six years.

Having considered some of the context in which *UUS* appeared, and some of the reasons why the Orthodox response has been so lacking, we are now in a position to consider what responses are extant as well as earlier writings on the papacy.

CHAPTER TWO

Orthodox Positions on the Papacy

Orthodox writings on the papacy increased dramatically in the twentieth century.[1] In order to discern the ecumenical progress made thus far, to determine the areas which still require work, and above all to determine what, if any, consensus exists in this literature, careful and systematic consideration must be given to every major work that has been written so far on the papacy by various Orthodox theologians and hierarchs. Special attention should go to those articles and books published in the years leading up to *UUS* as well as those articles originating as a direct response to the encyclical. What follows, then, is a chronologically ordered attempt to summarize and systematically analyze in one place the major Orthodox works from 1960 onward. In an effort to be comprehensive, I include as "Orthodox" those papers written by members of the so-called non-Chalcedonian Churches (the "Oriental Orthodox") as well as those (more numerous) papers by the "Eastern Orthodox." These works are first summed up and then a synthesis of them is offered which points toward the following chapter.

Literature, 1960–2006

John Erickson cautioned that "any attempt to pick out a single and altogether consistent and clearly defined 'position' must be held suspect."[2]

Nonetheless, certain similarities clearly emerge, certain problems are repeatedly highlighted, and certain solutions are frequently mentioned, allowing for a synthetic portrait of the papacy as it is found in Orthodox theology of the last fifty years.

However, I will deal with only those works commanding scholarly respect[3] and treating the papal *office* as such.[4] I will not consider works on attendant issues like the person, figure, and role of Peter, exegesis of texts such as Matthew 16, or the role of the bishop of Rome in the early Church, including among the Fathers and later Byzantine theologians.[5]

John Meyendorff

The first attempt by Orthodox scholars to deal with the papacy comes— not surprisingly—in the 1960s as the relationship between Catholicism and Orthodoxy began to thaw.[6] In this period, several scholars both in Paris and in New York published a series of essays on Petrine primacy which were edited by John Meyendorff, the Orthodox historian, and published in English in 1963 as *The Primacy of Peter: Essays in Ecclesiology and the Early Church*.[7]

Meyendorff's own contribution was to provide historical links between the role of the bishop of Rome in the early Church and later developments in that office at the start of the second millennium.[8] Meyendorff argues—in terms that will rapidly become very familiar in this review—that "the Byzantines unanimously recognized the great authority of the old Rome, but never understood this authority in the sense of an absolute power."[9] He does not develop his reflection on the office much beyond this, save to note that papal primacy would develop in new and increasingly unacceptable ways in the second millennium, particularly after the Gregorian reforms.

Later, in other places, Meyendorff turned to ecclesiological questions again and again, noting that "I see no way in which the Orthodox Church can fulfill its mission in the world today without the ministry of a 'first bishop' . . . based upon that 'privilege of honor' of which the Second Ecumenical Council spoke. We should all think and search how to redefine that 'privilege' in a way which would be practical and efficient today."[10] In an article on the Ecumenical Patriarch of Constantinople Meyendorff himself searched for how the Orthodox would define such a ministry of a "first bishop," noting that a "first bishop . . . would not be a pope with administrative powers *over* his peers but would possess sufficient authority to organize, channel and, in a sense, represent the conciliarity of the Church."[11] After stressing the "pragmatic and political origin of all the primacies" in the early Church Meyendorff goes on to argue that "universal primacy" is "not simply a historical accident reflecting 'pragmatic requirements' . . . but a sign that the Holy Spirit did not abandon the Church" (244). Universal primacy, he stresses "does possess a scriptural and ecclesiological basis" (243). The Spirit provides no "ultimate guarantee, no ultimate security" to the one exercising that primacy, but enables its incumbent to exercise "a special ministry, a special *diakonia* of universal primacy and that such a *diakonia* implies a particular *charisma*" (245).

Nicholas Afanasiev

Afanasiev's essay in the Meyendorff volume ranks among the most famous of his works, and one of the most influential pieces of Orthodox ecclesiology in the twentieth-century revival of what is now commonly called "eucharistic ecclesiology."[12] Afanasiev stresses that before considering the primacy of Rome attention must be given to the position of Rome, and then to the whole question of primacy, which means a further step back to the question of ecclesiology. Which ecclesiology? Catholic ecclesiology has been understood traditionally as universalist while the ecclesiology of Orthodoxy is ostensibly eucharistic, but, Afanasiev acknowledges, more often also universalist in practice. Catholics may claim this universalist ecclesiology—and its logical consequent, universal primacy—is ancient, but Afanasiev argues that a eucharistic ecclesiology is in fact older.

For Afanasiev, eucharistic ecclesiology does not exclude a primate, i.e., a head who presides over the Eucharist. In this light, "priority" (the term Afanasiev prefers to "primacy," which he calls "a legalistic expression, whereas priority is founded on authority of witness, and that is a gift God grants" [115]) is based not on power or honour but only love—"the church that came first among the local churches won its place by services rendered, and not by prestige." Such service did not confer "power" or "special rights" as the Churches were "not joined by law, but by love and concord. That is why a single church surrounded by many concordant churches only increases in authority by a corresponding increase in love" (113).

This single Church, Afanasiev acknowledges, was originally the Church of Jerusalem, but after the fall of Jerusalem, "the Church of Rome took over the position of 'church-with-priority' at the end of the first century," a movement that happened without "a formal transmission of priority"(124). Some of the earliest documents, including those of Clement of Rome, do not support the thesis that Rome had anything more than this "priority." Ignatius of Antioch is the next to recognize the role of Rome as the Church "'which presides in love'" while saying nothing about her bishop or power over other Churches. While this may seem "puzzling," it simply "proves that Ignatius had absolutely no idea of Roman primacy" (127). In the end, both Orthodox and Catholics must abandon their falsely universalist notions of papal primacy because "the mind of the Church has become unaware that the Church of God should be directed by a local church, one church among all others," except that Church "'which presides in love'" (143). Papal primacy, then, is an outrunning of one disciple in love rather than an overruling of all the disciples by one.

Alexander Schmemann

Until his early death in 1983, Alexander Schmemann remained one of the few consistently self-critical Orthodox theologians to avoid the siren song of triumphalism and to speak frankly on the topics to which he addressed himself. In his article "The Idea of Primacy in Orthodox Ecclesiology,"[13] he gives a forthright acknowledgment of the numerous "canonical and jurisdictional troubles and divisions" of recent Orthodoxy, in which the "absence of a clearly defined doctrine of . . . primacy" has been a "major handicap for . . . unity" (146–47).

Schmemann attempts a definition of primacy by first acknowledging that dealing with primacy is really dealing with power (147). Such power, however, must be carefully defined. If the Church is defined in terms of the Eucharist—if, indeed, the Church is constituted by the Eucharist—then "the essential corollary of this 'eucharistic' ecclesiology is that it excludes the idea of a *supreme power,* understood as power *over* the local church and her bishop" (153). Such power is thus excluded because it "would mean power *over* Christ himself," present in the Eucharist. Power in the Church, then, "can be defined and understood only within the indivisible unity of the Church, the eucharist and the bishop" (154). All of which does *not* mean that Orthodoxy rejects primacy: rather, it rejects a primacy defined as power over the bishop and local Church, hence over the Eucharist. Primacy that is reconcilable with a eucharistic ecclesiology (as seen, for example, in the famous sixth canon of Nicaea, which speaks of power [*exousia*] "understood as 'priority' or 'privilege' . . . , a *primacy of authority*") is much more acceptable for Orthodoxy, not least because such authority "cannot be defined in juridical terms" (162–63).

Schmemann argues vigorously that the early Church knew a form of non-juridical universal primacy, *pace* whatever modern Orthodox polemicists may say about this. This primacy exercised by Rome, evidence of which is "unanimously" to be found among the Fathers and early councils, has been interpreted incorrectly by both Catholics (the "ecclesiological error of Rome lies . . . in her identification of this primacy with 'supreme power,' which transforms Rome into the *principium radix et origio* of the unity of the Church and of the Church herself") and Orthodox, who "systematically belittled the evidence itself" (163). Roman theology tends to interpret the "evidence in *juridical* terms" while Orthodoxy, when not simply dismissing it, "is still awaiting a truly Orthodox evaluation of universal primacy in the first millennium of church history" (164).

In the meantime, this much is known: primacy is neither "supreme power" nor mere "chairmanship" but is exercised by a bishop who can and "must" speak for one Church, representing her unity precisely as a regular bishop and "not a 'bishop at large.'" In conclusion, Schmemann argues that such a role existed and was historically exercised by Rome—the "early tradition clearly indicates the primacy of the Church of Rome" as exercised without "jurisdictional power" (165).

Kallistos Ware

Few theologians are as well known inside and outside the Orthodox world as Metropolitan Kallistos Ware. He has treated the question of the papacy—more in passing than systematically—in a variety of places, including a 1969 lecture, "Primacy, Collegiality, and the People of God."[14] He begins with the observation that when Catholics and Orthodox last met together in council, at Ferrara-Florence in 1438/9, "they devoted about nine months (with some interruptions) to the question of the *Filioque,* and over two months to the question of purgatory; but on the problem of the papal claims they spent no more than two weeks."

Metropolitan Kallistos goes on to note a familiar refrain among Orthodox theologians on the question of the papacy—"what Orthodoxy rejects is not the Roman primacy as such, but simply a particular way of understanding that primacy." The problematic understanding is one that sees the papacy as possessing "a universal 'power of jurisdiction'" from which "the Orthodox feel compelled to dissent." If, rather, the pope is understood as "the *elder brother* within the family of Christ . . . [who] enjoys a position of leadership and initiative, but not of coercion: for the other bishops are his brothers, not his subjects or his servants," then the papacy presents no problems to the Orthodox.

In his most famous book, *The Orthodox Church,* originally published in 1963 and reprinted many times after that, most recently in 1993, Metropolitan Kallistos continues and amplifies this argument: "Orthodox believe that among the five Patriarchs a special place belongs to the Pope. The Orthodox Church does not accept the doctrine of Papal authority set forth in . . . the Vatican Council of 1870."[15] However, if Orthodoxy rejects that particular Roman definition of primacy, nonetheless Orthodoxy does not deny to "Rome a *primacy of honour,* together with the right (under certain conditions) to hear appeals from all parts of Christendom." This primacy assigned to the pope "does not overthrow the essential equality of all bishops. The Pope is the first bishop of the Church—but he is the *first among equals*" (28). As the first, "Orthodoxy recognizes that, in the early centuries of the Church, Rome was pre-eminent in its steadfast witness to the truth faith" (316). From here, Ware proceeds by way of affirmation rather than negation:

[I]nstead of saying what Orthodox will *not* accept, let us ask in positive terms what the nature of Papal primacy is from an Orthodox viewpoint. Surely we Orthodox should be willing to assign to the Pope, in a reunited Christendom, not just an honorary seniority but an all-embracing apostolic care. We should be willing to assign to him the right, not only to accept appeals from the whole Christian world but even to take the initiative in seeking ways of healing when crises and conflict arise anywhere among Christians. We envisage that on such occasions the Pope would act, not in isolation, but always in close co-operation with his brother bishops. We would wish to see his ministry spelt out in pastoral rather than juridical terms. He would encourage rather than compel, consult rather than coerce. (316)

Stylianos Harkianakis

Stylianos Harkianakis, an archbishop in the Greek Orthodox Church in Australia, authored an essay that first appeared in the 1971 collection *Papal Ministry in the Church,* edited by Hans Küng.[16] This collection, which solicited contributions from Christians of a variety of confessions, contains two Orthodox pieces. The first, by Harkianakis, argues that in evaluating the papacy, the Orthodox theologian actually has two tasks, the "idea of primacy as such" and the "primacy of Rome," both of which must be assessed "theologically." The former idea "of primacy as such has never been alien to Orthodox thought and is still acceptable today, whereas the primacy of Rome is still . . . a real obstacle on the way to Christian unity" (115). Roman primacy, properly exercised, is not an obstacle to Orthodoxy, whereas Roman primacy as conceived and executed, especially since the First Vatican Council, *is* an obstacle because of a "fundamental ecclesiological misunderstanding" (116). That misunderstanding, according to Harkianakis, can be clarified by asking the most important question about the structure of the Church: is it "monarchical or collegial?" (116–17). That question leads on to another about the nature of the Trinity, which provides an analogical model for understanding the relationship between the one and the many in the very nature of the Church. If, as the ecumenical councils worked out, the three Persons of the Trinity are all equal, then there is no room for any "idea of a *subordinatio*" among them (118–19). Only when seen in this light can we proceed to the question of whether there is a "first bishop" and, if so, what his relationship is like to all other bishops.

Just as the fundamental equality of the members of the Godhead does not detract from the *monarchia* of the Father, so too the fundamental equality of the episcopate—and, with it, the synodal nature of the Church—does not detract from "acknowledgement of one bishop as the first among the bishops" who exercises "primacy . . . not . . . in the sense of a *pontifex maximus* but rather in the sense of *primus inter pares*" (120). When understood thus, a primate "cannot do anything without the opinion of all the others, and the others cannot do anything without the opinion of the first." This method and model of primacy excludes "matters of jurisdiction and . . . the question of infallibility" and is, Harkianakis concludes, the only acceptable way for Roman primacy to be exercised without objection from the Orthodox. Indeed, such a primate performs "an essential service in the Church as a whole" (121).

Paul Evdokimov

In one of the last scholarly pieces he wrote shortly before his death in September 1970,[17] Paul Evdokimov, a French lay theologian and author of many prominent works in Orthodox anthropology, struck a note similar to Harkianakis: the primacy of the bishop of Rome must be situated in Trinitarian theology, and, when done so, will be understood not juridically but pastorally, with the bishop of Rome seen as equal to all other bishops and not above them as a "super-bishop" (124). Quoting Nil Cabasilas, Evdokimov notes that "'the Pope is bishop of Rome and the first among the bishops'" but that "this does not imply a juridical power of domination over the others, but a *care* exercised for the common good" (123). Given that "each Church" is "the *totus Christus*" any power over another bishop would ipso facto be power over Christ himself (124) and this possibility Orthodoxy categorically rejects. A universalist ecclesiology with such a super-bishop must therefore give way to a eucharistic ecclesiology and to the fundamental equality of all bishops expressed sacramentally and synodally. Only in this way can primacy be understood because only in this way is it really a reflection of the life of the Trinity. Insofar as a universal primate is like God the Father, "who presides in the love of the Trinity," and insofar as such a primate exercises "a charism of love in the image of the heavenly Father . . . devoid of all jurisdictional power over the others," he will be acceptable as an instrument of unity in both East and West (126).

Robert Stephanopoulos

In a short paper published in 1974,[18] Robert Stephanopoulos, now a Greek Orthodox priest and member of the North American Orthodox-Catholic dialogue, argued that "primacy as seen from an Orthodox perspective is not best explained as a juridical term, but rather as a moral authority" which is best exercised in the context of "conciliarity" so as to safeguard the authority of the local bishop and the autocephaly of the local Church (311). When understood thus, "the Petrine ministry . . . is a gift from God" (312) to be lived for the "good order" of the Church (313). Stephanopoulos concludes even more strongly by arguing that the pope is

> the elder brother among his fellow bishops and by mutual consent, as *primus inter pares,* exercises the Petrine ministry in the universal church. This solicitude is understood in terms of grace and spiritual freedom, of loving ministry and humble service. There is ample historical precedent for this. In the present moment, there is even a special need for it. . . . The Petrine ministry is integral to the mission and unity of all Christians and churches. (314)

Emmanuel Clapsis

Emmanuel Clapsis, a professor of systematic theology at Holy Cross Greek Orthodox School of Theology in Brookline, Massachusetts, authored a paper on the papacy in 1987,[19] just as almost all the various ecumenical dialogues in which Orthodoxy was engaged had come to

realize that the question of primacy in general was the most fundamental divide of all.[20] The JIC saw this perhaps more clearly than any
of the others.[21] It also saw, as Clapsis details, the necessity of treating
the papacy not as an isolable issue but in the context of the doctrine
of the Trinity and the Eucharist for "Trinitarian ecclesiology also develops the insight that there is one Church as there is one nature in
God, but the very best way to express the oneness of the Church is
the communion of the many local churches."[22] In other words, only
when the papacy is "debated, reinterpreted, and justified from the developing ecclesiology of communion" among sister Churches will the
Orthodox-Catholic dialogue be able to make genuine progress on the
question of the papacy (116).

Some progress has already been made, according to Clapsis's analysis of the JIC. Orthodoxy has no problem in affirming "the validity of
the claims of universal primacy of the Church of Rome. Orthodox theology, however, objects to the identification of this primacy with 'supreme power' which transforms Rome into the *principium radix et
origio* of the unity of the Church" (128). If Orthodoxy objects to papal
primacy on these grounds, it has still not settled the question of how
such a primacy would be otherwise exercised. Echoing Schmemann,
Clapsis argues that Orthodox theology also must further define for
itself "an ecclesiologically sound interpretation of primacy" (125).
Such an interpretation will require examination of models of primacy
as they currently exist in Orthodoxy, especially patriarchal primacy:
"[I]t is imperative from an Orthodox perspective to study the primacy
of Rome in the context of the primacies of the patriarchs of the East
and their role in the Universal Church" (124).

In general, patriarchs have very little of the power that the pope of
Rome does, and they exercise it only vis-à-vis their synods. Understood
in the light of the patriarchal synod, the Church manifests "its oneness
through a ministry which comprises *simultaneously* a *primus* and a
synod of which he is a *primus*. Thus from this perspective, it is possible
to accept a universal primacy of a bishop which, however, cannot be
conceived apart from the synod or over it." In other words,

> in a reintegrated Christendom, when the pope takes his place once more
> as the *primus inter pares* within the Orthodox Catholic communion, the

bishop of Rome will have the initiative in summoning a synod of the whole Church. The bishop of Rome, of course, will preside in such a synod . . . and his office may coordinate the witness of the Orthodox Catholic Church and be its spokesman in times of need. (127)

Vsevolod Majdansky

Continuing the theme of the bishop of Rome as patriarch,[23] the Ukrainian Orthodox Archbishop Vsevolod has been perhaps the clearest and most forthright contemporary Orthodox theologian to admit Orthodoxy's need of a certain form of primacy exercised by Rome. Vsevolod has argued that "the Roman Primacy . . . at its best . . . is a blessing for the Church."[24] In similar but even clearer terms a year later, Vsevolod argued not only that "Roman Primacy is and should be a gift of God to His Church" but that it performs a "service to the Church which we need,"[25] not least when one considers the "ludicrous" (230), "unbearable," and "unthinkable" (232) jurisdictional situation of Eastern Orthodoxy in the United States (a situation of "intolerable chaos" [241]). After the "great shock" in 1995 when Moscow and Constantinople broke communion with each other over the question of jurisdiction in Estonia, Vsevolod says he saw even more clearly that "the Church needs the Roman Primacy" (237). "Painful though it is," Vsevolod admits, "we need the primacy" (241).

Of course, Archbishop Vsevolod immediately qualifies this bold statement by arguing against acceptance of Roman primacy as it is currently constructed. The problem with such primacy, as Vsevolod points out elsewhere, is the unhelpful amalgam of offices that need to be differentiated; there needs to be a "clarification of the distinct roles of the Bishop of Rome as a Local Patriarch, first of the Pentarchy, and the Bishop of Rome as the universal primate" (244–45). Vsevolod argues that the Roman patriarchate as a patriarchate no longer exists: it has engaged in an "unending aggrandizement . . . at everyone else's expense" and such a "world-wide expansion"[26] as to become a super-sized monolith with the bishop of Rome acting as "the unique holder of a still higher position" (248) which enables him to "ride roughshod over the bishops" (250). The remedy for this situation lies in six changes that Vsevolod enumerates: first, "a clear, credible set of boundaries to the

Roman Patriarchate"; second, the "restoration of the canonical obligation of the Patriarch of the West, when he assumes office, to send his Profession of Faith to the other Patriarchs"; third, an "end to the practice of the Pope commemorating himself at the diptychs, and the restoration of the authentic practice of the commemoration of the Patriarchs when the Pope celebrates the Eucharist"; fourth, the "resolution of the discrepancy between the assurances given to the Orthodox in ecumenical dialogue, and the practical situation of the Eastern Catholics within the Roman Communion"; fifth, "a recognition that the primatial function of the Bishop of Rome . . . is not subject to habitual delegation" (255); and sixth, the erection by the Roman Church of "regional patriarchates"[27] to decentralize the behemoth Latin Church and assist in her better governance, as well as assisting Latin ecclesiology to become better acquainted with the patriarchal model of governance.

Archbishop Vsevolod returned to these theses in a longer article written about a year after their first articulation—and shortly after *UUS* was published—adding a sixth requisite change, viz., "a juridical guarantee that the terms in which Rome has defined the universal primacy will not be applied to our Churches."[28] He concludes hopefully that a "generous Orthodox response to *Ut Unum Sint*" may be had as Orthodoxy comes to realize that "there is no need to fear that we would emerge from such a conversation with the Roman Primacy in tatters." On the contrary, "the Roman Primacy is and should be a gift of God to His Church, a service to the Church which we need" (266–67).

Antonios Kireopoulos

Antonios Kireopoulos is an Orthodox theologian who served the U.S. Conference of Religions for Peace prior to joining the staff of the National Council of Churches U.S.A. in 2003. In his 1997 article, "Papal Authority and the Ministry of Primacy,"[29] Kireopoulos offers a very brief and incomplete survey of several Catholic and Orthodox ecclesiologies before proceeding to the central feature of his article, "a review of the current Roman Catholic debate on papal primacy," albeit a review in which he knows he will "only be scratching the surface" (46). His essay, then, is not so much an original contribution as a review—

selective and incomplete—of the positions of others. Nonetheless, he does provide a somewhat helpful summary of some key Orthodox arguments.

For all the Orthodox emphasis on the local Church, "we still ascribe to a ministry of primacy. And again after all, though our problems may be of a different nature, we certainly haven't worked out the solution."[30] The papacy, for Catholics, is a centre of unity in a practical sense but Orthodoxy does not understand unity to cohere in one person or office—"primacy does not constitute the origin of unity; rather it is the manifestation of the unity already inherent in the Church" (59). While acknowledging that "the East has always considered Peter as higher than the other apostles," Kireopoulos goes on to argue that nonetheless a universal primacy with "jurisdictional authority" is unacceptable for the Orthodox (56). The "only solution to be found . . . [is] by seeing the Church in terms of *communion*" (57). A Church lived as communion requires greater collegiality and also remains "in particular instances in need of one voice" (58).

Nonetheless, Kireopoulos ends pessimistically: a "universal ecclesiology" quite naturally and logically entails primacy exercised as "power" and into such a context one cannot simply drop a eucharistic ecclesiology of communion and expect the two to work things out. The only solution, he maintains, is for "Roman Catholic theologians . . . [to] re-think their entire ecclesiology" while Orthodox "need to do so as well" in order to deal with their problem of "'competing autocephalies'" (61–62).

Mesrob Krikorian

In 1997, a conference on the papacy was organized in Rome under the auspices of several ecclesiastical institutions brought together to commemorate the centenary of the founding of the ecumenically minded Society of the Atonement, a Roman Catholic religious order. Theologians from all the major Christian confessions engaged in what Pope John Paul II requested in *Ut Unum Sint,* viz., a "patient and fraternal dialogue" on the papacy. The results of this dialogue were then edited by James Puglisi and published in 1999.[31]

Fully one-third of the articles in this volume are from Orthodox sources. This can be taken as a measure both of the size and influence of Orthodoxy and also because there is no complete consensus in Orthodoxy on the issues of papacy, primacy, and related matters. Reflecting this diversity are four papers: one from an Oriental Orthodox—the Armenian Archbishop Mesrob Krikorian—and three Byzantine Orthodox theologians—Dumitru Popescu, Metropolitan John Zizioulas, and Nicholas Lossky.

Archbishop Mesrob's contribution[32] is notable here as being the only one from any of the so-called non-Chalcedonian Churches. He begins by debunking the romanticization of the "first millennium" as a time of unity, noting that "harmony among Churches prevailed only up to 451." Instead of looking back to this period, we must "continue the fraternal dialogue and try to formulate anew the Petrine office in such a form which would be acceptable to all" (91). In so doing, we need to get away from a primacy of domination and instead move toward "primacy as *a service of unity* whose aim and duty is *to admonish and caution*," a duty thus exercised that "hardly can be rejected by anybody, if it is practiced in conciliarity and collegiality together with bishops or patriarchs of other Churches" (93).

Quoting from the 1978 Fourth Ecumenical Consultation of Oriental Orthodox and Roman Catholic theologians, he notes that all bishops are of equal dignity; primates enjoy only a primacy of honour (whose content has to be decided upon by all concerned) and are on an equal footing with all other primates in the world; unity is manifested not through a person or office but through one faith; when a question is controverted, an ecumenical council is the only means to settle it because the "Oriental Orthodox will not be able to accept the sole and highest authority of the Roman pontiff in respect to ecumenical councils" (96).

Krikorian concludes with three affirmations: first, the primacy of the bishop of Rome is a fact "which nobody can ignore or neglect." Second, the primacy as exercised in the first millennium "had neither administrative nor authoritarian character." Third, in a united Church, the pope should be able to convoke ecumenical councils and to preside over them, either alone or with other patriarchs. The decisions are valid only when a majority of bishops endorse them: the pope has no veto. In sum, the office of bishop of Rome admonishes in the "service of unity" and is "exercised in charity" without any "jurisdictional power and authority" (97).

Dumitru Popescu

The Romanian Orthodox theologian Dumitru Popescu argues that the early Church accorded Rome nothing more than "a primacy of honour and not a juridical primacy."[33] Moreover, such primacy as exists and could exist again must not follow the monarchical model that became prevalent in the Roman Church from the Gregorian reforms onward— "the Church is not a monarchy; she is a communion whose life is guided, not by the judgment of a single person, *unius arbitrium,* but by the common law of the Catholic Church."[34] This law, "during the first Christian millennium," "was exercised within an ecclesiology of communion" (111). If today the "experience of the papacy can be of great importance for Christian unity" it will be so when "exercised in the context of an ecclesiology which situates communion both at the visible level and at the invisible level of the Church." As for today, "we need unity, but for this unity to be accepted by all, it must be founded on Peter's confession of faith in presence of Christ. As long as the Church remained faithful to this principle, she kept her unity; as soon as she abstracted from it, her unity was broken." Such unity, in sum, "is not only a Christological, monarchical unity, but also a pneumatological unity of communion" (112–13).

John Zizioulas

One of the most astute and important Orthodox theologians writing today, Zizioulas has written a great deal on ecclesiological questions in general.[35] On the papacy in particular, he has authored two important papers, both given at symposia in Rome. In the first paper,[36] in 1997, Zizioulas notes that the topic of the papacy has traditionally been treated in one of two ways. The first is by a "*historical* method" which, while once used extensively, "has led to no fruitful result" (117). The second means is "the *theological* one" used by JIC. This method can "bear fruit if it is followed with consistency by both sides." Thus, for Zizioulas, the "primacy of the Bishop of Rome has to be theologically justified or else can be ignored altogether" (123).

Zizioulas undertakes such a theological exploration of the papacy, arguing that "a theology of the primacy in the Church can be summed up in the following observations":

- "the Church cannot but be a unity of the One and the Many at the same time";
- "the Church is local and universal at the same time";
- "the bishop is both a local and a universal ministry";
- "the synodal system is a 'sine qua non conditio' for the catholicity of the Church";
- "primacy is also a 'sine qua non conditio' for the catholicity of the Church." (118–21)

Primacy, Zizioulas argues, exists on three levels, at least. First, there is a primacy "*within* each local church" centred in the bishop. Second, there is a "regional" primacy based on the "*metropolitan* system . . . developed in close connection with the synodical institution" (121). Finally, there is the patriarchate. Problems arose when Rome was not satisfied with this form of primacy but wanted universal jurisdiction. Most Orthodox, of course, wish to ascribe to the pope only a primacy of honour, but Zizioulas argues that "'primacy of honor,' [is] a misleading term since . . . it is not an 'honorific' primacy but one that involves actual duties and responsibilities" (123).[37]

If neither Roman universal jurisdiction nor a merely honorific role is satisfactory, then what is? Zizioulas suggests that the traditional approach to the Roman primacy, the Byzantine pentarchy, "would seem to satisfy fully the Orthodox" but this raises other problems, chief among which is that "there are now parts of the world which are Christian and which were not known at the time of the Byzantine pentarchy. To whom will these belong in terms of primacy?" Moreover, how can one justify the pentarchy *theologically?* This solution, then, has considerable "weaknesses" resulting once more in an impasse (123–24).

However, according to Zizioulas, papal primacy *can* be acceptable to the Orthodox under the following conditions: it cannot be exercised as a universal primacy "of jurisdiction"; it "should not be the prerogative of an individual but of a *local church*"; it must be exercised "*in a synodical context* both locally and regionally as well as universally"; and it can only be "exercised *in communion,* not in isolation or directly over the entire Church." The pope "would be the President of all heads of churches and the spokesman of the entire Church once the decisions announced are the result of consensus" (124–25). If Roman primacy is exercised in this way, it will be "not only 'useful' to the Church but an ecclesiological necessity in a unified Church" (125).

These views were reiterated to some degree in a second paper given in Rome in 2003.[38] After emphasizing once more that the question of papal primacy cannot be decided solely on the basis of scripture or history, but only "as a common answer from theology" (244), Zizioulas went on to argue in favour of papal primacy by means of an analogy to patriarchal Orthodox structures: the "many" (the synod) cannot exist without the "one" (the patriarch) and each has crucial checks on the other (235). Further, "synods without primates never existed in the Orthodox Church, and this indicates clearly that if synodality is an ecclesiological, that is, dogmatic, necessity, so must be primacy. . . . The logic of synodality leads to primacy, and the logic of the ecumenical council to universal primacy" (243). For this reason, then, "there must . . . be a way of incorporating primacy into conciliarity if we are to arrive at a theologically sound position on this matter" (238). Such a theologically sound position would have to be based upon an "ecclesiology of communion" in which both Catholics and Orthodox recognize that "the Church consists of *full local churches* united into *One Church* without losing their ecclesial fullness, and that primacy at all levels is a necessary means to realize and guarantee this balance between the many and the one" (246).

Nicholas Lossky

Echoing Erickson's warning about easy consistency, Nicholas Lossky, a Russian Orthodox theologian teaching in Paris, points out that "it is not possible to speak of one, common attitude towards the conceptions of conciliarity, of primacy, or of the relation between the two among Russian theologians and Church people. Especially of late, there have been many different, often contradictory conceptions and opinions."[39] Much of the Orthodox rejection of primacy stems from "an excessive anti-romanism, based on a certain distortion of the office in the historical development of the Church of Rome." This distortion, when mixed with ecclesiological confusion among the Orthodox, often leads to a "simplistic anti-romanism and therefore anti-papism" which often "tends to reappear in the context of the local autocephalous church" whose members often "consider the patriarch to be something of a 'super-bishop'" (129), a view apparently held by "the present patriarch of Moscow, a few bishops and a few theologians" (128).

Notwithstanding its prevalence in both Catholic and Orthodox Churches, this is, Lossky says, a faulty view of primacy. No primacy can be exercised without a concomitant conciliarity exercised among the bishops. These two must be held in tension—"conciliarity without primacy tends towards either a form of fusion or a form of democracy which amounts to individualism, not personhood. Primacy without conciliarity tends towards a kind of concentration of episcopacy in one super-bishop above the community, a form of domination tantamount to dictatorship" (134). If this primacy-conciliarity antinomy were correctly maintained, then "many Orthodox theologians" would be prepared to recognize "Rome (on condition of course that full communion is restored) as the court of appeal (excluding intervention before an appeal) in disputes among bishops." They would also recognize a "primacy of Rome such as it was understood . . . during the first millennium," the best expression of which "is probably to be found in the Council of Constantinople of 879–880" for which Lossky pleads to have "a common reception as the Eighth Ecumenical Council" (135).

Olivier Clément

Clément—a theologian teaching with Lossky at l'Institut Saint-Serge in Paris—is a convert to Orthodoxy, not from a supposedly "native" French Catholicism as some imagine, but from atheism. His book, *You*

Are Peter: An Orthodox Theologian's Reflection on the Exercise of Papal Primacy, is written in a largely irenic and fraternal manner. For this reason, Avery Cardinal Dulles, in his foreword to the English edition, says that this book is "almost exactly the kind of response for which Pope John Paul II was hoping."

Unlike the others reviewed here, Clément has actually written not an essay but an entire book—albeit a short one—in response to John Paul's request.[40] Each of the twelve chapters is very short, averaging about seven pages. The first six chapters are taken up with a very brief historical overview of the first millennium and of the tension between the early ecumenical councils and an inchoate sense of Roman primacy. About this latter, he remarks that "the true greatness of the period of the ecumenical councils is precisely that the power of decision rested with no one: neither pope, nor council, nor emperor, nor public feeling."[41]

According to Clément, this greatness gave way "little by little . . . [as] Roman primacy showed signs of becoming contaminated by the problem of power," a problem that became acute as "apostolic Rome appeared to have taken over from ancient imperial Rome."[42]

In his next chapter (of two: the second is on reforms necessary in Orthodoxy) on necessary reforms to the papacy, he expresses the hope that "Rome, when God wills it, and by an operation of grace unique to her, will return to the authentic conception of primacy as the servant of communion, within a framework of genuine interdependence between her bishop and all other bishops" (75). An authentic exercise of primacy will require at least four structural changes. First, Clément argues that "it is in no way essential . . . that the bishop of Rome should appoint the bishops of the entire world." Second, it is equally unnecessary that the bishop of Rome's "administrative headquarters should be a sovereign territory . . . and in consequence maintain a diplomatic corps" (92). (To the suggestion that such an arrangement grants the papacy a necessary independence, Clément offers the rejoinder that "none of the great popes of the first eight centuries had at their command such a state. They bore witness to the independence of the Church through martyrdom if necessary. Today everything depends on the political and ideological situation of Italy and western Europe" [95].)

Third, there must be some clarification around the question of the councils held in the West since the end of the last truly ecumenical council (Nicea II in 787). They are plainly not "ecumenical" in the way the West continues to insist but were instead—as Pope Paul VI offhand-edly remarked in a letter to Cardinal Willebrands in 1974—simply "general synods" of the Latin Church. Their decrees, therefore, carry a significantly different degree of authority and this must be clarified (94).

Fourth, there must be—as Clément quotes John Paul himself as saying—a papal primacy "with different gears" for different parts of the Church so that ultimately the relationship between Catholicism and Orthodoxy is not one of jurisdiction but of the plenitude of communion as sisters (92). Such an approach does not mean a gutting of the papacy—"this does not mean that the pope must be merely a spokes-man," Clément says. Rather, the pope would have significant authority as one to whom a "certain right of appeal" could be made together with his responsibility for the "convocation of councils" over which he would preside and whose decrees he would ratify (93). In sum, then, Clément argues that "the one essential would be to pass from a situation where the hierarchical dovetailing of power structures has legal back-up to one where tensions are held in balance without predetermined juridical solutions" (93–94).

John Erickson

In a September 1997 address to the North American Academy of Ecumenists, Erickson, who was dean of St. Vladimir's Seminary in New York until 2006, took grateful note of the "tremendous advance" represented by *Ut Unum Sint,* not only in its tone but also in its ecclesiological vision.[43] This changed situation "allows us to view the issue of primacy in a new light," the light of the Church understood as *koinonia.* However, Erickson is cautious about this process of re-evaluation, warning that "doctrinal agreement between Catholics and Orthodox on the subject of papal primacy . . . will not be achieved simply by a retrospective ecumenism that looks only to the mythic 'undivided Church of the first millennium'" (9) because "such appeals to history can be misleading or even dangerous" (8).

Bearing such cautions in mind together with a relativizing of the centrality of the papacy in the life of the whole Church, we will come to realize that papal primacy "is but one aspect of communion, and perhaps not the definitive one at that." Such primacy requires certain structures "if communion in its fullness . . . is to be maintained." Those structures include something that "most Christians—Protestants, Catholics, Orthodox—would agree on," namely a "'universal ministry of unity'" (3). However, any primate—whether regional, metropolitical, or universal—"remains first of all the bishop of a particular see. His prerogatives do not separate him from his brother bishops" (5). How, then, do we speak of primacy and what justification grounds it?

Primacy, according to Erickson, is "service in and for the Church" herself understood "as a communion in faith and love."[44] However, this does not mean that a primate is merely a titular or a primate "of honour"—"something more is involved in primacy. That something, I suggest, may be found in the concept of *phrontis, sollicitudo*—concern" (5). The primate is one who looks out for the welfare of everyone, who embodies an "all-embracing pastoral concern" better understood "in terms of leadership or love than in juridical terms." Such a concern is typically exercised "within a conciliar context" but a primate's concern "is continuous. . . . It does not come and go with the convening and adjourning of a council. In certain circumstances he may act to correct an abuse or to regulate an anomalous situation through a personal act, but he does so precisely as head of a college of bishops" (6–7).

John Panagopoulos

John Panagopoulos, a Greek Orthodox layman in the United States, wrote an extremely short response to *UUS,* which he recognizes as being "strongly marked by the spirit of openness, responsibility, living hope, humility and self-accusation."[45] For Panagopoulos, the papacy can only be acceptable "in the sense of *primus inter pares,* as was the case in the church of the first eight centuries, and not as a dogmatic question of faith." If this were so, "the way would certainly be open to communion, especially as the Orthodox cannot give up the notion of ecclesial primacy. In the sense of a primacy of honour, the supreme Magisterium would be attributed to the synodical structure of the church and not to a historical church, i.e. the See of Rome."

Vigen Guroian

The prolific Armenian Orthodox theologian Vigen Guroian, in a paper given at Aberdeen University, Scotland, for the conference "Commitment to Ecumenism: An Ecumenical Dialogue on *Ut Unum Sint*" in May 2005 has argued that

> the dialogue in which John Paul II called upon the churches to engage cannot simply be about how the Papacy is understood or understands itself; it must also be about how other churches define themselves as church. If we are going to get beyond the present impasse, it seems to me that this matter must be understood and respected by all parties.[46]

Guroian goes on to detail the honour and esteem in which Peter has been held in the Armenian liturgical tradition before detailing the treatment of the papacy in relatively recent Armenian theology, including that of Malachia Ormanian of the nineteenth century and twentieth-century Catholicos Karekin I. On this basis, Guroian concludes that

> there is no objection, indeed, there would seem to be a strong consensual affirmation within the Armenian tradition, that the Roman See ascended to universal primacy of honor at a relatively early date and that this *primus inter pares* was widely recognized and may still be not only desirable for the good of all but "necessary" to the success of the mission of the church in our time.

Such a claim is qualified by the need for "more discussion and clarification" about the role of the bishop of Rome as successor of Peter and whether that role "must . . . include the power of the Bishop of Rome to speak *ex cathedra* for not just his own church, but also for all of the churches" (20).

Guroian concludes by arguing that Rome needs to undertake the first step of kenosis, emptying itself of claims to "magisterial authority as defined by the Council of Trent and First Vatican Council over the other churches" (21).[47] If this is done, then while "there is no guarantee that the Orthodox churches would respond in the same spirit of charity and self-sacrifice" there is at least a chance that progress might be made (21).

David Bentley Hart

Hart's paper, "The Myth of Schism,"[48] is a characteristically pungent analysis that gets straight to the fundamental questions and engages in some "swamp-clearing" (to borrow a phrase of Stanley Hauerwas) by bluntly affirming several things that few Orthodox have said. Hart begins by arguing that *UUS* was an "extraordinary overture. . . . Indeed, it was so surprising a gesture that neither the Orthodox nor the Catholic Churches seems yet to know how to react to it." Hart suggests that "it may be the case that the one singular failure of the early Church was in not convoking a council to deal with the matter of ecclesiology as a properly doctrinal locus. It is here, perhaps, where all other problems come to rest" (1).

After noting that disagreements over papal primacy "remain at the very center of what separates us" (8), Hart raises an important question to which attention will be given here in later chapters: "What is the unique dignity of the apostolic office of patriarch, and what is its jurisdictional authority, and how does it relate to the pre-eminent patriarchate occupied by the bishop of Rome?" (9).

Thomas Hopko

Of all the literature reviewed here, Hopko's paper is *sui generis* because of its exact specifications detailing all the changes the Orthodox wish to see not just to the papacy but also to the liturgical, canonical, spiritual, and parochial structures and practices of the Roman Catholic Church. He himself seems to note this—"I can hardly speak on behalf of the Eastern Orthodox churches about the exercise of the Roman

papacy in our time" but, "encouraged by Pope John Paul's request for
forthright dialogue," he goes on to "list what I believe must happen if
the Orthodox churches would consider recognizing the bishop of
Rome as their world leader who exercises presidency among all the
churches of Christ."[49]

In compact fashion at the outset, Hopko argues that

> the Roman Church's current official teachings about papal privilege and
> power that are unacceptable to the Eastern Orthodox churches are the
> dogma of the pope's infallibility when speaking officially "from the chair
> of Peter (*ex cathedra Petri*)" on matters of faith and morals "from himself
> and not from the consensus of the church (*ex sese et non ex consensu ec-
> clesiae*)"; the binding character of the pope's infallible decrees on all
> (Catholic) Christians in the world; the pope's direct episcopal jurisdiction
> over all (Catholic) Christians in the world; the pope's authority to ap-
> point, and so also to depose, the bishops of all (Catholic) Christian
> churches; and the affirmation that the legitimacy and authority of all
> (Catholic) Christian bishops in the world derive from their union with
> the Roman see and its bishop, the Supreme Pontiff, the unique Successor
> of Peter and Vicar of Christ on earth. (3)

From here, Hopko moves directly—almost abruptly—to a long list
of further very specific changes that he thinks must be made. What is
especially unique about Hopko's paper is not only the extremely forthright nature of his proscriptions, but that they cover aspects of the
Catholic Church that are untouched by any other writer reviewed
here.[50] Only after having listed these desired changes does Hopko return to the papacy and begin to unpack some of his more condensed
requirements. He details the "structural and administrative changes
[that] must occur if the Pope of Rome will be accepted and recognized
as the bishop who exercises presidency among the churches and serves
as Christianity's world leader." These changes include the election of
the pope by the people and clergy of the Church of Rome and the
abolition of the College of Cardinals; the local election of all bishops
and the consequent abolition of papal authority to make episcopal appointments; the abolition of any congregation in Rome responsible for

taking disciplinary measures in matters of doctrine; the dismantling of most of the Roman Curia; and the end of the pope as an "official head of state" (8).

In contrast to his earlier "high octane" rhetoric, Hopko concludes his paper with studied understatement by noting that "enormous goodwill, energy and time would be necessary to refashion the papacy" along his desired lines. To his credit, he goes on to note that "the Orthodox churches would surely have to undergo many humbling changes" as well, being ready to "sacrifice everything, excepting only the faith itself, for the sake of building a common future together. . . . Like Roman Catholics and Protestants, they would have to be willing to die with Christ" (9).

Theodore Stylianopoulos

At a 2003 symposium in Rome organized to solicit Orthodox responses to *UUS,* Stylianopoulos, an emeritus professor at Holy Cross Greek Orthodox School of Theology in Brookline, Massachusetts, argued that "the Orthodox Church has long nurtured profound respect for a qualified primacy of the Church of Rome and its revered pontiff."[51] Stylianopoulos lists two qualifications on that primacy, noting that the first Orthodox "concern is about the nature and extent of that primacy. . . . The other concern is about the nature of the succession of Peter's dignity and function."[52]

Stylianopoulos then points out that the question of papal primacy cannot be adjudicated solely or simply on the basis of the Petrine texts in the New Testament. "Rather, the witness of the tradition as a whole must be taken into serious consideration as long as that tradition is judged to be not contradictory to the biblical witness" (42). In the end, we can speak biblically and traditionally about a "Petrine function, a special mandate and commission to Peter which is distinct in some undefined manner from that of the other disciples" (49). That lack of clear definition means that "Peter is a preeminent figure in the New Testament but not the only one. No single apostolic figure enjoys universal dominance or exclusive authority in the New Testament. In other words, the 'primacy' of Peter is not power over other apostolic figures but an authorized leadership in the context of shared apostolic authority in the common life of the Church" (61).

Stylianopoulos concludes his research by arguing that "the practical challenge of unity, as well as the theological urgency behind it, favor the value of a visible universal leader, just as they favor a visible local leader in the person of the bishop." That universal leader, however, must exercise an office "fully based on the principles of shared authority, love, and service, rather than on exclusive status, rights, and jurisdiction" (63).

Nicolae Durā

At the same 2003 symposium in Rome, the Romanian Orthodox theologian Nicolae Durā presented a paper on the papacy, a question he did not hesitate to recognize as "the most difficult to solve" of all those facing the Orthodox-Catholic dialogue.[53] Durā begins by noting that part of that difficulty stems from the complexity of offices which inhere in the papacy, arguing that sorting out papal from patriarchal roles remains "an area still open for our common work to find satisfactory answers and solutions" (164). Additional questions to be asked include "under what kind of primacy are placed the members of the churches interested in the restoration of full communion with the bishop of Rome. Is it a 'primacy' of charity, of service for unity, or a primacy that 'is more than government'?" (167).

After his review of the canonical literature, Durā concludes that in searching for data on the concept and practice of a "Petrine ministry," "it is evident that no canon makes any mention or allusion to it. This legislation speaks neither of the 'Petrine ministry' nor of a primatial office of the bishop of Rome as successor of Saint Peter" (185). From this, however, Durā warns against concluding that there is not and should not be any such thing as a Petrine ministry. On the contrary, he argues for expanding horizons and that "the whole tradition of the Church, Orthodox and Catholic—biblical, liturgical, patristic, historical, and so forth—must be taken into account, from the apostolic period up to our own time, in order to better discover the principal role of the bishop of Rome at the service of the unity of the ecumenical

Church" (186). In sum, what is still wanting, Durā says, is a "compara-tive study that can evaluate—*sine ira et studio*—all Orthodox and Catholic ecclesiological data" about the Petrine primacy.

Vlasios Pheidas

Also at the 2003 symposium Vlasios Pheidas of the Greek Orthodox Church, who teaches theology at the University of Athens and in the Institut de Théologie Orthodoxe d'Etudes Supérieures at Chambésy in Switzerland, presented "Papal Primacy and Patriarchal Pentarchy in the Orthodox Tradition."[54] After reviewing some of the relevant data, Pheidas argues that "the Orthodox canonical tradition has always con-sidered the papal primacy" within the threefold "framework" of "eu-charistic ecclesiology," "the extraordinary prerogatives due to the *prima sedes* in the canonical institution of the patriarchal pentarchy," and "the operation of the conciliar institution, notably of the ecumenical coun-cil." On this basis, Pheidas concludes that only by returning to the prac-tices which obtained in the first millennium will there be a sufficient basis for agreement about the papacy—"all that was not attested in the first millennium lacks the ecclesiological and canonical premises that are necessary to serve as a starting point for the dialogue" (81).

Hilarion Alfeyev

The Russian Orthodox bishop of Vienna and noted theologian Hi-larion Alfeyev, in a recently published book,[55] frankly acknowledges that Orthodoxy lacks a single centre of co-ordination and authority and that such a lack has created numerous problems for Orthodoxy, especially in North America. He acknowledges not only that there are "serious differences between the East and the West in the understand-ing of the primacy of the bishop of Rome" (53) but—perhaps echo-ing Schmemann—that the question of primacy generally understood is one that has not yet been adequately and satisfactorily resolved by and among the Orthodox—"at the pan-Orthodox level the principle of primacy (other than a primacy of honour) has not yet been wholly clarified, while the principle of catholicity exists without any stable mechanisms for its practical realization." Alfeyev therefore calls for "a serious and responsible discussion of the theme of primacy at an inter-Orthodox level" in order to enable the JIC to be able to come to one mind on this matter (55).

Alfeyev is reluctant to commit to a firm Orthodox position on papal primacy until such an inter-Orthodox discussion happens, but he does nonetheless suggest that, at a minimum, three things would need to be clarified: first, "the recognition of the primacy of the bishop of Rome must be preceded by the restoration of the unity of faith, the unity of the dogmatic tradition of the ancient undivided church" (53). Second, the claims of the universal "jurisdiction of the bishop of Rome over the bishops of the Orthodox churches in the case of the restoration of unity" must also be considered by the JIC and a consensus reached. Third and finally, the "dogma of the infallibility of the pope . . . is unacceptable to Orthodox sensibilities" and must be dealt with (54).

Toward a Synthetic Conclusion

Based on the foregoing, is it possible to arrive at something of an Orthodox consensus about the papacy? Are there points of convergence in these many theologians? Notwithstanding the important cautions of Erickson and Lossky about a diversity of Orthodox positions, clearly there are areas of consensus and agreement.

First, Orthodoxy endorses a certain primacy of Rome as an indubitable fact of history from which no one can dissent. In so doing, of course, Orthodoxy immediately insists that Roman primacy be sharply qualified and pared down from its current *plenitudo potestatis,* but at the very least Orthodoxy is generally prepared to grant Rome such primacy as was enjoyed in the first millennium and is prepared to grant to Rome, in a reunited Church, at least that much authority again.

Second, several Orthodox theologians recognize not only the historic reality of Roman primacy but the present necessity of it, not least in view of the jurisdictional chaos of Orthodoxy, especially in North America. The Roman primacy, then, is a clear way to re-establish the good of canonical order in the Church, a gift much needed by all.

Third, Orthodoxy embraces Roman primacy as having the character of a centre of appeal (following the Council of Sardica), of co-ordination, and, especially, of pastoral solicitude for all the Churches, particularly those in turmoil or undergoing persecution. The bishop of Rome, for most Orthodox theologians, would not be a toothless titular head of the Church but would have real responsibilities in summoning all the Churches together, cautioning the wayward, building up the bonds of brotherly unity, ensuring proper canonical procedures, witnessing to a unity of doctrine and morals even when unpopular, and promulgating the decisions of the synod of bishops of which he would be collegial (and not monarchical) head according to the model of a patriarch and his synod. He would, in other words, have more authority than the Ecumenical Patriarch but much less of the *plenitudo potestatis* the pope of Rome currently possesses.[56]

These three areas of positive consensus are matched by at least as many objections to current aspects of the papacy. Orthodoxy seems to be of one mind in rejecting at least three aspects of the papacy as it is currently constructed.

First, *universal jurisdiction* is both completely foreign to, and therefore totally rejected by, Orthodox ecclesiology and polity as based in the history of the early Church. There is not, and cannot be, any supreme *juridical power* or *domination* by one bishop over the other bishops, who are sacramental equals in their stewardship of the eucharistic mysteries. Metropolitan Kallistos is perhaps the clearest: it is "a universal 'power of jurisdiction'" from which "the Orthodox feel compelled to dissent."[57] Such jurisdiction is regarded as both historically and canonically unsupported and theologically unjustifiable. It is unacceptable to the East not only because of its culture and historical practice of local autocephaly, but also because such a claim is irreconcilable with Orthodox Trinitarian doctrine in the light of which Orthodox ecclesiology is to be understood. As Harkianakis and Clapsis make clear: "Trinitarian ecclesiology also develops the insight that there is one Church as there is one nature in God, but the very best way to express the oneness of the Church is the communion of the many local churches"[58] whose eucharistic unity is manifested concretely in a synodal and conciliar manner rather than in the oneness of an omnipotent and universal pope.

From Afanasiev onward, Orthodox ecclesiology in the twentieth century has been returning to its roots in the Eucharist, striving to purge any juridicism or universalism from within its midst and replace it with an *ecclesiology of communion*. The second point of wide agreement in Orthodoxy rejects any notion of papal primacy understood in a juridical or extra-sacramental way exercised without a corresponding relationship to a synod of brother bishops whose unity is manifested above all in the celebration of one Eucharist rather than in the functioning of one office. Such a synod would function along the lines of a patriarchal synod, with the two maintaining a tension between the one and the many, each of whose responsibilities would be clearly articulated.

The third point of consensus is that the pope is first and foremost a bishop and, to the extent that he exercises authority he does so sacramentally as a bishop and ecclesiastically as the first bishop and patriarch of the ancient and still venerable first see of Rome. Orthodoxy generally knows no other means for expressing primacy than the episcopal, metropolitical, and patriarchal offices, and to the extent that the current responsibilities and powers of the bishop of Rome are not clearly similar in scope to these three, Orthodoxy rejects them. Roman primacy must be tied to a clear exercise of conciliarity, synodality, and collegiality, and never exercised apart from these manifestations of fraternal episcopal relations.

These six areas of agreement—three positive assessments, three negative rejections—among Orthodox theologians on the papacy are not exhaustive of the entire Orthodox tradition. Each position is not an official one adopted by the respective Church of the theologian in question. Moreover, there is no complete agreement. Nonetheless, there is considerable consensus on the key points. What follows is an attempt to build on that consensus and extend it in a manner that, it is hoped, will be at once ecumenically sensitive and also responsive to Catholic concerns. For reasons laid out in the next chapter, the most plausible way of doing this seems to be through recovery of the patriarchal office as one crucial component in the reconfiguration of the Roman papacy.

CHAPTER THREE

A Renewed Roman Patriarchate

Catholic Perspectives

Although there are some differences among Orthodox theologians on acceptable models for papal primacy, in general Orthodox thought converges on the model of the patriarchate and upholds this as being not only central to Orthodox ecclesiology but a model whose resurrection by Rome could play a central part in reconfiguring the papacy in an ecumenically acceptable manner. What would be the best form of patriarchate or patriarchates for the papacy to take? Are there models of patriarchates among the Orthodox Churches that could, *mutatis mutandis,* form the foundation for the resurrection of the Roman patriarchate? In other words, which Orthodox patriarchate(s) most clearly resembles or embodies that form of leadership that the Orthodox themselves have insisted should be manifest in the papacy? While no one model would lend itself to reproduction or imitation by Rome, several models each contain singular features that, drawn together in a composite, could conceivably form a patriarchate at once recognizable to the Orthodox and also acceptable to the Catholic Church.

However, I begin with an apologia for undertaking this line of argument in view of the decision in March 2006 to abolish the title "Patriarch of the West" as it appears in the *Annuario Pontificio.*[1] This decision, which is still lacking a convincing rationale[2] (that is to say that the given rationale analyzed below is less than convincing and raises as many questions as it answers, and has also been presented with an unmistakeable if intangible sense of being only the first step in an unclear sequence), was an enormous surprise if not shock to virtually everyone. This decision would seem to undercut *rapprochement* with the Orthodox—as some Catholic ecumenists[3] thought immediately after the deletion was announced, and as some Orthodox fearfully suggested in print. This surprise decision, problematic though it is for some reasons—methodological as well as substantial—need not be regarded as destructive of the hopes for a resurrected patriarchal office in the papacy. My reasons for saying this are essentially twofold.

First, the statement issued by Rome to clarify this egregious decision noted that "if we wish to give the term 'West' a meaning applicable to ecclesiastical juridical language, it could be understood only in reference to the Latin Church. In this way, the title 'Patriarch of the West' would describe the Bishop of Rome's special relationship with the Latin Church, and his special jurisdiction over her."[4] I find nothing problematic in this statement and in fact it is a perceptive reading of the issues at hand. Indeed, the statement seems to suggest that the concept of distinguishing between the numerous papal roles[5] is still an important task, both for the internal life of the Catholic Church and for her ecumenical relations with other Christians, above all the Orthodox. The statement would seem to leave the door open to, at the very least, a patriarch-like role for the bishop and pope of Rome, a role captured in the title "Patriarch of the West" or, as I prefer, "Patriarch of Rome." Quite apart from the geographical ambiguity involved in the former rendition, it is completely *sui generis* to have one patriarch in the Church not clearly bound to a see-city.[6] All the other ancient patriarchs of the Church are clearly styled as patriarchs of their see-city: Constantinople, Alexandria, Antioch, and Jerusalem. The patriarchates of more recent origin generally follow this (e.g., Moscow) or, at most, claim to be patriarch of a given country with attachment to a particular see-city (e.g., the head of the Bulgarian Orthodox Church is styled the "Patriarch of Bulgaria and Metropolitan of Sofia"[7]). Only Rome retained an ill-defined title.[8]

The second reason given by the PCPCU in rationalizing this decision was that the Latin Church has for many centuries not operated as a patriarchate and today seems to be inclined to move toward greater reliance on episcopal conferences, in which, the statement says, the Church, seems to have "found . . . the canonical structure best suited to the needs of the Latin Church today."[9] This argument will be taken up in the fifth chapter, where I will propose that these episcopal conferences be reconfigured in such a way as to be established as patriarchates within the Roman Church.

A third and much more fundamental reason for persisting in arguing in favour of the resurrection of a patriarchal office for the bishop of Rome was itself given (somewhat incredibly) by Rome in abolishing the title: ecumenical sensitivity. The document issued by the PCPCU stresses—as did Achille Cardinal Silvestrini, former prefect of the Congregation for the Eastern Churches, in early comments[10]—that this decision has above all sought to "prove useful to ecumenical dialogue."

The usefulness of this decision is rather recondite; its capacity to stir up ecumenical dialogue is not. It has manifestly generated much discussion and not a little anxiety on the part of the Orthodox, all of whom have insisted that the decision is an infelicitous one and must be re-thought. Of all the papal titles to drop, this is the least likely candidate because it is the title most familiar to the Orthodox themselves. Hilarion Alfeyev, bishop of Vienna of the Russian Orthodox Church, was first off the mark to say that

> it is not at all clear how the removal of the title could possibly ameliorate Catholic-Orthodox relations. It seems that the omission of the title "Patriarch of the West" is meant to confirm the claim to universal church jurisdiction that is reflected in the pope's other titles, and if the Orthodox reaction to the gesture will not be positive, it should not be a surprise.[11]

Hilarion went on to say that the now abolished title was one that the Orthodox most clearly recognized. The other titles are the problematic ones: "In this context unacceptable and even scandalous, from the Orthodox point of view, are precisely those titles that remain in the list, i.e. Vicar of Jesus Christ, Successor of the Prince of the Apostles,

Supreme Pontiff of the Universal Church." The first is unacceptable because "according to the Orthodox teaching, Christ has no 'vicar' who would govern the universal Church in his name." The second "has been criticized in Orthodox polemical literature from Byzantine time onwards." And the third title,

> "supreme pontiff of the Universal Church" points to the pope's universal jurisdiction which is not and will never be recognized by the Orthodox Churches. It is precisely this title that should have been dropped first, had the move been motivated by the quest for "ecumenical progress" and desire for amelioration of the Catholic-Orthodox relations.[12]

Many of the same arguments were advanced in a letter written on 17 March 2006 by Archbishop Christodoulos of Athens and all Greece and in an announcement from Constantinople in June 2006. In the cordial letter of "deep concern" written to Pope Benedict "with the profoundest benevolent respect and in the spirit of fraternal love and mutual concern for the promotion of Christian unity," Archbishop Christodoulos speaks of the "unease of many who feel that by dropping the title of 'Patriarch of the West'" the JIC, about to begin meeting again in 2006, "will be deprived of a common basis upon which they could build the reunification of our Churches, a reunification that we all desire. For us Orthodox, the Pope of Elder Rome has always been the Patriarch of the West."[13] Given this long-standing history and recognition of the pope as patriarch, the archbishop underscores the point that "the title of Patriarch of the West is fundamentally important for the ecclesiology of the Orthodox Church" and then advances the argument that this title is also "important even in terms of the Catholic Church alone" and her polity and structures. The letter concludes by disputing one of the reasons given by the PCPCU in its clarification—"the argument that the title hinders the establishment of several patriarchates in the West and therefore should be suppressed is groundless."[14]

In early June, some of these arguments were put forth anew in a declaration from the patriarchal synod in Constantinople.[15] This longer, more detailed statement reiterates certain points from the two above-mentioned Orthodox responses, including the point that the removal of the title "Patriarch of the West" from the Pontifical Year-book of this year, as well as the retention of the above mentioned titles [Vicar of Christ, Supreme Pontiff of the Universal Church], have a particular importance for the relations between the Orthodox and the Roman-Catholic Churches, especially now in view of the reopening of the official Theological Dialogue between the two Churches, given that this Theological Dialogue will also deal with the issue of Primacy in the Church. (§1)

That this title has been abolished while others remain is a "point . . . of extreme importance to the Orthodox Church"; these titles "create serious difficulties to the Orthodox, given that they are perceived as implying a universal jurisdiction of the bishop of Rome over the entire Church, which is something the Orthodox have never accepted" (§5).

The statement goes on to note that "of all the titles that are used by the Pope, the only one that goes back to the period of the Undivided Church of the first millennium, and which has been accepted in the conscience of the Orthodox Church is the title of 'Patriarch of the West.'"[16] The statement offers some historical examples of the use of this title and the rationale for it before arguing that "the consciousness of the geographical limits of each ecclesiastical jurisdiction has never ceased to be a basic component of Orthodox ecclesiology" (§2). This emphasis on geography is stated differently a little later in the document, where the synod first insists that it would "be unthinkable for the Orthodox ecclesiology to denounce the geographical principle and to replace it with a 'cultural' one in the structure of the Church. The unity of the Church cannot be conceived as a sum of culturally distinct Churches, but as a unity of local, namely geographically determined, Churches."[17] Given such a geographic base,

the removal of the title "Patriarch of the West" must not lead to the absorption of the clearly distinct geographical ecclesiastical "jurisdictions" by a "universal" Church, consisting of Churches which are distinguished on the basis of either "culture" or "confession" or "rite." Even in today's historical circumstances, the one Church must, from an ecclesiological point of view, be considered as a unity of full local Churches. (§4)

The statement concludes by expressing the hope that, in this year of the recommencement of the JIC this decision will not jeopardize the progress toward unity—"the Ecumenical Patriarchate expresses its wish and prayer that no further difficulties may be added in the discussion of such a thorny problem, as that of the primacy of the bishop of Rome" (§6). In a final twist, the statement concludes by finding it

> appropriate to recall the view of Professor Joseph Ratzinger, now Pope Benedict XVI, published some years ago, that "Rome cannot demand from the East regarding the primacy issue more than what has been expressed and applied during the first millennium." If such a principle is accompanied by an ecclesiology of "koinonia–communion" through placing every aspect of primacy within the context of the synodical structure of the Church, this would greatly facilitate the effort to solve a very serious issue for the unity of the Church of Christ. (§6)

The decision to abolish the title has unwittingly unleashed a very great deal of ecumenical anxiety among the Orthodox who are not prepared simply to endure this abrupt and totally unexpected change without protest.[18] The Orthodox have made it clear that this decision has major implications not only for the dialogue but for the relationship as it now exists: the synodal statement argues that "by retaining these titles and discarding the 'Patriarch of the West' the term and concept of 'sister Churches' between the Roman-Catholic and Orthodox Church becomes hard to use" (§5). The decision cannot avoid being seen as a substantial ecumenical blunder, the solution to which the Orthodox have articulated: a reinstatement of the title.

Theological Literature on the Roman Patriarchate

A reinstatement is merely the beginning and but the minimum thing to do. What is really required is a serious and substantial reconfiguration of the papacy so that the papal and patriarchal roles are much more differentiated and, as a result, the "patriarch of the West" is not merely an empty ornament on the page of the papal yearbook but an actual office with serious responsibilities exercised in conjunction with the papacy for the unity of the Church of Christ. In favour of this differentiation of offices, a further reason arises to justify holding on to the title Patriarch of the West: the considerable body of *Catholic* theological literature of the last forty years represented by the following Catholic thinkers.[19]

Joseph Ratzinger

The first theologian to argue for such a differentiation was none other than Joseph Ratzinger himself, who was one of the first Catholic theologians of the twentieth—or, indeed, of any—century to write about the patriarchal office in general and, in particular about the need for that office to be disentangled from the papal. In many ways, he launched this trajectory in Catholic ecclesiological and ecumenical reflection in the postconciliar period—which makes the reasoning behind his actions as pope all the more obscure.

In a frank series of articles published from 1964 onward, Ratzinger admitted that the confusion between the pope as bishop of Rome and as patriarch of the West was "the starting point for the split between East and West."[20] The fault for this is to be found in both the exigencies of history and in an ascendant sense of Roman superiority—"the Roman church was even less able to distinguish between its Petrine responsibility for the whole Church and the specific position history had given it in the Latin West" (204). Such a failure to distinguish the offices of pope and patriarch led to "extreme centralization of the Catholic Church," the answer to which, Ratzinger concluded, is that "in the future they should be more clearly distinguished" (206). Ratzinger went so far as to suggest that "someday perhaps Asia and Africa should be made patriarchates distinct from the Latin church."[21]

The divisions between East and West, Ratzinger argued in more detail elsewhere, were sown early on as the bishops and Church of Rome came to mistake the deference shown them by the East on account of their orthodoxy *as a Church* (especially during the Arian crisis and later similar crises) for submission to a purported sense of primacy *of their bishop* that was thought to belong to Rome by right (whether apostolic or political). Thus did the Roman Church come to confuse not patriarchal and papal offices but, even more fundamentally, a primacy of orthodoxy and unity in faith for a primacy of administration.[22] In addition, over time Rome came to forget that "Rome is in principle the equal of the other Patriarchs on the same plane."[23] Having forgotten this, Rome then as now fails to "consider that a number of functions that we usually see today as flowing from the Primacy were originally understood as a result of the Patriarchal dignity, such as the right of liturgical legislation, participation in the nomination and deposition of Bishops, and similar areas of competency on the level of ecclesiastical discipline."[24] Even more bluntly, Ratzinger argues that "only the Faith is indivisible" while "everything else may be diverse, including even independent functions of governance, as were realized in the 'primacies' or Patriarchates in the ancient Church."[25] Ratzinger concludes that

> one must therefore consider it a task of the future to distinguish clearly once again the authentic office of the Successor of Peter from the Patriarchal office and, where necessary, create new Patriarchates without considering them any longer part of the Latin Church. To accept unity with the Pope does not mean, then, to belong to one administrative whole, but simply to be part of a unity of faith and of communion, recognizing that the Pope has the power to interpret in a binding way the revelation wrought by Christ, and submitting oneself to this interpretation when it is made in a definitive way. This means that union with Eastern Christianity does not need to change anything at all of the latter's concrete ecclesial life.[26]

Ratzinger was not alone in reflecting on the patriarchal office but he was certainly among the first and indubitably remains the most influential.[27] He would, to be fair, attenuate his thinking somewhat in certain places toward the end of the twentieth century, including in the book-length interview *God and the World: A Conversation with Peter Seewald,* but nonetheless strongly reiterated that "there is no doubt that we need such supra-regional associations, which can then take over some of the work from Rome."[28]

Yves Congar

Yves Cardinal Congar, a towering giant of twentieth-century Catholic theology and ecumenism, also reflected on the question of Rome as a patriarchate, which he called "une realité trop négligée." Congar's treatment, which he called "très modeste," argued that the idea of Rome as a patriarchate is "difficile et aussi neuf" to the point that not a few have said "c'est une fiction."[29] In Congar's words, "the notion of patriarch has been neither understood nor honored by Rome."[30] Nonetheless, Congar goes on to ask: "is it possible, is it reasonable, is it realistic to imagine the structure of a reunited Church in the form of collegiality concretized in the collegiality of patriarchs?"[31] Congar concludes by acknowledging that recognition of a distinction between patriarchal and papal powers of the bishop of Rome would not necessarily alter anything in the concrete life of the Latin Church but would nonetheless have enormous ecumenical value.

J.-M. R. Tillard

In his *Church of Churches,* the renowned ecumenist Jean-Marie Roger Tillard has spoken of the "quasi-identification" of the office of the "Bishop of Rome . . . and that of the patriarchal authority." He says flatly that these two "have almost become one and the same. . . . Since the exercise of the primacy assumes several of these characteristics of the exercise of the patriarchate, it can no longer be seen in all its purity. It appears under a disguise which no longer permits an adequate perception of its identity."[32] Tillard goes on to state that "the quasi-confusion of his authority as primate of all the Churches and his function as patriarch of the West, inducing him to act with the bishops of other patriarchates in the way which his title as patriarch of the West authorized him to do so in the West, has caused a problem" (271). The answer to this, Tillard argues, is that "the Bishop of Rome should not interfere in such a way that he would act like a super-patriarch. His primacy must be inscribed within the network of episcopal functions and hierarchies proper to these ecclesial bodies, without violating their dignity and the perception they have of being responsible for their own fidelity to a long tradition" (272).

J. Michael Miller

Archbishop Miller, who long served in the Roman Curia before taking up an appointment in 2007 as archbishop of Vancouver, wrote about the papacy and ecumenism for his doctoral thesis in 1980 and then again in 1995 in his *The Shepherd and the Rock: Origins, Development and Mission of the Papacy.*[33] This book, while striving to be an "apologetic" treatment of Catholic papal claims, is marked by a balanced and nuanced treatment of the Christian East, whose counterclaims are treated irenically.[34] In the concluding chapter of his book, Miller recognizes that the papacy has changed and will continue to change—"the theology of the Petrine ministry is still an uncompleted task and a continuing challenge" (346). In addition to the theology, the historical form of the papacy has changed and will continue to change in the face of challenges from other Christians (354–58). Miller, following Ratzinger, Hermann Pottmeyer, and others, frankly admits that "many powers and rights acquired over the centuries do not belong to the nature of Peter's ministry. If the good of the Church required it, they could be pruned. Innovative ways of discharging the Petrine ministry will undoubtedly be developed in the future" (359).

One such "innovation" that Miller especially highlights as necessary and important is his "thesis 16" that "the specific Petrine ministry of the bishop of Rome should be more clearly distinguished from his duties as patriarch of the West" (359). Miller notes that the pope exercises diocesan, regional, patriarchal, and universal jurisdiction and says that "the pope's jurisdictional primacy over the whole Church should be more clearly differentiated from his patriarchal authority over the Latin church" so that "when full communion is restored, the bishop of Rome would refrain from exercising his patriarchal authority over the East" (359–60).

Christopher O'Donnell

The Carmelite theologian O'Donnell, in an article published in 1996, began by recognizing that "a large measure of the misunderstanding between East and West centers on issues concerning patriarchs. Moreover, in recent years the notion of patriarch is seen to have major ecumenical significance."[35] O'Donnell reviews the history of the title before acknowledging that throughout history the "bishop of Rome had the title of patriarch" but never "had any real idea of what the patriarchal system represented" because "all power is subsumed in the papal primacy" (353). This, of course, is problematic, and O'Donnell argues that, pending further or more major reconfigurations to the papacy, at the very least "the Vatican . . . could attempt to act in the Latin Church in a more patriarchal way; at present the style of the Curia is perceived as bureaucratic, and occasionally as autocratic. Legitimate authority cannot afford to ignore even a false perception of itself if it is to be effective and life-giving" (354). O'Donnell goes on to conclude that

> the fusion of the canonically, if not indeed theologically, distinct offices of local bishop, Western patriarch, and Supreme Pontiff is perhaps not the best way forward for the renewed papacy that will be necessary if Christian unity is to be fostered. A self-conscious exercise by the bishop of Rome of his office as patriarch of the West could, in appropriate circumstances, only strengthen the patriarchal life of the Eastern Churches and gratify those Eastern Churches not in communion with the bishop of Rome. (354)

Hermann Pottmeyer

The contemporary German theologian Pottmeyer has written a very lucid and nuanced book on the ways in which the claims of the First Vatican Council in particular can be reconciled with the demands of ecumenism.[36] Following the early lead of Ratzinger, Pottmeyer goes on to reiterate that "many of the de facto papal functions developed originally from the position of the bishop of Rome as Latin patriarch— functions that have nothing to do with his office as successor of Peter. This realization would open the way along which reform can advance" (122). An advance in reform, Pottmeyer says, depends on dealing with the problem of "papal centralization. . . . In dealing with this problem, the separation of the pope's primatial and patriarchal competences is an important element of the solution" (124) so that what Pottmeyer quotes Ratzinger as calling the "'universal patriarchate'" of Rome is dismantled and its various components differentiated once again. Such a task must "be matched by a breaking-up of the functions of the Roman Curia" (134).

One other important element, Pottmeyer stresses, is the creation of genuinely "triadic" ecclesial structures, replacing the typical dipartite model of Roman ecclesiology—"the renewal and further development of the triadic form of church structure is, then, an essential condition for the church to regain its original distinctive form as a communion of churches" (134).[37] In this new model, there must be "regional ecclesiastical units, especially the patriarchal churches" (132).

Frederick Bliss

The Catholic ecumenist Frederick Bliss, a professor of theology at the Angelicum in Rome, has amplified the line of argumentation first set forth by Joseph Ratzinger. In his 1999 book, *Catholic and Ecumenical*, Bliss argues that a "serious reappraisal of the patriarchal function of the bishop of Rome" is needed, noting that "this precise ministry has not been taken seriously in the west" because episcopal (local), regional, patriarchal, and primatial roles have all been subsumed into the one papal office. Bliss argues that "distinctions among these roles need to be made, and visibility given to the patriarchal task within the Latin Church. If the east finds this happening, they will see implied in the action, at least, a growing respect for the patriarchal concept that is so important to them." Bliss then explicitly cites Ratzinger's argument about countering centralization and conceptual confusion in the papacy by arguing that papal roles must "'be more clearly distinguished'."[38]

George Nedungatt

In 2001, the Jesuit canonist, George Nedungatt, published a very lengthy and informative article, "The Patriarchal Ministry in the Church of the Third Millennium," providing a comprehensive overview of the office in both Catholic and Orthodox circles, both currently and historically.[39] Noting that Rome is only very rarely understood as a patriarchate, and that some would wish to see this title abolished altogether as an anachronism or a diminution of the powers of the papacy,[40] Nedungatt argues that "both the titles 'Patriarch of Rome' and 'Patriarch of the West' are historical, official, and meaningful" (12). Nedungatt goes on to say that even though the offices of patriarch of the West and pope have been absorbed down through the ages ("the patriarchate has come to be regarded as a non-issue in the Western Church" [46]), one really must, "for the future progress of ecumenism, . . . distinguish between these two offices . . . following the tradition of the first millennium" (13).[41] Failure to do so places

> the ecumenical future of the Church . . . in jeopardy. . . . For the ecumenical future of the Church it is important to appraise the patriarchal ministry seen as an episcopal ministry and succeeding to the apostolic ministry in the *kairos* of the Church: an ecclesiological vision that still awaits deepening and development in the light of the collegiality of the Second Vatican Council. (85)

Myriam Wijlens

The canonist Myriam Wijlens published an article in 2001 about the place of intermediate structures in the Catholic Church.[42] While examining those structures, Wijlens undertook to note that an important ecclesiological and ecumenical task consists in "identifying what the role of the Patriarch of the West is. That then in turn could provide a clarification on the position of the Roman Pontiff: what belongs to the office of Roman Pontiff and what to the Patriarch of the Latin Church? The answer to these issues could be useful to the dialogue with the other churches."[43] Wijlens then speculates on the reasons why the papal and patriarchal roles have not been differentiated and the fact that the latter role was totally ignored by Vatican II, the 1983 *Code of Canon Law,* and by nearly all Latin ecclesiologists and canonists—"from an ecclesiological perspective, the patriarchate of the West plays virtually no role in the structure of the Latin Church." Nonetheless, "still today many functions ascribed to the Roman Pontiff belong to the Patriarch of the West. An example of this concerns the appointment of bishops" (123). Wijlens concludes that it remains important to differentiate these roles—"a serious study of the role and function of the Latin patriarch is called for" (124).

Waclaw Hryniewicz

The ecumenist Waclaw Hryniewicz has recognized the importance of kenotic reforms to the papacy for it to be acceptable to the Orthodox, saying that mere "moral reform" will be insufficient when what is required "concretely . . . [is] the structural reform of the papacy." Such a reform, he has suggested, should manifest a differentiation between papal and patriarchal roles. As things stand now, the Church suffers from "ecclesiastical centralism and has remained one huge Western patriarchate." Consequently, "many papal actions and decisions, apparently primatial, belong in fact to the power of the Pope as Latin Patriarch, and concern only those within his patriarchal jurisdiction. Theoretically speaking the West could surely have developed more patriarchates."[44]

Hryniewicz recognizes that simply carving up the Western patriarchate, or creating new patriarchates, is not a simple proposition in a world where the geopolitical distinctions "East" and "West" have long since lost almost all meaning and peoples of all traditions are scattered in almost all lands. Nonetheless, he suggests that "one could . . . imagine a new structure of the reconciled Church in the form of a concrete collegiality of patriarchates both already existing . . . and those which should still be established. . . . Is this merely a utopian vision? It is surely not when one thinks in light of the ecclesiology of the ancient Church" (18).

Walter Kasper

The need for such a study is highlighted by many others writing on this topic, including Cardinal Kasper, former president of the PCPCU. Recently Kasper said that Ratzinger was correct in underscoring that "the issue—wrongly considered obsolete—of the place of Rome as patriarch of the West" is still an open question worth considering.[45] "[T]he issue is to disentangle the functions which have accrued to the papacy in the course of time. The important thing is to distinguish the essential and therefore indispensable duties of Petrine ministry from those duties which pertain to the Pope as the first bishop (patriarch or primate) of the Latin church, or have accrued over time" (83).

Patriarch Gregorios III

The Melkite Greek-Catholic patriarch of Antioch and the East, of Alexandria and Jerusalem, Gregorios III (Laham) has recently written in general terms about the usefulness of the "patriarchal principle" for Catholic-Orthodox unity, which he describes in terms of antinomic balance:

> The patriarchal principal, a balanced model of unity and synodality, of local autonomy and a system of integrated communion, rests on an ideal that must always inspire and assist us to find ecclesiological solutions for the new situations which confront the Church in the twenty-first century.[46]

In more particular terms, Gregorios argues that while we do not often hear the title "Patriarch of the West," and that it largely remains hidden or irrelevant—"l'évolution ecclésiologique de l'Occident Chrétien, le titre de 'Patriarche d'Occident' apparaît donc de nos jours comme passablement obsolete" (15)—amidst the complexity of papal history, nonetheless it is a legitimate and useful title with a demonstrable history—"Il paraît en effet incontestable qu'il ait existé un Patriarcat d'Occident dans les premiers siècles de l'histoire de l'Église" (14). Over time, however, especially into the early and high Middle Ages, that Roman patriarchate would be ignored and obscured in what Gregorios calls "une véritable absorption du rôle patriarcal de l'Évêque de Rome par son rôle primatial," an absorption that has ended up confusing the papal role with the patriarchal, and the patriarchal with the papal—"Les légitimes prérogatives primatiales du Pape de Rome, acceptées explicitement ou tacitement en Orient telles qu'elles sont exprimées en particulier par le canon 13 du Concile de Sardique (343), ont été justifiées, par certains papes, avec des arguments de juridiction directe qui relèvent en soi du rôle patriarcal" (15). To clear up some of this confusion of roles, it is necessary, with "une nuance d'ordre historique" (15) to differentiate the roles—"Tout d'abord, il nous apparaît capital de faire une distinction nette entre le ministère du Pape en tant qu'il a juridiction sur les fidèles de tradition latine, et son ministère pétrinien, voué à la préservation de la foi et de l'unité de l'Église" (27).

Such a differentiation of roles must have practical consequences and manifestations. In the first instance, "the centralized model proper to the *ad intra* functioning of the Latin Church cannot be applied to relations between the patriarchal or *sui juris* Churches."[47] In addition, Patriarch Gregorios calls for the creation, "around the person of the pope of an assembly of Oriental Catholic patriarchs whose role would be that of a kind of 'senate of the papacy' for a certain number of subjects."[48] In the end, Patriarch Gregorios suggests, reform of the papacy and differentiation of roles should have as its goal the possibility of a "patriarchal papacy"—"One can imagine a sort of 'super-patriarchate' that would bring together the different patriarchal Churches from the Roman communion."[49] Such a "super-patriarchate" will have its own unique character—it will not be a simple "Byzantinization" of Latin ecclesial models and structures—and will assist in realizing the goal of Christian unity:

> On the other hand, greater decentralization of the Roman Church, which could build on the patriarchal structure, would better define the exercise of the Petrine ministry and, in so doing, would render it more acceptable to other Christians. There is no question of our attempting to impose an Oriental ecclesiological model. But we want to imagine an ecclesiology for the twenty-first century that is neither Oriental nor Occidental but really Catholic: communion of autonomous Churches, synodality linked to a centre of unity, and collegiality . . . [that] is a living reflection of the divine Trinity.[50]

Michel Dymyd

The Ukrainian Greco-Catholic canonist and theologian Michel Dymyd has recently written a very sanguine article suggesting that the decision to abandon the title "Patriarch of the West" need not be a negative one and can portend positive changes in the structure of the Catholic Church. Dymyd, drawing heavily on Pottmeyer's work as well as Ratzinger's, advocates nine possible changes. First, a fresh attempt at separating papal from patriarchal powers must be made. Second, the Church today needs new regional centres of unity and thus there may be the possibility of creating new patriarchates in the East and the West, while third, the Latin Church should be divided into new patriarchates that conform to the cultural, geographic, and political realities of today's world. Fourth, a role for each individual bishop in the governing of the universal Catholic Church must be allowed, and fifth, a reinterpretation of the Vatican dogmas on the papacy and its relationship to the episcopate must be made. Sixth, a renewal of the Eastern traditions of theology, canon law, and pastoral life in conformity with their original ecclesial identity is needed. Seventh, there must be a greater emphasis on the Church as communion in every aspect; eighth, a new triadic structure to the Church must be developed; and ninth, a new emphasis on service must be given as the key manifestation of supreme authority in the Church. This should lead to an eighth genuinely ecumenical council for the reunion and renewal of all.[51]

Antoine Lévy

The Dominican theologian Antoine Lévy has recently suggested—albeit in a somewhat vague and romantic way—that the so-called college of patriarchs from the early Church should be revived today and used again as a vehicle for the expression of the collegiality and communion of East and West. Lévy, however, proposes that the usual model be stood on its head:

> We propose to invert the profound logic of the councils of union (Lyons 1274, Florence 1439). . . . In place of uniting the oriental patriarchs to the Roman see, while preserving the privileges of these patriarchs, we propose to re-establish communion between the oriental patriarchs and the Roman see while preserving the privileges of the bishop of Rome. . . . In place of an assimilation without condition of the patriarchs to the Church

of Rome, we suggest the re-establishment of a veritable collegial organism between the diverse patriarchs who make up the universal Church. In other terms, if the bishop of Rome wishes that his specific charism in favor of the communion of the Churches be received by the other patriarchs, he must himself first recover his identity as patriarch of the West. He will also be a member of the patriarchal college on an equal footing with those who, like him, represent their Church as both father and as head.[52]

Gisbert Greshake

The contemporary German theologian Gisbert Greshake, whose writings have been clearly influenced by Ratzinger's, has argued similar things, calling for the recovery of a triadic structure in the Church and renewed appreciation of the patriarchal office.[53] Greshake, however, goes "far beyond"[54] Ratzinger, in amplifying this argument and in calling for a triadic structure without which the "Church falls (and fell) into the danger of becoming sick."[55] He begins by saying that "through the loss of genuine Patriarchal structures, the Roman Catholic Church suffered a real loss of catholicity and of her incarnational structure."[56] The Churches of the East have also suffered a real loss though for different reasons. The answer to both losses is the same. In a passage well worth quoting *in extenso,* Greshake diagnoses both dangers and then offers a solution:

> In a merely dual structure, in the face of a strong primatial power—the danger of the West!—the weight and the meaning of the fullness of catholicity and synthesis demanded by the multifaceted incarnational character of the Church becomes weakened or even destroyed in favor of a Roman uniformity and centralization that impoverishes itself. *Or*—the danger of the East!—in the face of a *weak* or *contested* papal primatial power lies the threat that the Church will disintegrate into a multitude of local or particular (autocephalous) Churches that no longer realize any effective unity among themselves. Only a triadic . . . Church structure— one which realizes itself on these levels: local Church with her Bishop, principal Church with her *Protos,* universal Church with the Pope— guarantees that neither will the communion of the universal Church dis-

integrate into a multitude of local Churches . . . nor will [it] be . . . unable to bring the weight of catholicity to bear in the face of papal Primacy.[57]

A. Raphael Lombardi

Lombardi's recent book, *The Restoration of the Role of the Patriarch of the West,* is an exceedingly simple treatment entirely derivative in method and consisting of an attempt to balance "pro" and "con" arguments about the restoration of the patriarchate of the West.[58] His goal was to answer why the concept and role of patriarch in the West declined in the second millennium, and to inquire as to whether this decline was a contributing factor to East-West division (3). Lombardi notes that today any "proponents of such a model can expect to encounter a certain amount of inertial resistance from the centralizing bureaucrats of the Vatican" (7). In the end, Lombardi suggests on the one hand that the patriarchal model is a relic of history that is not part of "the mind of the Church today" (112) but concludes that "this multifaceted and complex problem of healing the schism among the Christian Churches seems to require further study and research" (113).

Geoffrey Robinson

The Australian Geoffrey Robinson, retired auxiliary bishop of the Roman Catholic Archdiocese of Sydney, has recently published *Confronting Power and Sex in the Catholic Church: Reclaiming the Spirit of Jesus,*[59] a work that addresses various issues connected to the scandal of sexual abuse of children by a small number of Roman Catholic priests. The book's larger purpose is to examine structural issues in the Catholic Church and her governance, and to that extent is useful for our purposes. Robinson is far more comprehensive in his vision for structural reform than anyone else examined here. He is not content with reforming the papacy and curia, but wants dramatic changes brought into Rome, the bishops, national and local churches, and even into parish governance.

Robinson proposes several things for reforming Catholic structures, including the necessity of moving to a tripartite and widely diffused structure involving many "players" and forms, of which I treat only the first two.[60] His "first level" consists of what he calls a "Peter-figure" who would still have overall responsibility for episcopal vigilance over the Church on questions of faith and morals (268–69). This "Peter-figure" would retain many of his current responsibilities and would be assisted by a revamped Roman Curia whose culture would need to be changed so that it no longer acts to boss other bishops around. Robinson proposes that the best way to change this culture is to ensure that none of its employees are bishops or cardinals, but simply priests and deacons, or lay people. Robinson argues that this Peter-figure "must not be reduced to a mere figurehead" but he is not specific on what exactly this figure would or would not do, save to note that "there should be legislation that clearly sets the Peter-figure within the church and accountable to the church. . . . Among other matters, it should set out when the Peter-figure must have the consent of, or at least consult with, the bishops and/or the whole Church" (269).

Robinson's second level is much more interesting and detailed and pertains to the episcopate. Here he proposes five new bodies whose existence would in fact have great ramifications on the papacy. First, the current synod of bishops needs to be changed to downgrade the number and role of Curialists in its deliberations and in its secretariat; its modus operandi should be changed to allow for less speech-making and more honest, open, freewheeling deliberation and frank discussion of "practical and pastoral matters" whose results should be a series of resolutions voted upon by all bishops of the world and then published directly (rather than being used as material for a post-synodal *papal* document, as currently happens) (273).

Second, he proposes "a council of the Church" should meet regularly—in varying forms Robinson does not specify—and this council, while likely composed in the majority by hierarchs, should not exclude lay people as well as "lower" clergy. If the synod of bishops deals with practical and pastoral matters, this council, like other ecumenical councils, should be charged with an examination of "matters of faith and morals" (273).

Third, and most interesting, Robinson proposes that Latin ecclesial structures be further divided and clarified beyond the simple local-universal dichotomy in place today. Here Robinson proposes "a system of government for the Latin Church based on that of the Eastern patri-archs," a system he awkwardly calls that of the "patriarch-president" (275)[61] who would be "elected by the bishops of that region and then appointed by the pope" (276).[62] He goes on to argue that

> there is no reason why the Latin Church could not be divided into a num-ber of different areas, with each of these areas having its own patriarch-president. There is no reason why each continent or, indeed, each nation could not have its own patriarch-president and the same level of auton-omy in running its own affairs as the Eastern patriarchs have. In other words, there is no reason why a system of government that is already highly respected within the Catholic Church could not be extended to the whole church. (255–76)[63]

Even more striking, Robinson goes on to suggest that "the roles of pope and patriarch of the Latin Church are two quite distinct roles *and there is no necessity that they both be held by the one person.*"[64] In other words, he proposes that the "person appointed to the office of patriarch of the Latin Church" need not be concomitantly the pope and bishop of Rome, but that these offices could be not merely differentiated—as everyone in the survey above has suggested—but actually divided and clearly separated so that the Latin patriarch would be simply one more patriarch alongside the "patriarch of the Copts or Melkites" (275). There would be numerous "Eastern" patriarchs in communion with the bishop of Rome, and numerous "Western" patriarchs as well. Robinson proposes not only the differentiation of papal and patriarchal roles, but the division of "the West" into multiple patriarchates, not exclud-ing the possibility of having even national patriarchs. The rationale for these latter, Robinson suggests, is that "there are occasions when the whole church of a particular nation *must* speak and act together" (277).[65] These patriarchs would "have a role of governance together with the pope," though in ways Robinson does not explicate (279).[66]

Michael Magee

The final and by far the most substantial and important treatment of patriarchates by a Catholic theologian comes in Michael Magee's recent, vast, and exacting work, which has superlatively teased out from history, beginning in the Old Testament period, progressing through the New Testament, Fathers, Ecumenical Councils, and continuing down to the present day, an understanding and a definition of "the patriarchal institution" as he calls it. All the other authors reviewed here have treated this question of patriarchates in short essays or in passing references: Magee alone has given the question sustained treatment. His careful and painstaking work gives detailed consideration to serious problems of historiography and the complexity of the task of treating the history of Rome as a patriarchate, noting that historically Rome has only rarely been understood or functioned as a patriarchate and that the origins of the institution itself are largely hidden since in the early Church roles were not yet well defined.[67]

The documentary evidence of even the very title ("Patriarch of the West" or "of Rome") is sparse and infrequently encountered, seemingly limited to a handful of references over the course of the last two millennia.[68] This is not surprising when one considers two facts: first, the origins of the patriarchal institution in general terms are largely hidden in history and therefore any attempt to pinpoint how exactly they were first defined or when they were first used is likely to be an impossible task.[69] The second reason why such references in Western ecclesiastical literature are so rare—why, that is, the title has almost never been invoked authoritatively—centres on the unique developments in and challenges to the Church in the West. The bishop of Rome, after the loss of the city's imperial status early in the fourth century and after the collapse of the city following various sackings, was often the only central authority, both ecclesial and "secular," and so sought to bring order using whatever claims to authority and power he could muster. In such a context it is not entirely surprising that the bishop of Rome did not often style himself as "Patriarch of the West" but instead reached for a seemingly more authoritative or more authoritative-sounding title or titles with which to emphasize unambiguously his authority—a kind of subsidiarity in reverse whereby "lower" titles, or titles pertaining only to a local area, were set aside in favour of such higher or more maximalist claims such as "universal bishop," "vicar of Christ," "*rector om-*

nium fidelium" and "*pater regnum,*" titles invoked during papal corona-
tions and other solemn occasions.[70] Magee explicates the matter for us:

> If the interventions of Roman Pontiffs within the West outside the local
> Church of Rome might conceivably have been justified on the basis either
> of universal primacy or of his Patriarchal role, it is not surprising that
> Popes acting in moments momentous enough to have been recorded for
> later history would have invoked the more exalted of their titles. . . . To
> invoke one's personal prestige on account of a higher role even while act-
> ing in a lower capacity seems simply consonant with human nature, and
> does not necessarily indicate more than this even if such a tendency can
> be shown to have become somewhat habitual in the West.[71]

After Magee's monumental work, what then remains in treating the
question of Rome as a patriarchate as distinguished from the Roman
papacy? Even if one could surmount enormous historical hurdles to
trace each and every instance of the title, one would still be left with the
fact that the title is rarely encountered and even more rarely invoked
explicitly. One would still be left with the *functional* problem of how, in
the present, to give an ancient title new meaning and applicability by
differentiating it from the papal office. Magee has himself concluded
that a great deal of work remains to be done not on the level of history
but instead that of ecumenism and ecclesiology:

> It would seem that what is needed at the present time is an inquiry into
> how the patriarchal institution might be understood so as to be reconcil-
> able with defined Catholic dogma, in a manner acceptable also to our
> separated Eastern brethren because of its rootedness in sources shared by
> them, supported by the facts of the first millennium, fully consistent with
> the significant developments in ecclesiology provided by the Second Vati-
> can Council, and open to the new possibilities that the future affords.
> (444)

Magee's study laid the groundwork for understanding the patriarchal institution in Catholic terms and within the Catholic Church.

He made it clear that in conceiving of Rome as a patriarchate—whether in historical or possible future terms—it is extremely important to have a sufficiently broad, sophisticated, and nuanced conception of ecclesiastical authority to be capable of discerning the outlines and functioning of an office when it is not explicitly labelled or differentiated as "patriarchal" or when that title has not yet been pressed into service. For this reason, Magee constantly uses the somewhat cumbersome but helpful phrase "patriarchal institution" to help recognize a form of authority in the Church that has varied greatly across centuries and places, and even within individual Churches. He proposes a different and more sophisticated approach that is sufficiently open to recognize that Rome's functioning as a patriarchate is not going to be exactly similar to the other patriarchates in the Church. There is, as Magee and others have found, no single model of "the" patriarch against which to compare Rome's functioning—"the specific prerogatives possessed and exercised by the Eastern Patriarchs varied from one to another, and in some cases did not remain constant even within a single Patriarchate" (444). Notwithstanding this diversity, Magee, after a long survey of the terms and their cognates in the Old and New Testaments, the Fathers, councils, canons, and other crucial sources up to and including the Second Vatican Council, comes to define a "patriarchal institution" thus:

> The *Patriarchal* institution may be described as that ordering of the communion of the universal Church . . . by which each of the supra-local *particular Churches* (encompassing hierarchically ordered groupings of local Churches with their respective Bishops) is headed by a *Protos* (usually the Bishop of the principal See claiming an *apostolic* or otherwise long-standing and venerable foundation) enjoying an habitual administrative "*primacy*" within the particular Church, in union with the Bishops of the same particular Church, in union with whom the Bishops of the same particular Church exercise *collegial* stewardship of the complex of liturgical, canonical, theological and spiritual traditions that are formative of their believers' faith.

Such Churches so governed enjoy a *"relatively autonomous* ecclesial identity"* (473–74).

––––––––

This overview of these Catholic theologians demonstrates that the argument about the importance of distinguishing the papal from the patriarchal offices is not an exclusively Orthodox one. It is, rather, grounded in the theology of some of the foremost Catholic theologians, ecumenists, and canonists of the postconciliar period.[72] Almost as one, they have said that this remains an ecclesiologically and ecumenically crucial task even as they have acknowledged that it is a task that remains unfulfilled.[73] In an attempt to fulfill that task we begin by looking at how patriarchates are defined and how they function, first with Catholic canon law on patriarchates and in the next chapter with actual Orthodox polity as reflected in the functioning of patriarchates today.

Patriarchates According to the 1990 *CCEO*

Caveats

One of the fruits of the Second Vatican Council was the promulgation first, in 1983, of a new *Code of Canon Law* (based on the 1917 Pio-Benedictine code) for the Latin Church and then, in 1990, of the *Code of Canons of the Eastern Churches*.[74] After centuries of living in a situation of piecemeal and often incoherent and contradictory laws, the Catholic Church sought, in the *CCEO* (to use the recognized acronym from the Latin title), to introduce some measure of coherence and consistency into Eastern law, a feat not previously accomplished by the Christian East itself.[75] In turning to this latter code for clues as to how Rome understands patriarchs and their office, we keep several caveats firmly in mind.

First, what follows is less an exhaustive analysis and more a summary or descriptive survey of how patriarchs are described and portrayed, which powers they are understood to have, and what their relationship is with both the bishop of Rome and their own synods.[76]

Second, the treatment of patriarchs in the *CCEO* is acknowledged to be questionable in many ways and thus any interpretation of it, as here, must be cautious and circumspect, especially for two reasons: the code is transitory and non-exhaustive. The code was not intended, by the "chief legislator" himself, Pope John Paul II, as being anything other than a transitory document. (Eastern Catholic law has been promulgated in a series of incomplete steps from the late nineteenth century onward.[77]) It is a serious code, to be sure, but it does not pretend to be completely, exactly, and exhaustively reflective of all Eastern realities, and it is not intended as the utterly definitive and final word on these matters. The evidence for this assertion is twofold: first, the code recognizes the difficulty, not to say impossibility, of legislating for all twenty-two Eastern Catholic Churches of very diverse background, history, structure, and traditions, and therefore allows each Church *sui iuris* to proceed with the drafting of its own particular as well as "special" legislation (*ius speciale ad tempus*) alongside of (and not in contradiction to) the general laws of the *CCEO*. Second, canon 2 states that "the canons of the Code, in which *for the most part* the ancient law of the Eastern Churches is received or adapted, are to be assessed chiefly by that law."[78] Thus the non-exhaustive nature of the code ("for the most part") is recognized and the possibility of critical responses ("to be assessed") to it is opened if its canons do not conform to ancient Eastern law. (There has been no shortage of these.) Also recognized is that there are some aspects of the code about which matters are not settled but on which decisions had to be taken nonetheless by those who "for the most part" tried to balance competing theories and claims in a transitory document intended to deal with an ecclesiologically anomalous situation (that is, a situation where Eastern Churches are separated from each other and from their "mother Church," and where disunity still reigns between Catholics and Orthodox).[79]

The code exists as an interim document pending the achievement of full Orthodox-Catholic communion and unit—"the canons of the *Code of Canons of the Eastern Churches* . . . remain in force until abrogated or changed . . . for just reasons. The most serious of those reasons is the full communion of all the Eastern Churches with the Catholic Church."[80] A door is left open to revision or abolition of or additions to this code pending the achievement of Christian unity.[81] This, Michael Fahey argues, is a point perhaps insufficiently understood by ecumenists and Orthodox critics—"the code . . . is by no means intended to be a blueprint for the life of Eastern Christians after the final restoration of unity between East and West. The code is meant to have a short, but hopefully useful, lifetime."[82]

Finally, this code finds its inspiration in *Orientalium Ecclesiarum* of the Second Vatican Council,[83] and that document, laudable though it was in many respects, was, as Schmemann and others argued, nonetheless unwittingly "tainted" with a Latin ecclesiology particularly when it came to describe patriarchs, which were viewed through a quasi-papal lens as having powers that Eastern ecclesiology generally does not assign to them.[84] This same problem besets the *CCEO* according to many ecumenists and Orthodox critics.[85] The argument about "Latinization" actually cuts both ways here: the purpose of this survey is to see how *Rome* understands patriarchates. If Rome's understanding is "Latinized," that nonetheless illustrates the point of this exercise in showing what, exactly, Rome understands canonically by a "patriarch" and "patriarchate."

Patriarchs in the CCEO

After the office of the Roman Pontiff has been described, the patriarchal office itself is treated especially in canons 55–101. After recognizing that a patriarch is part of the "most ancient tradition of the Church" (c. 55), the code says that he presides over his Church "as father and head" (c. 55) and in this capacity "enjoys power over all bishops including metropolitans and other Christian faithful of the Church over which he presides according to the norm of law approved by the supreme authority of the Church" (c. 56). All patriarchs are equal but some have a precedence of honour by virtue of occupying more senior sees (c. 59). All patriarchs are elected by their respective synod of bishops (cc. 63–77).

The *CCEO* describes as "ordinary and proper, but personal" the power a patriarch exercises over his Church (c. 78, §1). Inter alia, this entails the "right" to "issue decrees" on matters of local law and canonical observance (c. 82, §1); promulgate "instructions to the Christian faithful of the entire Church" for the purpose of promoting "sound doctrine, fostering piety, correcting abuses, and approving and recommending practices which foster the spiritual welfare of the Christian faithful" (c. 82, §3); and "issue encyclical letters to the entire Church" on various matters, which letters he can order clerics and hierarchs to read and explain throughout the territory (c. 82). The patriarch is exhorted, "in all matters which concern the entire Church over which he presides or more serious affairs" "to hear the permanent synod, the synod of bishops of the patriarchal Church, or even the patriarchal assembly" (c. 82, §3). In conjunction with this synod, the patriarch can "establish provinces and eparchies, modify their boundaries, unite, divide, suppress, and modify their hierarchical status and transfer the eparchial see" (c. 85, §1). The patriarch is also competent to appoint and move auxiliary bishops and to ordain and enthrone other bishops, especially metropolitans (c. 85–86).

The general relationship between the patriarch and bishops is described thus: "Bishops of the patriarchal Church must show honor and obsequium to the patriarch and must render due obedience to him; the patriarch shall show to these bishops due reverence and treat them with brotherly charity" (c. 88, §1). This relationship is more expansively described in canons 102–113, on the synod, which it is the patriarch's prerogative "to convoke . . . and to preside over" (c. 103). The decision to convoke the synod is not, however, exclusively patriarchal: it must, according to canon 106, be convoked when there are "matters . . . to be decided which belong to the exclusive competence of the synod of bishops" or when "at least one-third of the members request it." It is the responsibility of the patriarch to "transfer, postpone, suspend and dissolve" (c. 108) the synod and also to prepare its agenda.

The synod enjoys certain responsibilities and rights exclusive to it. According to canon 110, it has exclusive legislative authority, it is the sole tribunal for the patriarchal Church, and it is the sole electoral body for the choosing of a new patriarch. It is also the synod's role to determine when its legislation is to be promulgated (c. 111) but the actual promulgation itself is the "competence of the patriarch" (c. 112), who is also responsible for the interpretation of the laws.

If the synod has exclusive legislative authority, the patriarch has exclusive administrative authority according to canon 110, section 4. Part of his administration consists in having a patriarchal curia (cc. 114–24), "which is comprised of the permanent synod, the bishops of the patriarchal curia, the ordinary tribunal of the patriarchal Church, the patriarchal finance officer, the patriarchal chancellor, the liturgical commission" and any other relevant local commissions (c. 114). The permanent synod (*synodus permanens*) "is comprised of the patriarch and four bishops designated for a five-year term" (c. 115) and must meet at least twice a year at a time decided upon by the patriarch (c. 120).

In addition to all this, there is a "patriarchal assembly" (*conventu patriarchali*) (cc. 140–45) which is a "consultative group of the entire Church" (c. 140) required to meet when the bishops or patriarch request it, and at least "every five years" (c. 141). As with the synod, the patriarch convokes this assembly and determines to "transfer, postpone, suspend and dissolve" its sessions (c. 142). Unlike the synod, however, this assembly is not composed solely of hierarchs, but is also to include lower clerics, monastic superiors, rectors of major academic institutions, and "from each eparchy at least one presbyter enrolled in the same eparchy . . . as well as two lay persons, unless the statutes determine a greater number" (c. 143, §1.6).

Finally, on the question of territory, the *CCEO* says that a patriarch presides over a certain territory in which his powers are most fully exercised; for faithful and clergy of his Church who live outside this territory, the patriarch enjoys certain lesser powers, some of which are superseded by the Roman Pontiff (see cc. 146–50).

Deviations

The treatment of patriarchs in the *CCEO* is not without substantial problems, as canonists, ecumenists, and others have noted. There are two rather glaring problems with the *CCEO*'s treatment, and then several problems of lesser weight.

The first major problem is that patriarchs are defined in a subordinate relationship to the Roman Pontiff. The structure of the *CCEO* is significant here: the patriarchal office in the *CCEO*, under "Title IV," comes immediately *after* "Title III: The Supreme Authority of the Church," which treats of the Roman Pontiff, whose office is "given in special way by the Lord to Peter, first of the Apostles and to be transmitted to his successors," conveying upon them the titles "head of the college of bishops, the Vicar of Christ and Pastor of the entire Church on earth; therefore, in virtue of his office (*munus*) he enjoys supreme, full, immediate and universal ordinary power in the Church which he can always freely exercise" (c. 43).[86] This full papal power also entails a "primacy of ordinary power over all the eparchies and groupings of them by which the proper, ordinary and immediate power which bishops possess in the eparchy entrusted to their care is both strengthened and safeguarded" (c. 45, §1). This papal power can be exercised in a variety of ways, but it is the pope's "right, according to the needs of the Church, to determine the manner, either personal or collegial, of exercising this function" (c. 45, §2). Thus he can choose to use the assistance of others (including the Curia) in exercising his office (c. 46, §1), and may, but is not bound to, seek "the participation of patriarchs and other hierarchs who preside over Churches sui iuris in the synod of bishops" according to "special norms established by the Roman Pontiff" (c. 46, §2). When he does exercise his power, it is final—"there is neither appeal nor recourse against a sentence or decree of the Roman Pontiff" (c. 45, §3).

This relationship of patriarchal subordination to the Roman Pontiff comes out again in canon 92, on the question of ecclesiastical communion between the two. The ancient custom of patriarchs sending to each other proof of their fidelity to the apostolic faith and a request for intercommunion is replaced by the expectation that the patriarch is required to "manifest hierarchical communion with the Roman Pontiff, successor of Saint Peter, through the loyalty, veneration *and obedience* which are due to the supreme pastor of the entire Church" (§1; emphasis added). In addition, in case the many other repeated references to this are missed, the third and final section of this canon states that "within a year of his election and then often during his tenure in office, he is to make a visit to Rome to venerate the tombs of the apostles Peter and Paul and present himself to the successor of Saint Peter *in primacy over the entire Church* (§3; emphasis added).

The power of the Roman Pontiff is emphasized elsewhere in the code when canon 57 says that "the erection, restoration, modification and suppression of patriarchal Churches is reserved to the supreme authority of the Church." Insofar as "supreme authority" is a euphemism for the Roman Pontiff,[87] such a power is, of course, unprecedented in the experience of patriarchs in the undivided Church of the first millennium. Equally unprecedented is the pontiff's ability to interfere in patriarchal elections. In canon 72, section 2, provision is made whereby, after fifteen days of electoral deadlock, "the matter devolves to the Roman Pontiff." This does not necessarily indicate an appointment— the method of resolving the situation is left to papal discretion—but it does indicate an unprecedented level of interference in the life of an Eastern Church.

In addition to the major problem of the relationship between the patriarch and the Roman Pontiff, there are other problems of lesser weight in the *CCEO*. In some respects, these problems are ones of nuance or of new situations that the compilers of the *CCEO* had to deal with as best they could. The noted canonist Ivan Žužek has said that delineating the administrative powers of the patriarch in the code raised many problems as canonists struggled to find "a healthy equilibrium between the collegiality which is practiced in the synods and the exercise of the administrative power of the patriarch."[88] Žužek argued that the *CCEO* struggled to resist the Latinizing and "papalist" tendency (first noted by Schmemann in his reflections on patriarchs in the documents of Vatican II) toward "concentration of power in the person of the patriarch" at the expense of genuinely synodal government.[89]

Such views are among the reasons why Catholic canons on patriarchates are often greatly criticized by Eastern Christian theologians, canonists, and ecumenists. Given these contestable points in the *CCEO* as well as its transitory nature, one must be extremely cautious in drawing any lessons from it as to the actual functioning of a patriarchate and the powers of a patriarch and synod and the relationship between them.

CHAPTER FOUR

Patriarchates

Orthodox Perspectives

Since Rome has only rarely been understood as the Patriarchate of the West, most Catholics lack a functional concept of it as a patriarchate, and only a very attenuated and Latinized concept of patriarchates in general. This is perhaps one reason why, of all the theologians reviewed above, none went beyond mere advocacy for differentiating papal from patriarchal structures to provide an actual, detailed sketch of how such a differentiated structure would function—what, that is, a Roman patriarchate would look like and would practically entail. Given this lack of detailed understanding of how Rome might function as a patriarchate, this chapter seeks to provide some insights into how patriarchates function or how they are envisaged as functioning. For such insights I draw on select patriarchates and polity in the Orthodox Churches according to current canons and statutes.

This survey of Orthodox patriarchates demonstrates that there is no one single model of patriarchate but rather a wide diversity of models of patriarchal leadership. The canonist George Nedungatt, after reviewing the office of patriarch in an array of Orthodox Churches, concluded rightly that "given the wide spectrum of patriarchs, it is not possible to delineate the juridical figure of *the* patriarch."[1] The recent and out-

standing study of Michael Magee also noted that "the specific prerogatives possessed and exercised by the Eastern Patriarchs varied from one
to another, and in some cases did not remain constant even within a
single Patriarchate."[2] Among Orthodox patriarchates, as John Erickson
argued, "the line between legitimate primacy and 'neo-papalism' has
not been drawn."[3] Lewis Patsavos's survey of some patriarchates noted
that "it is evident that diversity of practice exists."[4] Finally, a patriarch
himself, Gregorios III of Antioch, has observed that

> the ecclesiological usages of the Christian East did not appear in their
> integrity one day like Athena emerging fully armed from the thigh of
> Jupiter. They have themselves been the object of a complex genesis and
> process of development. On the other hand, they are far from being as
> uniform as the expression "Orthodox ecclesiological ethos" would pre-
> suppose. The practices of the Christian East are varied according to time
> and place.[5]

Some patriarchates are, not unlike Rome, extremely centralized and
clericalized, and maintain a very close control over their Churches with
a heavily attenuated role for synods and bishops, and no role at all for
lower clergy and lay people. Others, by contrast—and these are much
more numerous—have considerable place for lay involvement including especially in the election of the patriarch and often the bishops also.
No one model can claim to be normative given this diversity, and there
would seem to be few, if any, norms—and certainly no universally
agreed upon norms—as to what a patriarchate must be and how it
must function. In perhaps the most extreme example of this lack of
norms, Nicholas Ferencz tells us that after the abolition of the patriarchate of Moscow "in 1723, the other Eastern Patriarchs recognized
this bizarre college [the Russian Holy Synod set up by Czar Peter the
Great in 1721 under a government official, the *oberprocurator*] as 'their
beloved brother in Christ'"![6] Within some extremely general parame-
ters, which seem, perhaps deliberately, not to have been fully worked
out let alone written down in an authoritative manner universally recognized by all Orthodox Churches, each patriarchate is free to function

in its own unique context as it sees fit and without risk to the ecclesial communion it shares with other patriarchates.[7] The "Eastern" ethos allows for considerable local diversity, flexibility, and variety in how patriarchates are structured and function and in reaction to historical and cultural changes.

I underscore the point about diversity of models for several reasons. The first is to dispel stereotypes that patriarchs are merely "first among equals" without real power. Some Catholics seem to fear that if the bishop of Rome begins functioning as a patriarch, he must therefore abandon his strong control over the Latin Church, risking greater division and dissension than there already is at present.[8] Some Orthodox also share this fear that ecumenical advances may require the "gutting" of the papacy, thereby weakening the Catholic Church.[9] Nobody has put this more perceptively or sharply than the Orthodox theologian Patrick Reardon in an article published during the visit of Pope Benedict XVI to Ecumenical Patriarch Bartholomew in Constantinople in November 2006. Reardon argues that if you "take away the centralized doctrinal authority of Rome, . . . the Roman Catholic Church today would be without rudder or sail in a raging sea" and therefore even less attractive to Orthodox Christians.

> [T]o Orthodox Christians, such a "solution" to the problem would seem very attractive. In fact, however, one fears that it would be no solution at all. Such a weakening of the papacy would be an utter disaster for the Roman Catholic Church as it is currently constituted. To many of us outside that institution, it appears that the single entity holding the Roman Catholic Church together right now is probably the strong and centralized office of the pope.[10]

These concerns can be allayed by considering that several Orthodox patriarchs have very considerable power and exercise very close control over their Churches. If they can do so, there is every reason to believe that a Roman patriarchate could be designed in such a way also, avoiding unnecessary weakening over the Latin Church.

It is important to underscore the diversity of models for a second reason, and that is to allay fears that a Roman patriarchate would be forced into some unsuitable model that fails to take account of its unique situation—that, in other words, Roman ecclesiastical structures would be "Byzantinized." The examination of a possible model for the government of the Roman Church is not an attempt to force a "foreign" model upon Roman structures. On the contrary, this model has enough flexibility to allow Rome to function, if so desired, as a very centralized patriarchate, governing the Latin Church very closely while at the same time acting as the centre of communion with and for the Orthodox Churches, with which a much different relationship would obtain—primacy "with different gears" as Pope John Paul II himself is reported to have said.[11] The diversity of extant patriarchates allows us to avoid the worry that one model might be too narrow and insufficiently accommodating of the singular nature of the Roman Church. A Roman patriarchate would be a patriarchate with significant differences from the rest but nonetheless recognizably patriarchal in nature and function.

In looking at patriarchal models in the Orthodox world, the survey below has been constructed to fulfill three goals. The first goal is to display examples of highly centralized patriarchates to allay Catholic fears about excessive decentralization in a Roman patriarchate.

The second goal of the survey is to focus on three areas that have most often been the object of criticism from the Orthodox against the Roman papacy. Thus I have sought first to inquire into how each patriarchate handles the questions of jurisdiction (is it purely local? regional? or "extra-liminal"?) and "canonical territory." Second, I have looked at the relationship between the chief hierarch and his fellow bishops and between him and the synod, whose own powers, as well as "checks" on patriarchal powers, are briefly enumerated. Third, I examine the question of episcopal and patriarchal selection.

The final goal of the survey is to see if there is among the Orthodox patriarchates any one model that could be useful, *mutatis mutandis,* to the project of reconfiguring the papacy by dividing papal and patriarchal functions. There is indeed one such model in the Armenian Church, and the survey concludes with a more detailed examination of her structures to understand how they function with two patriarchates within two catholicosates within one Church.

When one comes to search for recent scholarship on the question of Orthodox polity, one discovers a lacuna in the literature: there is no one, recent, accessible source that details such information for every Orthodox Church.[12] There are, of course, some well-known and often outstanding introductions to the Orthodox Churches written in *general* terms and therefore only touching superficially—if at all—on questions of polity and structure.[13] There are occasional studies that typically fall into one of four categories: general studies about ecclesiastical organization in broad terms;[14] particular studies of the structure and polity of *individual* Orthodox Churches;[15] episcopal and patriarchal genealogical studies;[16] and individual studies about particular organizational issues within a given Church.[17] In the end, however, we have little recent, comprehensive scholarship covering all the canonical Orthodox Churches on the particular question of their polity. What lies below, then, is an attempt to begin filling this lacuna by focusing on the four ancient "Byzantine" patriarchates (Constantinople, Alexandria, Antioch, and Jerusalem), three "modern" patriarchates (Moscow, Bucharest, Sofia,), and three non-Chalcedonian patriarchates (the Syriac, Coptic, and Armenian).[18] Much of the originality of this study comes from drawing on a new source of information only recently made available and not much analyzed to date: the patriarchates' self-descriptions on their official websites.

The Ecumenical Patriarchate

Jurisdiction and Canonical Territory

Of all the Orthodox patriarchates, none has quite so unique a role as that of the "archbishop of Constantinople, New Rome, and Ecumenical Patriarch," as he is officially styled.[19] This office, next after the papacy, has received the most scholarly attention and been the object of the most concern in Christian history.[20] Much of this attention has to do with the fact that the Ecumenical Patriarchate is *sui generis* among the Eastern patriarchates.[21] Until the transfer of the imperial capital[22] in the fourth century AD and the resultant elevation in status bestowed by the famous third canon of the first Council of Constantinople in 381 ("Because it is new Rome, the bishop of Constantinople is to enjoy the privileges of honour after the bishop of Rome"[23]), Constantinople was, as Fortescue rather archly put it, an "insignificant little diocese of Byzantium" and its "little bishop . . . *parvenu* of the *parvenus*."[24]

The fortunes of the Ecumenical Patriarchate have risen and fallen throughout history, and so has the extent of the authority and jurisdiction it claims for itself, which is disputed not just by other Orthodox but even increasingly by secular Turkish courts.[25] This is a phenomenon common to all patriarchates and centres of ecclesial authority: different periods of the Church's life have seen different configurations of authority depending on political, social, theological, and historical factors and circumstances. I will not focus extensively on how the patriarchates have changed in their structure and functioning but concentrate on *current* polity. After Constantinople became the imperial capital, her patriarchs not infrequently undertook a campaign of self-aggrandizement at various periods and with varying levels of success. These actions, combined during the High Middle Ages with the "enfeebling of the other Patriarchates of the East," meant that the "Patriarch of Constantinople was rather more than 'first among equals'; his influence over Orthodox Christendom was extremely powerful."[26] At times, the Constantinopolitan patriarchs have acted in ways that numerous commentators have explicitly labeled "papal."[27]

The Ecumenical Patriarchate today is not nearly so "monarchical" or "papal" in its pretensions, but it is arguably the most centralized patriarchate extant. It alone of the patriarchates surveyed here allows for no lay involvement whatsoever in episcopal and patriarchal elections and maintains an extremely tight control over its dioceses and bishops.

The immediate geographical territory over which the patriarch himself directly presides today is extremely small and has been shrinking for decades. The Ecumenical Patriarchate's website admits that the archbishopric of Constantinople "consists of 37 communities, 28 parish priests, 2 parish deacons" along with a handful of other institutions like high schools.[28]

Beyond this territory in the archbishopric itself, the Ecumenical Patriarchate also claims "immediate jurisdiction" over many territories around the world. The vast exodus of Greek Christians from Turkey in the twentieth century to Australia and North America,[29] along with immigration from Greece, Crete, and Cyprus, has resulted in the creation of eparchies in those lands, over which the Ecumenical Patriarchate also maintains "canonical jurisdiction."[30] The immediate jurisdictions are listed as including—beyond Constantinople itself—four other metropolitanates in Turkey, seven metropolitanates in the semi-autonomous Archdiocese of Crete, five metropolitanates in the Dodecanese Islands, eight metropolitanates plus one "direct archdiocesan district (New York)" in the United States, and then eighteen archdioceses, exarchates (new Churches), or metropolitanates in Canada, South America, Western Europe, and Asia.[31] Beyond these, the Ecumenical Patriarchate also has seven stavropegial monasteries (that is, monasteries not answerable to the local bishop but under direct jurisdiction of the patriarch) in Britain, Greece, and the United States, as well as several other "patriarchal foundations outside of Turkey" (primarily academic centres) and "patriarchal organizations outside of Turkey" (primarily offices for liaison with governments, the United Nations, and similar bodies).[32]

The Ecumenical Patriarchate, then, exercises a form of "universal" or transnational jurisdiction and does so in an extremely centralized way. As Nicholas Ferencz has demonstrated in considerable detail, the Ecumenical Patriarchate's Greek Orthodox churches, dioceses, and other centres in North America—and one sees no reason not to extrapolate to the rest of the world—are the most "extreme" in their centralized nature, with everybody and every structure and issue being "completely subject to the Ecumenical Patriarchate . . . with all diocesan organization and administration requiring patriarchal approval." There is only a "minimum of authoritative input from the lower clergy and laity," often through assemblies and similar meetings, all of which are subject in the end to approval (or not) from Constantinople.[33]

The most recent example of such "assemblies" as of 2009 may be seen in a proposal for the Ecumenical Patriarchate to exercise some control over not only its own direct territories and subject dioceses, but

over *all* Orthodox Christians everywhere in the world—or the "diaspora" as the Ecumenical Patriarchate insists on calling it. This proposal, made during the fourth "Pre-conciliar Pan-Orthodox Conference" at Chambésy in June 2009, would see the establishment of new
"episcopal assemblies" in various regions of the world, to "be chaired
by the first among the prelates of the Church of Constantinople."[34]
These assemblies are said to be a "temporary"[35] solution pending a
pan-Orthodox "great and holy synod" to restore the ancient canonical
practice of "one bishop to one city."[36] All canonically recognized, active
Orthodox bishops in a given territory would be voting members and
responsible simultaneously to the assembly and to their own individual
synods. The responsibilities of these assemblies would be fivefold: to
seek unity among the Orthodox themselves; to co-ordinate on practical
questions, such as liturgical translations or catechetical publications; to
build relations with other Christians; to relate to governments on social
questions; and to prepare the ground for long-term Orthodox unity.[37]
It remains to be seen how many of these assemblies are actually established, and how well they function. While their motives seem com-
mendable, the fact that they are chaired by hierarchs of the Constantinopolitan throne may lead to a further inflammation of the unsolved
issue of what role, if any, that patriarchate has outside its territory and
over other Orthodox Christians.

Powers, Checks, Balances

There is no complete agreement among Orthodox canonists and theologians today as to the exact nature or justification of the Ecumenical
Patriarchate's powers.[38] The official website provides some insights
into how Constantinople currently understands its status.[39] We are
told that the "privileged position of the Ecumenical Patriarchate . . . is
solely dependant on written canonical stipulations."[40] In witness of
this "privileged position," the document cites several examples of Constantinople doing what no other patriarchal see or ecclesiastical centre
in the Church has done or can do. There is its "practice of purviews
outside its jurisdictional boundaries, namely the jurisdiction of the
Diaspora." In addition, it is said to enjoy "supreme juridical authority

in the institution of appeals. The canons do not allow any other Throne to practice the right of . . . jurisdiction outside their boundaries" (§2).

The Ecumenical Patriarchate further has "the right and responsibility of the commencement and the coordination of actions of inter-Orthodox importance, according to historical and theological reasons." These are less clearly defined, especially in canonical terms, but are thought to include responsibility for missionary endeavors in new territories, such as the Balkans and Slavic lands at the end of the first millennium (§3); taking the initiative to condemn "the tendency of 'racial nationalism' as a dangerous innovation" along with ethno-phyletism (the heretical belief that one must be of a certain ethnic group in order to belong to a particular Church) as they both appeared in the nineteenth century (§3);[41] and taking the initiative in ecumenical endeavors.[42] Other matters aimed at unity include

> the numerous inter-Orthodox meetings; the unhampered and fruitful preparations for the convocation of the Holy and Great Synod; the solid unity of the Orthodox peoples in the treatment of new historical challenges that happen in our own times—an example of this is the historical meeting of the leaders of the autocephalous Orthodox Churches in the sacred Centre of Orthodoxy, in March 1992. (§4)

Finally, and perhaps most controversially, Constantinople claims for itself the role and right of granting of autocephaly to new Orthodox Churches, beginning with Russia in 1589 (§5).[43] Perhaps because of this controversy, the website merely notes that the Ecumenical Patriarchate "has presided over the restoration of the Autocephalous Church of Albania and Autonomous Church of Estonia."[44]

A later section on the website devoted ostensibly to the biography and background of Bartholomew, the current patriarch of Constantinople, gives further insights into how that see and its incumbent currently understand themselves and their roles. Here we are told that he

> presides in a fraternal spirit among all the Orthodox Primates. The Ecumenical Patriarch has the historical and theological responsibility to initiate and coordinate actions among the Churches of Alexandria, Antioch,

Jerusalem, Russia, Serbia, Romania, Bulgaria, Georgia, Cyprus, Greece, Poland, Albania, The Czech Land and Slovakia, Finland, Estonia, and numerous archdioceses in the old and new worlds. This includes the convening of councils or meetings, facilitating inter-church and inter-faith dialogues and serving as the primary expresser of Church unity as a whole.[45]

We are also told that the patriarch "has three times convened the leaders of the self-governing Orthodox Churches around the globe, challenging them to vigorously pursue solutions to the challenges of the new millennium." He is described as the "primary spiritual leader of the Orthodox Christian world and a transnational figure of global significance."

Selection of Patriarch and Bishops

The Ecumenical Patriarchate is governed by a "holy and sacred synod" under the presidency of the patriarch. This, of course, is the "synodos endemousa" whose history, according to most authors, goes back to the very origins of the patriarchate, although its form, composition, and authority have grown and shrunk over the years.[46] Numerous synodical committees also participate in governance or assist the bishops with various tasks.[47]

This synod was changed recently, seemingly unilaterally by the patriarch himself, according to Ron Roberson.

> Since 1920 it had been made up of twelve active metropolitan bishops whose dioceses were within Turkey. But in February 2004 Patriarch Bartholomew directed that it would henceforth be composed of six metropolitans from Turkey and six from outside the country. There has been no direct lay participation in the administration of the Patriarchate since a mixed council was abolished in 1923.[48]

The Ecumenical Patriarchate is almost alone among Orthodox patriarchates in having almost no lay participation, above all in the election of the patriarch and other bishops.[49] The patriarch is elected by the "endemousa" synod which is said to take account of the views of bishops who are not members of this synod.[50] The other bishops are elected by the synod alone.[51]

The Patriarchate of Alexandria (Chalcedonian, Greek)

Jurisdiction and Canonical Territory

The Church and see of Alexandria has a long, distinct history.[52] One of the three most ancient sees in the Church, its claims of far-reaching authority (sometimes the subject of jealousy or dispute by other sees[53]) were the model used by the first Council of Nicaea in an attempt to come to terms with questions of jurisdiction.[54] The exact early nature of Alexandrian Christianity is generally regarded by most scholars as "notoriously obscure"[55] and this applies no less to the earliest origins of Alexandrian polity and jurisdiction. Nonetheless, it is clear that from early on the bishop of Alexandria was able to command "unlimited powers comparable to those of Caesar in politics," and was given much latitude by other bishops to do so in order not to undermine the struggle against various persecutors and then against Arianism.[56]

Since the Council of Chalcedon in 451, Alexandria has been rent by division and disunity because of differing positions on the nature of Christ.[57] Ecclesiastically, this division has been evident "from the seventh century [when] the Monophysite Church was organized independently of the Orthodox Church of Alexandria."[58] As a result, there arose two rival claimants to the throne, the Coptic or so-called non-Chalcedonian, and the Greek (Byzantine) or Chalcedonian bishop, both of which tended toward a "system of monarchy" in a "highly centralized system" in which the bishop enjoyed "enormous authority and responsibility regarding the administration of the Church."[59]

Powers, Checks, Balances

The contemporary Greek successor to this see, with the title "Pope and Patriarch of Alexandria and All Africa," enjoys jurisdiction over the entire continent.[60] He governs the Church together with a synod of bishops, composed of eighteen metropolitans and six diocesan bishops.

> [T]he Patriarchate is governed on the basis of a series of regulations that were originally adopted at the end of the 19th century. It established a synodal system of administration in contrast to the previous governance by the Patriarch alone, and provided that the Patriarch should be elected by both clergy and laity. The Holy Synod . . . must meet at least once a year, but ordinarily gathers every six months.[61]

The relationship between patriarch and synod is supposed to be one of mutuality, neither acting without the other. This is seen concretely in the fact that the "patriarch has the right to suspend publication of any synodical decree whose formulation in his judgment is incomplete. He must, however, justify his action at the next meeting of the synod. If the synod insists upon its publication, it then becomes obligatory for the patriarch to conform to the decision of the synod."[62]

Selection of Patriarch and Bishops

The patriarch and bishops are both elected by the synod though there seems to be very little literature or documentation on the history or actual practices of election.

The Patriarchate of Alexandria (Coptic)

Jurisdiction and Canonical Territory

The Coptic Church[63] has historically styled its chief hierarch as "pope," and claims this title came into common usage for the Alexandrian patriarch long before it was commonly applied to the bishop of Rome—likely sometime around the middle of the third century. The Coptic Church is governed by a pope-patriarch who, like many Orthodox hierarchs, retains the traditional see-city in his title even though he is resident elsewhere: in this case, in Cairo.[64] The pope-patriarch claims to be the successor of Saint Mark the Evangelist in the see and has the title "Head of our priests, the Pope Abba . . . Pope, Patriarch and Archbishop of the great city of Alexandria." He thus reigns as bishop over Alexandria as well as Cairo.[65] His territory includes eleven metropolitanates and nearly sixty dioceses in Egypt and abroad. He governs these territories alongside nearly thirty auxiliary, exarchical, abbatial, and general bishops.[66]

Powers, Checks, Balances

Unlike the Roman papacy, the Coptic claims no infallibility nor universal jurisdiction—"the patriarch enjoys great authority but he is not the highest authority: all decisions of the Church are taken by the Holy Synod."[67] The patriarch is assisted by his synod as well as other bodies. The synod is the highest decision-making body in the Church and is "composed of the Patriarch, metropolitans, bishops, khoeri-episcopos [chorepiscopus, a rural bishop], abbots of monasteries, and stewards of the Patriarchate."[68]

In the 1985 election, at which the current Pope Shenouda III was elected, the constitution of the synod and Church specified that the one just elected enjoyed several rights and duties: he is the head of the synod which meets only at his summons and with him in the presidential chair (save for those emergency situations when the pope is sick or when he refuses a request by more than half the synod to meet); he supervises monasteries and appoints their abbots; he is the liaison with the state and other Churches; and he alone consecrates holy myron (holy oil).[69]

Selection of Patriarch and Bishops

The patriarch is responsible for seeing that episcopal vacancies are filled through proper election. He is able to appoint on his own "general bishops" to assist him in any capacity and with what authority as he designates; he consecrates all new bishops and raises some of them to metropolitical status, and neither consecration nor promotion can take place if the patriarchal see is vacant.[70]

The Coptic Church also enjoys considerable lay involvement in its official structures alongside the patriarchate and synod. Patriarchs have "from the very beginning . . . been . . . elected by both the clergy and the laity."[71] This level of lay involvement has changed over the centuries but even today, when "the Patriarch passes away or if the Patriarchal Throne becomes vacant for any other reason, the Church Synod and the General Council shall convene and jointly select a Bishop for the office of 'locum tenens'." What happens next has varied several times in the twentieth century alone, not least because of varying levels of governmental involvement, but the most recent procedures specified indicate that a nominations committee assembles a list of candidates and then an "electoral committee consisting of the 'locum tenens' Bishop, three clergymen and three notable Coptic laymen, will conduct the voting at the Patriarchate." The names of those three who receive the highest number of votes are announced and then the following Sunday at Saint Mark's Cathedral in Cairo the new patriarch is chosen by lot, "an old practice of the Coptic Church dating back to the 8th century" and recently revived after a long period of disuse.[72]

The Patriarchate of Antioch (Chalcedonian Orthodox)

Jurisdiction and Canonical Territory

The patriarchate of Antioch, the third-most senior see in Christian history—bumped to the fourth position after Constantinople was added to the "pentarchy"—is today based in Damascus, Syria, with jurisdiction over that country along with Lebanon, Iran, Iraq, Kuwait, and "parts of Turkey"[73] where the ancient city of Antioch is itself based. The patriarchate also has jurisdiction over dioceses in Australasia and North America[74] (the claims of other patriarchates to the same territories notwithstanding).[75] As with other patriarchates, its method of governance has changed over the centuries and today Antioch is not nearly as "monarchically" run as it once was.[76]

Powers, Checks, Balances

The patriarchate is governed by the patriarch and also by a synod consisting of "all the ruling bishops" who meet twice yearly, in spring and autumn, to consider general matters and also to elect a new patriarch.[77] The synod "has the function of electing the Patriarch and other bishops, preserving the faith and taking measures against certain violations of ecclesiastical order." The synod and patriarch tend to "balance" each other in several ways. The patriarch, e.g., is "obliged to publish any law, regulation, or decision ratified by the Holy Synod within a month of its last meeting. In the event he does not, this obligation is undertaken by the metropolitan first in rank according to seniority." The senior metropolitan also has the right to convene the synod if the patriarch fails to do so according to the appointed schedule for regular meetings; this same metropolitan would also preside over the synod if the patriarch would not. The patriarch, however, also has certain "checks" on the synod, enjoying the "right to request the revision of any decision of the Holy Synod. However, the revision is defeated if an absolute majority vote favors retaining the original decision."[78]

In addition to the synod and patriarch, a third body assists in governing the Church—"a general community council is made up of the Holy Synod and lay representatives. Meeting twice a year, this body is responsible for financial, educational, judicial and administrative matters."[79]

Selection of Patriarch and Bishops

When a new patriarch is to be chosen, the "general community council" selects three candidates, one of which is then elected by the synod.[80] Bishops are elected by the synod.

The Patriarchate of Antioch (Syriac, non-Chalcedonian)

The so-called non-Chalcedonian Patriarchate of Antioch of the Syrian or Syriac[81] Orthodox Church is today based in Damascus and headed by Patriarch Ignatius Zakka, who traces his lineage, like the Roman papacy, all the way back to Saint Peter, considered "the first Patriarch of the Apostolic See of Antioch." This patriarchate, like many in the region, has moved around depending on political circumstances, and settled in Damascus in 1959. Much of its population has since moved to Western Europe and to North and South America, where this Church has a substantial presence.[82] Political persecution and consequent peregrinations on the part of patriarch and people seem to be common features of ecclesial life outside the Roman Empire, and this Church along with the Armenian Orthodox Church has developed in a unique way by having two major centres of authority—a patriarchate and a catholicosate—within one Church.

Jurisdiction and Canonical Territory

Historically the jurisdiction of the Patriarchate of Antioch is said to have "extended from the Greek Sea in the West to the far end of Persia and India in the East, and from Asia Minor in the North to the frontiers of Palestine in the South. . . . His authority was dominant over all the Christians in these districts, irrespective of their nationality, race or language." Today the Church has "followers" in "Syria, Lebanon, Iraq, Jordan, Turkey, Egypt, Europe, North and South America, and Australia," all of whom are united under "the common father of all Syrian Orthodox people wherever they are," viz., "Moran Mor Ignatius Zakka I Iwas, the 122nd successor to St. Peter in the Apostolic See of Antioch" who heads a Church which styles itself "the Universal Syrian Church."[83]

Power, Checks, Balances

This Church has evolved into two major centres of authority and numerous derivative ones. There is the "Patriarch of Antioch and All the East and the Supreme Head of the Universal Syrian Orthodox Church" based in Damascus and then there is the Catholicos in India. What is most interesting and perhaps even counterintuitive is that the patriarch outranks the Catholicos in India. The Church has recently published

extremely detailed and exactingly descriptive statutes in its "Constitution of the Syriac Orthodox Church of Antioch."[84]

Article 2 of the statutes pertains to the patriarch, who is described
as the "Supreme Head of the Church and its Holy Synod, the General
Supervisor of all religious and administrative affairs." Later on, in article 7, he is more fully described as "the defender of its faith, doctrine,
and apostolic traditions. The symbol of its unity, its representative and
spokesman everywhere. The general supervisor of all its affairs, and the
spiritual father of all Syrian Orthodox people worldwide. He must be
obeyed by the Catholicos, Metropolitans, priests, monks, nuns, deacons and all laity." We are told elsewhere that the patriarch can only
be removed if he lapses into "heresy, . . . deviates from the canonical
laws, suffers from mental disorder or is found guilty of a serious mis-
conduct."[85]

Article 12 states that administratively the patriarch is to supervise
all "religious, administrative, and financial matters" of the local "archdioceses," whose "local bylaws and . . . final budgets" he approves. Additionally, he is responsible for all "agreements, documents, treaties,
contracts . . . and letters . . . that relate to the affairs" of the Church and
for sending representatives to ecumenical bodies as well as to internal
bodies like parish or diocesan councils (art. 16). He sends a "patriarchal
envoy" to "vacant or brand newly established archdioceses" (art. 18).
Finally, he "has the right to examine, correct, scrutinize, eliminate or
introduce new church rites" and also to exercise supervision over other
historical and theological texts about whose publication he has "the
sole right" to decide (art. 21).

The third article balances the power of the patriarch by repeating
the use of the word "supreme" to declare that "the Holy Synod, headed
by H. H. the Patriarch, is the supreme religious, spiritual, legislative
and administrative authority of the Syrian Orthodox Church of Antioch." This synod is convened by the patriarch, who "presides" over all
sessions and "sanctions and announces its decisions" (arts. 13, 14). This
patriarchal synod presides over thirty-one archdioceses around the
world, including the Catholicate of the East, headquartered in Kerala,
India (art. 4).

The patriarch must "confer necessarily" with the synod in six areas:

A. The approval of the election of the Catholicos, Metropolitans, and their ordination.
B. Moving Metropolitans from one Archdiocese to another.
C. Removal of the Catholicos, and Metropolitans, and the acceptance of their resignations.
D. Altering the geographical boundaries of Archdioceses.
E. Creating, establishing or abolishing Archdioceses.
F. Selling part or all of the Patriarchate's real estates and endowments (art. 22).

The synod is to meet at least "every two years, and whenever deemed necessary." If the patriarch fails to call the synod, it can meet on its own under the most senior metropolitan (art. 99). All metropolitans are expected to attend and absences can be punished (art. 101). The synod has four main functions: to elect and induct the patriarch, approve patriarchal nominees for bishop, investigate and impeach the patriarch or metropolitans, and investigate and punish heresy or other violations of tradition and discipline (art. 103). Such synodal investigations and punishment, including deposition from the clerical state, can include, under special statutes, the patriarch himself (art. 104).[86]

There are two forms of synod in the Syrian Church: the patriarchal synod, described above, and then another called the "General Synod" which includes both the patriarch and his bishops and the Indian catholicos and his bishops (art. 100).

Besides the patriarch and synod, the other major figure is the Catholicos in India. He is described in the eighth article as ranking "second after the Patriarch" and is "elected only by the Metropolitans under the jurisdiction of the Catholicate See." He is elected locally, but only ordained and installed "lawfully" by the patriarch (art. 15). In the liturgical diptychs, the patriarch's name is always mentioned first, the catholicos second, and the local metropolitan-archbishop (whose role is described in article 9) third (arts. 8 and 9).

Selection of Patriarch and Bishops

Article 7 of the statutes uses very "Roman" language to describe the patriarch as "the legitimate successor of St. Peter the Head Apostle. He is the Pontiff." This patriarch, who must be at least forty years of age at time of election (art. 35), is elected by "the Catholicos, the Metropolitans of the Archdioceses, the Metropolitans Patriarchal Vicars[87] in the Archdioceses, and the Metropolitan Assistant Patriarch" (art. 7). This election, which takes place in secret session in the patriarchal cathedral (art. 37), must take place no later than thirty days after the death of the previous patriarch (art. 33). The electors themselves are apparently not allowed to elect as patriarch the Indian Catholicos, the "Metropolitan of the Knanaya Archdiocese, the Metropolitans of the churches of the Antiochian Apostolic See in India, and the Metropolitan of North America of the Malankara Archdiocese. All above shall elect but may not be elected" (art. 36, §1).

Metropolitan-archbishops are chosen via a dual election-appointment system. After the previous metropolitan has died or resigned (situations covered in arts. 79–83), the patriarch appoints a "patriarchal envoy" to run affairs in a circumscribed manner until a new metropolitan is elected. A metropolitan is to be chosen from among the hieromonks (monks who are also priests), and is "nominated by H. H. the Patriarch" before being "elected by the majority of the clergy and the faithful of the Archdiocese for which he is nominated" (art. 86). If, however, the local election cannot take place for some reason or other by this fuller convention of clergy and laity, then the situation devolves to "the Archdiocesean clergy, Boards of Trustees, church institutions and active committees [who] will elect him, and submit his name to H. H. the Patriarch, who in turn must consult with members of the Holy Synod. If he receives the majority of their votes, he then ordains him" (art. 86). If the local archdiocese is completely unable to elect a metropolitan, then the situation devolves entirely to the patriarch and synod who, after six months of vacancy, will together exercise "the right to choose and ordain a metropolitan" (art. 91).

The Patriarchate of Jerusalem

Jurisdiction and Canonical Territory

There are today three patriarchs *resident* in Jerusalem, including an Armenian[88] (treated below) and a Latin Catholic "patriarch" (who is merely an archbishop with an honorific title[89]). Other Christians have, of course, had a great interest in the Holy City and have had a presence there, sometimes officially and sometimes unofficially, but almost always controversially, for many decades or centuries.[90] The focus here is on the Greek Orthodox patriarch of Jerusalem.

This patriarchate, according to Sotiris Roussos, "was established in 451 AD," is based at the Brotherhood of the Holy Sepulchre in Jerusalem, and has jurisdiction over the monastery, holy places in the city, Israel, Jordan, and areas controlled by the Palestinian Authority.[91] It also (and controversially) has sixteen parishes and monasteries in the United States.[92]

Powers, Checks, Balances

The patriarch governs the Church in conjunction with a synod and a "mixed council." The synod includes all bishops as well as "titular bishops and archimandrites appointed by the patriarch" provided that the total synodal membership does not exceed eighteen. The patriarch presides over the synod, but if he is absent any member of the synod can preside. A majority vote decides all matters in the synod, with the patriarch breaking a tie.[93]

Selection of Patriarch and Bishops

The patriarch also presides over the mixed council, which allows for lay input in the Church, including especially in the election of the patriarch. The council includes delegates from among the laity and lower clergy. This council works jointly with the synod in the election of the new patriarch: the council picks three names, one of whom the synod then elects. Bishops are not elected but are appointed by the patriarch, which helps to perpetuate the Greek stranglehold over the patriarchate.[94]

The Patriarchate of Moscow

The Patriarchate of Moscow is the largest in the world, a fact that has sometimes led certain of her members to assume that Orthodox preeminence should belong to Moscow and not Constantinople, and to act accordingly.[95] The size and importance of the Russian Church has also ensured that it has been the object of prolonged study. In addition, this Church takes questions of polity, jurisdiction, territory, and organization very seriously and the happy result is a recently promulgated exacting and detailed set of statutes.

The history of the Russian Church has often been a turbulent one, and even today questions of the relationship between Church and state are in most respects as controverted as they always have been if in different ways.[96] Historically, changes in the structure and polity of this Church have usually been concomitant with changes in the Russian political system and a desire by various autocrats for greater control over the Church. This was never more clearly seen than in the changes forced upon the Russian Church in the Soviet era.[97] There was, of course, appalling persecution against many Christians in the Soviet Union, but aside from such barbaric acts, the state exerted a quieter but no less powerful influence on the Russian Church by co-opting many of her clergy and hierarchs[98] and then by re-creating her patriarchal structures in a fashion that left them easily malleable to political purposes. This fact is clearly visible in the 1945 "Statutes of the Russian Orthodox Church,"[99] on which a brief reflection is necessary in order to understand the post-Soviet constitution of the Russian Church.

The 1945 statutes were brought in to regulate the patriarchate, established in 1589, abolished in 1700, and restored only in 1917[100] but then vacant until after World War II when Stalin permitted an election with the resulting choice of Alexy I as patriarch. Given the constraints of time and circumstance, those re-creating the patriarchate in 1917 were not able to define that office with much precision and on balance the patriarch was not as powerful and unifying a figure as some had hoped or as the Soviet government would later desire for its own purposes.[101]

When the Church proved its patriotic service during the Second World War, restrictions on it were eased up somewhat and a *sobor* was permitted from 31 January to 2 February 1945 at which a new patriarch was elected and the new statutes promulgated.[102] While ostensibly the hierarchs had elected one from among their number and produced and promulgated these statutes themselves, the government had arranged these matters in advance according to its liking.[103] The government intervened because it "realized that the Church as a whole could not be used in the interests of the Communist state while it was scattered in small and disunited groups without a central control." The government therefore decided to give the Church "a united and centralized organization" that was in many respects modeled after certain "peculiarities of the Soviet constitutions" in which "authority is based on centralization and subordination."[104]

According to Bogolepov, in the 1945 statutes, the patriarch enjoyed extensive and unprecedented powers while the Church was allowed to retain only "an external façade of the conciliar system (sobornost)" (26). Thus the Russian patriarch, and he alone, had subordinate to him not only other organs within the Church, but also the bishops—"he is not 'primus inter pares' but is the immediate authority over them" and manifests this authority by unilaterally appointing, translating, or removing bishops without reference to, or input from, any other ecclesial body (27–28). Bishops were required to make annual reports to the patriarch, whose "vicars" they were thought to be. The patriarch was too busy controlling a vast Church to govern his own diocese, and so he appointed a vicar-bishop (like the cardinal-vicar of Rome) in his stead (29–31). While there was ostensibly a synod of bishops, the patriarch alone convened it, determined the scope of decisions it would be permitted to make, decided the agenda, and promulgated only those decisions of which he approved (31–32).

The Russian Church was able to amend these statutes and regulate her own internal life only once Communism began to crumble. Thus in 1988, and then again in 1990 and 1994, councils of the Russian Church promulgated new statutes governing ecclesial affairs.[105] Gone are many, but by no means all, of the monarchical powers ascribed to the patriarch,[106] who is now more clearly regarded as one authoritative person alongside three other organs: the Local Council, the Bishops' Council, and the Holy Synod (statute I.7).

Jurisdiction and Canonical Territory

According to the modern statutes, the patriarch is styled "His Holiness the Patriarch of Moscow and All Russia"[107] and has "primacy in honour among the episcopate of the Russian Orthodox Church and shall be accountable to the Local and Bishops' Councils" (IV.1). The one elected to the patriarchal office "for life" (IV.11) must already be a bishop with academic qualifications, administrative and pastoral experience, and of an age not less than forty (IV.17). Election to this office ipso facto entails the offices of bishop of Moscow as well as "archimandrite of the Laura [or Lavra, a prestigious monastery] of the Holy Trinity and St. Sergius and of a number of the Moscow monasteries of particular historical importance" (IV.10). He also governs other stavropegial monasteries.

The patriarch is enjoined generally to exercise "care for the internal and external welfare of the Russian Orthodox Church and shall govern it together with the Holy Synod as its chairman" (IV.4). The relationship between patriarch and bishops is said to be "determined by Canon 34 of the Holy Apostles and Canon 9 of the Council of Antioch" and is manifested concretely in ways that could be considered broadly "executive." The patriarch presides over all sessions of the synod, implements its decisions as well as those of the other councils, submits to those councils reports on the life of the Church in the times between councils, supervises the various employees and departments in the Church bureaucracy, writes encyclical letters to all the faithful, signs documents approved by the synod, communicates with other patriarchs and primates, liaises with the state when necessary, receives appeals from diocesan bishops "of the self-governing Churches" (that is, the Latvian, Moldovan, and Estonian Churches, as well as the Ukrainian Church [VIII.16–17]), issues decrees on episcopal and other appointments, ensures replacements when dioceses are permanently or temporarily deprived of episcopal leadership, has the "right to visit in necessary cases all dioceses of the Russian Orthodox Church," gives advice to bishops "both to their personal life and the exercise of their archpastoral duty," mediates in disputes between bishops and makes a binding decision, bestows honours to bishops, clerics, and laity, and consecrates holy myron (IV.7).

Powers, Checks, Balances

There are "checks" on the patriarch, including the fact that "the right of judgment on the Patriarch . . . as well as the decision on his retirement shall belong to the Bishops' Council" (IV.12). High authority in the Russian Church is also shared among three other bodies: the Local Council, Bishops' Council, and Holy Synod.

Selection of Patriarch and Bishops

The Local Council is, in fact, the largest and most powerful body in the Russian Church, acknowledged in the statutes as the "supreme power in the field of doctrine and canonical order in the Russian Orthodox Church" (II.1) and being composed of the patriarch (as head), diocesan bishops (ex officio), and elected clerical, monastic, and lay delegates (II.4). This council has responsibility for such things as general doctrinal instruction, resolution of "canonical, liturgical and pastoral matters" in order to secure "the unity of the Russian Orthodox Church and preserving the purity of the Orthodox faith, Christian morals and piety," approval of the decisions of the bishops on doctrinal and canonical matters, canonization of saints, determination of the relations between the Church and state, election of the patriarch, and general solicitude for "contemporary problems" (II.5).

The next largest body is the Bishops' Council, composed of all diocesan and assistant bishops. It is to meet at least once every four years, and always on the eve of a meeting of the Local Council. There seems to be overlap in the responsibilities of the bishops alongside the Local Council, but the bishops are differentiated from that body not only by additional responsibilities but also by what seems to be the "juridical" and "administrative" nature of their authority in having what could be broadly summarized as responsibility for the "institutional" aspects of the faith and life of the Church.

Thus they have responsibility for the "agenda, programme, rules of procedure . . . and structure of the Local Council . . . as well as . . . the procedure of the election of the Patriarch of Moscow." The bishops are also charged with the "supervision of the implementation of the decisions of the Local Council" and of the Holy Synod, whose decisions they are to approve. The Bishops' Council, moreover, is to establish and dissolve "the bodies of the church governance" including ecclesiastical courts, and to see that the finances and property of all such bodies are kept in good order. This council also acts as "ecclesiastical court of final appeal" (II.5).

The Bishops' Council is additionally charged with "adoption of the Statute of the Russian Orthodox Church and introduction of alterations and amendments to it"; "competent interpretation" of the canons and other rules; maintenance of relations with other Orthodox Churches; "establishment, reorganization and dissolution of the self-governing Churches, exarchates and dioceses, and determination of their boundaries and names"; and "establishment, reorganization and dissolution of the Synodal institutions" (III.3).

The third largest body in the Russian Church, meeting between sessions of, and reporting to, the Bishops' Council, is the Holy Synod, which is composed of "seven permanent members and six temporary members from among the diocesan bishops" (V.3). The patriarch, as chairman, proposes the agenda which is then approved or amended in the first session. The synod attempts to work by consensus but will resort to voting whenever needed and nobody may abstain (V.16–17). Members can speak freely to voice complaints or problems with decisions, and the patriarch does this in a special way by means of a temporary veto presented orally at the start of a session and then in written form "within seven days. On the expiry of this term the Holy Synod shall consider the matter again." If the patriarch is still not in agreement, the decision is suspended pending a full meeting of the Bishops' Council. If, however, "it is impossible to postpone the consideration of the matter and the decision must be taken immediately, the Patriarch of Moscow and All Russia shall use his own discretion" but must later submit his decision and actions to the Bishops' Council "for consideration, on which the final solution of the matter shall depend" (V.20).

The synod has overlapping responsibilities with the Bishops' and Local Councils, but additionally is charged with regulation of liturgical and disciplinary matters, evaluation of ecumenical relations and progress, and promulgation of teaching documents to all the faithful (as well as liturgical and catechetical materials of all types). Its most distinctive duties are "episcopal" in that the synod elects and appoints bishops (as well as rectors and abbots of other institutions, and the members of many commissions for all manner of practical issues in the Church, from social work with the poor to the quality of liturgical vestments) and "in exceptional cases" can transfer and retire them; it also determines the remuneration of bishops and supervises them through the synod and considers "the reports by the bishops on the situation in the dioceses and take decisions on the reports" (V.24–28).

The Patriarchate of Bucharest

Jurisdiction and Canonical Territory

Numerically the second-largest Orthodox Church in the world, the Romanian Church enjoys a patriarchal status that is one of the youngest, recognized as such only in 1925. The Romanian Church came together, as the modern nation-state of Romania was doing so, in the nineteenth century.[108] As with many other Orthodox Churches, the influence and interference of the state in matters of ecclesial polity has been frequent. Only since 1989 has the Romanian Orthodox Church been ostensibly free of state interference in determining its own direction and function.[109]

The Romanian Church is comprised of six metropolitanates within Romania, along with "3 metropolitan sees and 2 Dioceses (in Europe), and an Archdiocese (on the American continent)." There are also Romanian parishes in Bulgaria, Israel, Australia, and New Zealand which are all "under the direct jurisdiction of our Patriarchate."[110]

In 1885, the Romanian Orthodox Church was recognized as autocephalous by Ecumenical Patriarch Joachim IV, and in February 1925, following unification of Romania in the postwar period, the Romanian synod decided to raise the metropolitan to the rank of patriarch.[111] This decision was recognized by the Ecumenical Patriarch Basil III in July 1925.[112]

Powers, Checks, Balances

The role and responsibilities of the primate-patriarch have changed over the years, according to Romania's most prominent canonist Nicolae Dură. In general, Dură argues that the patriarch enjoys wide and extensive powers, which he divides into three categories: the power of *teaching* (chiefly to preach missions and send pastoral letters to his flock—as authorized by the synod—and also to undertake correspondence and discussions with other Orthodox and Christian Churches [149]), the power of *consecration* (chiefly of new bishops and metropolitans, as well as holy myron, but also including power to canonize saints and regulate and amend liturgical services [150–51]), and the power of *jurisdiction* (147). In this latter category, the patriarch has extensive rights and responsibilities—Dură lists sixteen—almost all of which pertain to his relations with his clergy. Thus the patriarch convenes and chairs the synod, and can even, in emergencies, arrogate unto himself the right of immediate decision in matters that would otherwise be under synodical jurisdiction. The patriarch supervises the election of new bishops and their exercise of diocesan responsibility (and rebukes them when they fail), hears appeals from lower clerics as well as other bishops in ecclesial litigation and decides their punishment, and can overrule other bishops not only to create stavropegial monasteries but also to draw into his service clerics of other dioceses even without release from the diocesan bishop. The patriarch also issues the laws of the Church and supervises their enforcement. Finally, he alone acts as liaison with the state and no other cleric can do so without his permission (148–49).

In addition to the patriarch, the Romanian Church is also governed by a "holy synod" of all active bishops and then a smaller "permanent" synod consisting of the patriarch, functioning metropolitans, and the secretary of the synod.[113] The full synod is "the highest authority . . . for all dogmatic and canonical matters of any kind."[114]

In addition to this synod, and meeting between its sessions, is a smaller body, sometimes called the "standing" and sometimes the "permanent" synod, "which consists in the Patriarch and the appointed metropolitans"[115] who number four, along with one bishop who is assistant to the patriarch and acts as secretary.[116]

Two other bodies exist alongside both synods and play a role in governing the Church. The first of these is the Church National Assembly consisting of three delegates from each diocese (one cleric and two laity). The National Assembly has responsibility for "all administrative and economical issues as well as those that are not dealt with by the Holy Synod."[117]

The second body is the Church National Council consisting of "three clergy and six lay persons, elected by the Church National Assembly for four years."[118] It is counted the "supreme administrative body, both of the Holy Synod and of the Church National Assembly."[119]

Selection of Patriarch and Bishops

A substantial number of lay people (up to two-thirds of some local assemblies) and "lower" clergy participate in the election of both diocesan bishops and the patriarch. The patriarch is elected by the Church National Assembly after the synod of bishops has vetted two, and often three, candidates.[120] The same pertains to the election of bishops: the synod vets candidates, and then the respective local or diocesan assembly will elect one from the list.[121] In general, the Romanian Church recognizes "an important role for the laity, but that there are given limits for the role."[122]

The Patriarchate of Sofia

Jurisdiction and Canonical Territory

The Bulgarian Church has enjoyed a "considerable measure of autonomy" since 870.[123] By 927, "the autocephalous status and patriarchal rank of the Church of Bulgaria to which it had elevated itself ten years earlier at a local council in Preslav" was recognized by Byzantium.[124] This was not to last, and there have been frequent changes in the status and independence, as well as territorial jurisdiction, of the Bulgarian Church down through the centuries. Most recently, the autocephalous status was recognized again in February 1945 by Constantinople while the patriarchal rank was again self-declared by a local council in Sofia in 1953[125] and not recognized by Constantinople until 1961.[126]

The statutes of this Church were revised and promulgated in 1953 under communist influence—an influence much less marked, it would seem, than in Russia and elsewhere. They were to have been updated in the post-communist period, but internal divisions in the Bulgarian Church seem to have precluded that for now.[127] The very recent history and development of this Church has not been a happy one, rent as it has been by rival patriarchal claimants and synods.[128]

The Church is composed of eleven dioceses within Bulgaria, two overseas dioceses (North America, Australia), several international parishes (Constantinople, Budapest, Vienna, and Bucharest), and one monastery on Mount Athos.[129]

Powers, Checks, Balances

The Church is governed by a patriarch alongside two other major bodies and several derivative, secondary bodies, all of which are much later developments than the patriarchal office itself. The major authoritative body in the Church is the "Holy Synod, which functions in two bodies: the Full Synod . . . and the Little Synod, which serves as a standing body to deal with current issues."[130] The full synod meets twice yearly and more often if necessary. The little synod is elected by the full synod for four years. Both are chaired by the patriarch, whose additional responsibilities include that of liaison with state authorities and other Churches. The patriarch is said to enjoy "primacy by honour and dignity. He or his deputy holds the executive power."[131]

Selection of Patriarch and Bishops

In addition, there is within the full synod a "Supreme Church Council" consisting of two clerics and two laity and having responsibility for "economic matters."[132] Finally, there is what appears to be an ad hoc electoral body, known in some sources as the National Council, and in others as the "Patriarchal Electoral Council of the Church and the People" and consisting of all bishops as well as representatives—both clerical and lay—of diocesan assemblies and other central ecclesial institutions, and having the responsibility to elect the patriarch. This body can also be called into service to decide "upon basic policy and long-term questions" and to "make amendments to the Statute of the Bulgarian Orthodox Church."[133] Lay people are thus able to participate in the highest echelons of the Church's life.[134]

The Armenian Apostolic Orthodox Church

We come finally to the Armenian Church which, alone among all Orthodox Churches—Chalcedonian or otherwise—has preserved an utterly singular structure and polity.[135] Like almost all ecclesial structures, its origins lie in the intersection between political circumstances and ecclesiastical necessity.[136] In some respects, Armenia, universally acknowledged as the first Christian nation,[137] pioneered the concept of "accommodation" or "symphony" between Church and state and their respective structures though sometimes this was less a "symphony" and more a situation in which the Church became a "surrogate government," as one scholar has recently put it.[138] This Church-state relationship, the catholicos of Cilicia has recently argued, has allowed the

Armenian Church to develop as "a people's church par excellence, a participatory community in its way of life and particularly in its decision-making processes which give a decisive role to the laity."[139]

The Armenian structures are unique insofar as they have two patriarchs within a catholicosate, and two catholicosates within one Church.[140] All major hierarchical offices in the Church—the papacy, the patriarchate, and the episcopate—have been widely studied, but there is still very little scholarship on the origins and nature of a catholicosate as such. Hratch Tchilingirian sketches some of the history of this terminology and how it is sometimes equivalent to "patriarch" but sometimes not. On this latter score, he notes that "unlike a patriarch, a catholicos is the chief bishop and head of a national Church, whose authority is not necessarily confined to a geographical area. 'The Catholicos is the ecclesiastical head of a *people*' while a 'patriarch is an ecclesiastical head who occupies an apostolic see and claims jurisdiction over a geographical area.'" The Armenian Church's four "hierarchical sees are not separate churches, but are part of the 'One, Holy, Apostolic Church' and are one in dogma, theology, liturgy."[141] No other Church in the world has a structure like this, and it is instructive to consider in some detail how these four bodies exist in interdependence. This structure has, at the very least, considerable "symbolic" importance in ecumenical terms, illustrating as it does the possibility, hitherto unrealized in the Roman Church or any other, of differentiating roles, of creating and living with multiple patriarchates, while also preserving unity within a single Church.[142] As Peter Cooke has argued, "of all the Eastern Churches, the Armenian Apostolic Church is perhaps the best fitted, by virtue of its history and particular characteristics, to play the leading role in ecumenical dialogue as a mediator both between the various Churches of the East themselves, and between the Churches of East and West."[143]

Jurisdiction and Canonical Territory

In the Armenian Church, the two patriarchates and two catholicoi[144] collectively exercise jurisdiction over "350 parishes and churches in some 40 countries around the world . . . serving an estimated 7 to 7.5

million Armenians."[145] Such a structure does not seem to have been by design but was forced upon the Armenians by political persecution, internal division (including sometimes outright schism[146]), and similar pressures which cumulatively forced the movement of the catholicoi ten times between 314 and 1441.[147] Some have seen in the Church's willingness to allow such an unusual structure evidence of a "pilgrim" or "migrating" Church that has made the best of often difficult or even deadly political circumstances.[148] At the very least, such a dispersed structure has made it much more difficult for this Church, which has been heavily persecuted throughout history, to be completely destroyed: when one see is under duress, the others have sometimes been able either to offer assistance or to assume primacy until the situation changes.[149] As a result of such patriarchal and catholicosal peregrinations, the boundaries of the Church, especially of the catholicosate of Etchmiadzin, "have never been defined, nor the extent of his jurisdiction clarified 'in any clear and systematic manner' until the 19th century, when state-imposed church 'constitutions' were established for the Armenian Church in tsarist Russia (1836) and the Ottoman empire (1863)."[150]

Of the two patriarchates there is, first, that of Jerusalem, which was established in the early 1300s though there would seem to be evidence of an Armenian presence going as far back as the seventh century "when caravans of Armenian pilgrims began to arrive."[151] The patriarch of Jerusalem "along with a Synod of seven clergymen elected by the Brotherhood, oversees the Patriarchate's operations" and enjoys jurisdiction over churches in Israel, the West Bank, and Jordan. He is assisted by a vicar. This patriarchate, unlike the others, has no "involvement of lay representatives" in the election, which is the exclusive prerogative of the monastic Saint James Brotherhood.[152]

The second patriarchate is that of Constantinople. Both it and Jerusalem are considered "autonomous in the internal affairs of their Patriarchate and pledge canonical allegiance to the Catholicate [*sic*] of All Armenians."[153] It was established in 1461, in the aftermath of the Ottoman conquest of 1453.[154] In 1517 after the Ottoman capture, Jerusalem came under Armenian Constantinople's control, which grew for the next four hundred years until it became "the most powerful Hierarchical See in the Armenian Church" as the patriarch was made not just ecclesial leader but also "the head (ethnarch) of the Armenian 'nation' (millet)," a system that lasted until the 1930s.[155] Currently this Armenian patriarchate of Constantinople enjoys jurisdiction over its dioceses in Turkey alone, and these—as with other Christian leaders in Constantinople—are subject to severe restrictions by the state.

In addition to these two patriarchates, there are two catholicoi.[156] The first and foremost is the Catholicosate of Etchmiadzin, which moved to Cilicia in the tenth century after Armenia was overrun by Seljuks and many Armenians fled. This lasted until 1375 when Cilicia was destroyed but Armenia had recovered and was enjoying relative peace. By 1441,

> a new Catholicos was elected in Etchmiadzin in the person of Kirakos Virapetsi. At the same time Krikor Moussapegiants (1439–1446) was the Catholicos of Cilicia. Therefore, since 1441, there have been two Catholicosates in the Armenian Church with equal rights and privileges, and with their respective jurisdictions. The primacy of honor of the Catholicosate of Etchmiadzin has always been recognized by the Catholicosate of Cilicia.[157]

The Catholicosate of Cilicia (otherwise known as "Sis" or the modern name of Antilias in modern-day Lebanon[158]) enjoys jurisdiction in Syria, Cyprus, and Lebanon. It also exercises jurisdiction over churches in the United States, Canada, Greece, Venezuela, Kuwait, and the United Arab Emirates.[159]

The oldest and "supreme" see is the Catholicosate of All Armenians in Etchmiadzin, established by Saint Gregory the Illuminator in the fourth century.[160] The Catholicos-Patriarch is considered the "worldwide spiritual leader of the Nation, for Armenians both in Armenia and in the Dispersion. He is Chief Shepherd and Pontiff to nearly 9 million Armenian Apostolic Orthodox Christians, dispersed throughout the world." The patriarch-catholicos is usually chosen from among existing bishops and is elected by the entire Church. He is officially styled "Supreme Patriarch and Catholicos of All Armenians" though this is an abbreviated version of the full title, which is: "Karekin II, Servant of Jesus Christ, by the Mercy of God and the Will of the Nation, Chief Bishop and Catholicos of All Armenians, Supreme Patriarch of the Pan-National Pre-Eminent Araratian See, the Apostolic Mother Church of Universal Holy Etchmiadzin."[161]

Etchmiadzin enjoys jurisdiction over Armenia proper alongside Russia, Iran and Iraq, and Europe.[162] It also has care for "the spiritual and administrative headquarters of the worldwide Armenian Church."[163] This see also commands a certain primacy over the other catholicosate and patriarchates (though this is not always fully accepted or realized in practice[164]): "the Catholicos of Etchmiadzin divides the supreme jurisdiction of the Church with the patriarchs of Constantinople and of Jerusalem and the Catholicos of Sis, without derogating from the primacy of the see of Etchmiadzin and in hierarchical unity of the Church."[165] The other catholicosate and patriarchates are allowed to "administer to the Dioceses under their jurisdiction as they see fit, however, the supremacy of the Catholicosate of All Armenians in all spiritual matters remains pre-eminent."[166] Even if the catholicos allows the other jurisdictions to conduct their affairs "as they see fit," nonetheless the "catholicos also has the . . . right of confirming decisions and elections in the dioceses under his jurisdiction."[167]

Powers, Checks, Balances

After both catholicoi came into existence due to unexpected circumstances, the Armenian Church made a decision in 1441 to retain both of them "with equal rights and privileges, and with their respective jurisdictions. The primacy of the Catholicosate of Etchmiadzin has always been recognized by the Catholicosate of Cilicia."[168] The sees of Jerusalem, Constantinople, and Cilicia are said to enjoy "local autonomy" even as they recognize "the supreme authority of the Catholicosate of All Armenians."[169] Concretely this "supreme authority" of the Catholicos of Etchmiadzin is manifested in several ways.

[He] represents the centralized authority of the Armenian Church. He is the supreme judge and the head of the legislative body. He is President of the Supreme Spiritual Council as well as the College of Bishops. Ordination of bishops, blessing of Holy Chrism, proclamation of Feasts, invitation and dismissal of National-Ecclesiastical Assemblies, issuing decrees concerning the administration of the Armenian Church and establishing dioceses are part of his responsibilities.[170]

In general terms, then, the "catholicos is the chief administrator of religious, spiritual, ecclesiastical, and administrative matters and oversees the decision-making processes over dogmatic, liturgical and canonical issues. . . . In the Middle Ages, the catholicos also anointed the kings of Cilician Armenia."[171]

Selection of Patriarch and Bishops

Further distinguishing the Armenians is the fact that almost all clerics, from the Catholicos of Etchmiadzin down to many diocesan bishops and even parish clergy, are chosen by elections in which the "lower" clergy and especially laity have a prominent role.[172] The election of the Catholicos of Etchmiadzin is done in the National Ecclesiastical Assembly, which is "convened in the Mother See of Holy Etchmiadzin" and "elects the Catholicos for life"[173] by means of a "secret ballot."[174] This assembly is composed of delegates elected by and from dioceses around the world. Thus does the "universal" leader have a universal electorate which chooses him[175] though there are historical instances in which political powers have intervened to force an appointment, or in which a catholicos has "appointed and consecrated their own successors as co-adjutors (*at'orakic'*)."[176]

Once again the Armenian Church is singular in its habit of "consecrating" the new catholicos *even when he is already an ordained bishop.* This consecration follows the same pattern of anointing as for a priestly or episcopal ordination[177] and is rationalized as being the form through which the catholicoi "would acquire legitimacy for their office" especially in cases in which "the mode of their appointment [was] often left in doubt. Thus the catholical ordination became the decisive act by which a bishop succeeding to the primacy would be vested with the proper authority by the Lord Christ and the Holy Spirit through the laying on of hands of bishops, irrespective of the manner of his election or appointment."[178]

Two other bodies participate in the governance of the Armenian Church: a council of bishops and a "supreme spiritual council." The former is "an administrative-deliberative body presided over by the Catholicos of All Armenians. It makes *suggestions* on the dogmatic, religious, church, parish and canonical issues to be discussed as agenda items during the National Ecclesiastical Assembly." The latter is "the highest executive body of the Armenian Church" and has the Etchmiadzin catholicos at its head. This body was established by Catholicos Gevorg V Soorenian in 1924 "to replace the Synod of Bishops."[179]

The laity, then, have a very substantial role to play in the Armenian Church—arguably more so than in any other Orthodox or Catholic Church. They are prominent in their parish councils and assemblies (the latter a larger body which selects the smaller council to meet regularly) as well as in diocesan councils and assemblies, from which delegates to the National Ecclesiastical Assembly and the Supreme Spiritual Council are elected. As Catholicos Aram I has recently shown, "in the election of the catholicos . . . the diocesan bishop or pastor, the laity has the deciding vote." This is a practice of great antiquity—"from the beginning our church has opted for a people's authority that is expressed through a well-established conciliar process. A monarchical or pyramidal concept of authority has virtually no place in the thinking and practice of the Armenian church."[180] Lay people are, however, confined to electoral and more practical matters while "decisions concerning faith, dogma, liturgy or spirituality remain in the exclusive domain of the College of Bishops of the Church through 'conciliarity.'"[181]

The Armenian Church, then, remains singular in its structure and polity. Its quadruple structure of two patriarchates and two catholoci is duplicated by no other ecclesial body in the world. This makes the Armenian Church of great ecumenical significance because it demonstrates the possibility of maintaining unity within one Church while also having more than one patriarchate and more than one catholicosate.[182] No other Church has been bold enough to attempt such an "experiment" in structural diffusion, but the fact that the Armenians have done so and that their Church remains clearly united is good reason to suggest that the Armenian "model" could be not duplicated but certainly followed in attempting reconfigurations of the Church of Rome and her chief hierarch. There is, with the Armenian structure, enough flexibility, local adaptability, and autonomy, on the one hand, and enough central authority in one particular see, on the other, so that the Church is neither too centralized nor too localized but has achieved about as much balance as possible. Here is a Church with clearly and sufficiently differentiated roles that have been changed according to time and circumstance. Here is a Church whose patriarchates and catholicosates have enough authority to function in their own local jurisdictions while also having strong enough ties to the "mother see" of Etchmiadzin, which itself has enough authority, both within its own territory and over the other sees, to maintain clear and substantial unity of doctrine and life. It is important to underscore this point to counter the idea that decentralization necessarily entails the destruction of unity or of doctrinal coherence.

The Armenian Church, moreover, maintains the highest level of lay involvement of any Church, Catholic or Orthodox, in the regular councils of the Church and especially in the electoral assemblies by means of which local bishops, national primates, regional patriarchs, and a "universal" catholicos are chosen.[183] These two factors, lay involvement and multiple structures, are all the more interesting when one considers that they operate in a Church that is, notwithstanding such seemingly "progressive" practices, extremely traditional and "conservative" theologically and liturgically. This point bears mentioning if only to counter the idea among some Catholics that "popular" election of bishops, including the bishop of Rome, would somehow result in, or at least be concomitant with, a liberalization and destruction of the Church.[184]

What, in sum, are we to make of the Armenian example? It is mentioned here at some length not to suggest that it is a model that must be slavishly imitated in dealing ecumenically with the papacy but only to demonstrate the simple point that it is possible to have numerous patriarchal or similar structures in one Church while maintaining unity of faith: division of structures and consequent decentralization do not necessarily entail divisions of faith or destruction of unity and communion in the Church. It is also possible to have a strongly "democratic" polity, with lay people and "lower" clergy involved in episcopal, patriarchal, and catholicosal elections and in regular bodies of deliberation and decision making. I draw attention to these factors in an "instructive" way and do not suggest that they are or need necessarily to be "normative." That is to say, following Robert Taft's dictum that "history is instructive but not normative,"[185] the Armenian Church has been "displayed" here as an example from which certain helpful and instructive lessons might be drawn but it is not proposed as a norm that must necessarily be followed in the project of differentiating papal and patriarchal roles.[186]

Toward a Differentiation of Roles: Synthesis and Summary

The survey in this chapter shows the enormous diversity in the actual functioning of patriarchs and patriarchates and suggests that it would be possible for a Roman patriarchate to be, if desired and so designed, very centralized *as a patriarchate* and yet also to exercise very different, far less centralized "papal" authority in a united Orthodox-Catholic Church. There is a very wide range of patriarchal "styles" and structures, ranging from what could be called the "very centralized" (Constantinople) to the "moderately centralized" (Moscow, Bucharest, Alexandria [both Greek and Coptic]) through to the "decentralized" (Sofia, Antioch) and finally the "very decentralized" (Armenia).

Is it possible to attempt a synthesis and specify what, broadly, a patriarchal office entails? It seems that there are three features generally common to almost all patriarchates in Catholic and Orthodox terms.

First, a patriarch never governs alone and never possesses sole or unimpeded power. He always functions in some relationship to and with a synod (of varying size and powers) to "balance" or "check" the powers of the patriarch. Stated somewhat differently, the patriarch today (unlike in the past in some Churches) very rarely acts alone in a "monarchical" or unilateral fashion. The patriarchal Church, then, in whatever configuration, attempts—and sometimes less clearly and consistently in practical terms—to give place to both primacy and synodality, with neither the primate-patriarch nor the synod having complete power.

Second, each patriarchate is centred in its see-city and has primary jurisdiction over that territory. In the case of more recently created patriarchates, that territory may include the rest of the modern nation-state in which the see-city is found or it may include a larger geographical circumscription reflecting more ancient realities as in the case of the Greek Orthodox Patriarchate of Alexandria, which claims all of the African continent as its territory.

Each patriarchate, however, also has parishes, dioceses, metropolitinates, or other organizations and bodies (e.g., monastic communities) in other countries over which it exercises jurisdiction. In some cases, this jurisdiction is not as "full" or immediate as that which is exercised over the home territory, but in other cases it is.

Third, patriarchs and bishops usually have very limited say over their "brothers" and successors, that is to say no patriarch appoints his successor and neither patriarch nor bishop has an exclusive say in the selection of other bishops in their own dioceses or in the Church at large. Selection of hierarchs, then, is not the exclusive "gift" in the purview of some sovereign authority but usually arises out of an electoral process. This process involves, at a minimum, the metropolitans and permanent synod; more often, the full synod of bishops; and more often still—among the Orthodox but not, regrettably, among Catholic patriarchal synods—involving an electoral assembly that includes members of the "lower" clergy and laity.

What remains now is to attempt to sketch in fuller and more detailed terms how a Roman patriarchate could function and what it could look like. That is the burden of our final chapters.

CHAPTER FIVE

Patriarchates within the Latin Church

Institutional Implications and Practical Applications

The Necessity of Practical Reforms

Proposals calling for differentiation between the patriarchal and papal offices are quite numerous in the postconciliar period. None of these, however, has ever actually examined in any serious detail what this differentiation would practically entail; none has ever developed the idea of how such a patriarchate would function and with what authority vis-à-vis the papal office. I propose to do that here in some detail, breaking new ground by suggesting several practical ways for the papacy to be reconfigured.

In an article published on the eve of the first meeting of the JIC, John Meyendorff rightly lamented that "in discussing issues of ecclesiology, the temptation is always great to manipulate concepts and doctrinal definitions, while avoiding a critical approach to their application in practice."[1] That is a temptation which this chapter seeks to resist by specifying some of the practical changes to the papacy consequent to a differentiation between patriarchal and papal offices. While there are dangers in specifying "practical applications," there are also dangers in leaving the proposed reforms of the papacy vague and undefined. This latter danger is one that has, to my mind, limited the usefulness of almost all recent proposals for reform of the papacy.[2] To use a common colloquialism from the Orthodox that is no less forceful in its import because of the informality of its expression, "It is not the pope we fear but the pope's helpers!"[3] That is to say, mere theoretical proposals for reform of the papacy that do not also attend to such profoundly important practical questions as the role of papal "helpers" in the Roman Curia will remain proposals rightly intolerable to the Orthodox, who continue (and not without reason) to regard the Curia as a severe problem.

There need to be practical reforms, a view much underscored by numerous other authors. Waclaw Hryniewicz has noted that "ecumenism demands a critical attitude towards historical and present modalities of exercising the Roman primacy" and such a critical attitude must help to bring about "an effective reform of . . . church structures."[4] Such a reform should be undertaken on the basis of "the biblical concept of *kenosis*" and kenosis "would also concretely mean the structural reform of the papacy. The lesson of history should not be forgotten. A purely moral reform would not be sufficient to bring about a real change."[5]

The inadequacy of a "moral" reform has also been articulated by several others, including Yves Congar, and perhaps most concretely by retired Archbishop John Quinn.[6] In his own way, and perhaps most authoritatively, Cardinal Kasper, president of the PCPCU, has also acknowledged that discussions about reforms to the papacy cannot remain at an abstract level. In an article in 2006, Kasper reiterated that the question to which *Ut Unum Sint* is seeking an answer is that of the manner in which the papal office is exercised—"clearly the pope does not want to bring into question the petrine ministry and the dogma of primacy and infallibility. He wants to look for *new forms* of exercising the petrine ministry. . . . Thus the encyclical letter distinguishes between this unchangeable essence and the changeable forms."[7] Kasper ends his article by expressing his "hope . . . that, as was the case in the first millennium, the petrine ministry may take a form that, although differently exercised in the East and in the West, could be recognized both by the East and by the West within a unity in diversity and a diversity in unity."[8]

This theme of hopeful searching for new forms for the exercise of the Petrine or papal ministry comes through also in the 1998 "Reflections" of the Congregation for the Doctrine of the Faith entitled "The Primacy of the Successor of Peter in the Mystery of the Church," where the second section is entitled "The Exercise of the Primacy and Its Forms." The document acknowledges that "the primacy of Peter's Successor has historically been expressed in different forms of exercise appropriate to the situation of a pilgrim Church in this changing world." The document then makes two crucial points:

> the fact that a particular task has been carried out by the primacy in a certain era does not mean *by itself* that this task should necessarily be reserved always to the Roman Pontiff, and, vice versa, the *mere* fact that a particular role was not previously exercised by the Pope does not warrant the conclusion that this role could not in some way be exercised in the future as a competence of the primacy.[9]

Given such a recognition at the highest levels of the Church—from a pope himself, to his Congregation for the Doctrine of the Faith, and the PCPCU—to new forms of exercise of the papacy, I suggest both newly reconfigured and new forms of exercise of a papacy in which the patriarchal role is differentiated from the papal and *both* are strengthened by being more clearly defined. Put more simply, I ask and answer two questions: What would a Roman *patriarchate* look like and what would its responsibilities be as differentiated from the papacy? And what would the *papacy,* in turn, retain as its own unique responsibilities?

Caveats and Cautions

In what follows, I seek a balance between leaving the call for reform at a purely theoretical or "moral" level, on the one hand, and an overly detailed, prescriptive application of proposals for reform on the other. A balance is sought so that these proposals are neither too vague, lacking all specificity and applicability on the one hand, or on the other, so descriptive or, worse, prescriptive, as to constitute a presumptuous list of "job descriptions" or canonical-organizational "terms of reference." It is not for any one scholar to prescribe dramatic changes to the papacy, the polity of the entire Latin Church, and then the Orthodox Churches themselves in their relations with the papacy! These are all extremely serious and very weighty matters, and any changes to them can only come about through the most careful and prayerful consideration of the Church in conciliar fashion under the guidance of the Holy Spirit, seeking always to ensure that whatever recommendations are proposed respect history and sacred Tradition, and are undertaken always and only in response to the call to and prayer for unity made by the Head of the Church Himself. What follows are simply recommendations to the Churches for their consideration.

I try to find what Olivier Clément has called "a creative tension" in the papacy, a tension between openness to the Spirit in unforeseen and uncertain situations and the creation of offices and juridical structures in anticipation of certain problems.[10] I do not pretend that my suggestions are the only possible, logical, or appropriate ones. At several points, I am aware of some alternatives to what I suggest, which I will briefly note before going on to describe why one of them seems better than others. Even in suggesting that one structure or proposal seems better than others, I will not presume to suggest all the details for how that structure should be established—those are details that can and must be determined only by those who will live with and under them. There are no universally accepted norms for patriarchal structures in particular, and each Church is generally given considerable latitude in establishing its structures as its situation requires. The Roman Church should thus be extended wide latitude in setting up her own structures, and for that reason I will suggest *some* practical reforms, but by no means all, leaving always the final decisions to the judgment of those who enjoy the charism of the episcopal office and, in the meantime, being entirely open to further suggestions of other theologians. At no point, then, have I seen this as an exercise in "structural engineering" a practice Michael Magee has rightly decried.[11] While trying to be reasonably practical in some suggestions, I have equally tried to avoid capriciously cobbling together colourful tiles to fabricate some kind of ecclesiastical *bricolage*.

To avoid this danger of reconfiguring the Church in my own image, as it were, or at least in view of my own limited concepts, I have sought at every point to propose, where possible, not new creations dreamt up in my imagination but historically and theologically justifiable reconfigurations of existing or historical institutional forms so that these forms can more fully embody both their own history and their current theology. I have always had in mind Congar's "great law," quoted in the introduction and worth recalling once more—"the great law of Catholic reform will begin with a return to the principles of Catholicism. It is necessary to interrogate the tradition and to dive back into it, understanding that 'tradition' does not mean 'routine' nor even, properly, 'the past'."[12] I propose, wherever possible, reconfigurations in keeping with the principles and historical practices of Catholic tradition. Only after the potential of such reconfigurations is exhausted do I suggest—with, I hope, caution and restraint—the importance of creating new forms that, while new, are not created entirely *ex nihilo* but are in fact grounded in the principles of synodality and primacy and seek to give expression to those principles in creative but faithful ways.

Possible Objections to a Roman Patriarchal Structure

Much of what is proposed below will inevitably raise anxiety on the part of certain Catholics for whom the papacy is and must always be (in their perception if not in reality) an adamantine "rock" that does not break and will not move in the chaotic upheaval of our time inside and outside the Church. There is concern on the part of some primarily but not exclusively Catholic observers that any changes to the papacy—including, presumably, the "resurrection" of the patriarchal office at least insofar as it is thought to require a decentralization in the Latin Church—will destabilize if not simply destroy the Church. Change to the papacy, for those of this mindset, is perceived as weakening the Church's ability to respond to the various crises in the Church today, most of which have to do with the particular exercise of magisterial teaching authority on moral questions especially.[13] Since this is one of three concerns frequently voiced, I consider it important to briefly examine these arguments and respond to them.

The first argument is perhaps the simplest one and therefore dealt with most briefly, that the creation of patriarchal structures in the Latin

Church would be an artificial "Easternization" or "Byzantinization" of uniquely Latin ecclesial structures that are singular in nature. While it is true that the Western Church has never fully understood what it means to be a patriarchal Church and that patriarchs are much more numerous and common in the Eastern Churches, it does not follow that the patriarchate is a completely extraneous and alien institution having no foundations in the West. To this, on the contrary, I can make two replies. First, as I shall demonstrate in this chapter, there is abundant evidence of the pope functioning in a patriarchal fashion, especially through his regular and close collaboration with an authoritative Roman synod that shared authority with him for the overall good of the Church on questions of liturgy, episcopal appointments, and related administrative, doctrinal, and moral matters.

Second, there is the ongoing existence of actual figures called "patriarchs" in Western ecclesial communities and in the Latin Church, including the patriarch of Jerusalem, the patriarch of Venice, and the patriarch of Lisbon, all of whom hold that title to this very day.[14] While these are all recognized as having only a "prerogative of honour" (*CIC* canon 438), they are significant in demonstrating that the title is *not* foreign to the Latin Church as some might seem to think. Presumably, these sees could have been given another title to distinguish and embellish them, but it was recognized on the part of the papacy and the Latin Church that "patriarch" was a singular honor than which nothing higher—save, of course, for the papacy itself—could be conceived.[15] Western familiarity with, and recognition of, the singular and superlative nature of this title is surely a motivating factor behind not just West-Roman use of the title, but also Protestant. The Czechoslovak Hussite Church, founded in 1920, has designated its chief hierarch as "patriarch," a decision made all the more curious by the fact that they began ordaining women to the episcopate in 1999.[16] Among some Anglicans there has been long-standing discussion as to whether the archbishop of Canterbury should be designated a patriarch.[17]

A second argument one sometimes hears is that moving away from strongly centralized Roman government in the person of the pope and toward a more decentralized form of government in which local and regional bodies have greater autonomy will introduce a dangerous element of "democracy" into the Church or may lead to a revival of "conciliarism."[18] What this argument fails to consider is the example of the Eastern Catholic Churches, who have for many years exercised increasing levels of self-government without thereby in the least introducing doctrinal disorder into their Churches and without in the least succumbing to democratic "populism" in some base sense. This argument can be turned on its head to ask the question: if Eastern Catholics can be trusted to regain and exercise patriarchal and synodal governance and be entrusted with the election of their own hierarchs, why are Roman Catholics "forbidden" to do so?[19] If these synodal practices are good enough for some constituent members (Churches *sui iuris*) of the Catholic Church, why can they not be enjoyed by all? As for conciliarism, nothing that is proposed here suggests that the government of the Church should be turned over *exclusively* to councils or synods. Monarchical "papism" is to be rejected just as much as headless "conciliarism" is.

The third argument in various forms is perhaps the most serious and most substantial and merits more careful consideration. That argument, in brief and to state the matter baldly, is that any changes to the papacy will unleash moral, doctrinal, and disciplinary chaos in the Church. The noted English Dominican Aidan Nichols has argued that "at the present time, the Catholic Church, in many parts of the world, is undergoing one of the most serious crises in its history, a crisis resulting from a disorienting encounter with secular culture and compounded by a failure of Christian discernment on the part of many people over the last quarter century from the highest office-holders to the ordinary faithful."[20] In such a context, as Meyendorff hinted many years ago, seeking drastic changes to the papacy, no matter how legitimate and ecumenically necessary they may be, *ostensibly* might create deleterious consequences for both Catholics and Orthodox.[21] Nobody has put this more perceptively or sharply than—ironically enough—the Orthodox theologian Patrick Reardon in an article published during the visit of Pope Benedict XVI to Ecumenical Patriarch Bartholomew in November 2006. Reardon argues that if you "take away the centralized doctrinal authority of Rome . . . the Roman Catholic Church today would be without rudder or sail in a raging sea."

Given this reality, Reardon counsels that

if an Orthodox Christian, then, loves his Roman Catholic brothers and sisters, he will not wish for a diminished papacy. Indeed, he will devoutly pray for a very strong papacy. Otherwise he may be failing in proper Christian love for those whose spiritual well-being requires this strong papacy. It is a singular irony that our prayers for an effective and vibrant papacy, though motivated by a loving concern for our Roman Catholic brethren, would hardly seem, on the face of it, to further the healing of our ecclesiastical division. However we got into this mess, only God can get us out.[22]

Reardon voices some concerns that, on their face, seem legitimate and certainly reflect the concerns of certain Catholics as well,[23] but his article fails to withstand greater scrutiny. He does not deal with numerous obvious objections. First, he has nowhere demonstrated that a less centralized papacy would result in even greater disorder in the Catholic Church, and indeed he cannot do this because none of us can predict the future. Second, such a claim calls into doubt the sustaining guidance of Providence in the Person of the Holy Spirit, whose presence has not been lacking in protecting Reardon's own Orthodox tradition that itself has no heavily centralized leadership and yet has maintained an admirable and compelling coherence in doctrine. Third, a claim that a weakened papacy always results in greater doctrinal incoherence—heresy even—in the Church is not really borne out by the relevant history. Reardon forgets—as do many others—that the current, strongly centralized papacy, with the pope acting as global teacher, is a role that is barely more than a century old.[24] During much of papal history, the Church's core doctrine held together even under sometimes severely emaciated, persecuted, decadent, or outright wicked papal leadership.[25] Fourth and perhaps most damning, Reardon overlooks the fact that the currently strongly centralized papacy has itself presided over, and in many ways *doubtlessly contributed to,* the several crises he laments. If Reardon is concerned about the depressingly low calibre of too many bishops today, about the sexual abuse in the priesthood,[26] or about the often dodgy theology being taught in the name of the Church,[27] it is fatuous in the extreme to imagine that an unreconstructed papacy is going to solve these problems or prevent similar ones from arising in the future when *all of these crises are directly (if partially) attributable to the current modus operandi of the papacy.*[28] Fifth and finally, he fails to account for the possibility that a differentiated papacy with a patriarchate or patriarchates in its direct jurisdiction, and in union with the other (Orthodox) patriarchates, may in fact be enormously *strengthened* and enhanced precisely in this form. Those who attack the pope or papal teaching would be given pause to reconsider their position if the pope were to be firmly and clearly backed up by his brother patriarchs around the world, who would thus present a unanimous or strongly united front to doubters and dissenters. Reardon's fears, in sum, are not really credible. We have little to fear, and potentially much to gain, from differentiating roles and reconfiguring papal authority in an ecumenically sensitive and ecclesiologically sound way.

Consider the following additional arguments to ease the minds of those still anxious about a presumed "weakening" of the Church through a reconfiguration of the papacy. As Yves Congar hinted many years ago, distinguishing between patriarchal and papal offices would not necessarily alter very much in the actual life of the *Latin* Church.[29] Congar does not elaborate on this point, but I take him to suggest that a Roman patriarchate could be set up in such a way as to maintain the same highly centralized control over the *Latin* Church that the papacy has today. (As we saw in the previous chapter, there are no norms universally binding as to how a patriarchate is to be structured, and not a few of them have often been extremely centralized in ways very similar to Rome.) In other words, there would be a differentiation of patriarchal and papal roles, but this could in most ways be a differentiation without a difference *for the life of the Latin Church* if its patriarchate(s) were designed to maintain the same level of centralization and direct, constant Roman control. Only those "Eastern" Christians in communion with the Church of Rome but not a part of the Roman patriarchate would notice the difference in concrete ways because that direct, constant Roman control would not pertain to them.

I think, however, that merely differentiating the papal and patriarchal roles, without endowing the latter with concretely differentiated forms to manifest its life in substantially authoritative ways, would be a fruitless exercise both for relations with the Orthodox and for the very life of the Latin Church. As Michael Magee has noted, the collapse of patriarchal into papal roles has had damaging internal consequences for the Latin Church, placing her "in danger of losing sight of her own venerable particularity, and of defending her own sacred traditions on tenuous grounds, as if they were consecrated by their universal necessity rather than by their belonging to her own unique legacy among others of apostolic provenance. One logical result . . . would be a certain proclivity to intolerance of other traditions,"[30] a proclivity amply demonstrated in history. To counteract a possible revival of this dangerous and destructive proclivity, to answer *Ut Unum Sint,* and to put forth a model that is both recognized by and, it is to be hoped, acceptable to the Orthodox, I propose that the Roman patriarchate be more clearly and concretely differentiated from the papacy in four ways.

Establishing Latin Patriarchal Structures

My first proposal concerns the size of the Latin Church. This Church, numbering more than one billion members, very much stands in need of genuine regional units that will function between the diocesan or local Church and the universal Church. I propose the creation of six proper patriarchates within the Latin Church.[31]

Second, there needs to be a fully functioning synod not only governing each individual patriarchate, but also a synod for the life of the Latin Church as a whole. There was operative in the Latin Church for more than a thousand years a proper synod that shared authority with the bishop of Rome. Today, with modifications, such a synod, building on the modest attempt at synodal governance set up in 1965 by Pope Paul VI, needs to be revived both to strengthen the life of the Latin Church and also to embody its ecumenical seriousness in the search for unity with the Orthodox.

Third, there needs to be within each patriarchate a functioning, smaller *permanent* synod to resume responsibilities for *daily* administration and so take over most of the functions of the Roman Curia. I propose that the permanent synod of each patriarchate be composed of the patriarch together with the heads of the episcopal conferences that make up that patriarchate. There is evidence in the life of the Roman Church of a kind of "permanent synod," vestiges of which are seen today in the College of Cardinals. Here again, then, I am proposing less of a new creation and more of a revival and reconfiguration of a venerable tradition rooted in the deepest and earliest parts of Roman ecclesial history.

These three proposed changes—regional patriarchates, a full synod, and a permanent synod—all pertain to how the Latin Church and the pope would function in a patriarchal manner. Only once the internal life of the Latin Church has been thus reconfigured in a patriarchal manner can we see what "papal" tasks would remain to the bishop of Rome as universal pontiff with solicitude for all the Churches of Christ, East and West. After examining these three proposed changes, I will conclude the chapter by proposing a new institution, also synodal in nature, to co-ordinate the life of all the Churches, to bring together all the patriarchs, and to share, with the bishop of Rome, in the responsibility for unity of the entire Catholic Church properly so called. I shall propose the creation of an "ecumenical synod" comprised of all patriarchs, Eastern and Western, under the presidency of the pope, acting not with reference to the Latin Church, but for the good of the universal Church. I will, finally, articulate the remaining responsibilities of the pope *qua* pope, returning to *Ut Unum Sint* for a concluding word on those very responsibilities newly understood.[32]

"Canonical Territory" and "Universal Jurisdiction"

My first proposal for changes to the Latin Church concerns the creation of new patriarchates. This proposal has been raised often (if superficially) in the postconciliar period by numerous and important theologians, but it has never been given thoroughgoing consideration as to how such patriarchates would be set up, where they would exist, and how they would operate. I propose to do those three things here.

I begin with the question of regional patriarchates in the Latin Church for several reasons. First, I think that this system as I outline it will avoid two very severe problems confronting not just the Latin Church but other Christians relating to that Church today. Those problems are the size of the Latin Church in demographic terms—which is noted with concern not just by the Orthodox but by many Protestants also, especially in official ecumenical bodies—and the limitless territory of the Church in geographic terms. In demographic terms, the Latin Church is the largest Christian body in the world, numbering well over one billion members, far outstripping any other Christian group. In geographic terms, the "Western" Church has no boundaries whatsoever and has parishes, dioceses, and provinces on six of the world's seven continents. Moreover, the bishop of Rome acknowledges no limits to his territory but, indeed, precisely as pope, lays claim to "universal jurisdiction" over the entire world, which is thus all regarded as his *de facto* "canonical territory."

These issues of "canonical territory" and "universal jurisdiction" are incredibly vexing and hugely complicated.[33] We have long since moved from the relatively simpler days of the early Church, when questions of jurisdiction and territory were purely practical ones. Today, these questions are invested by some with a theological, political, and even "psychological" significance far beyond practical considerations: today questions of jurisdiction and territory have been almost sacralized in practice even as, in theory, neither phrase has ever, to my knowledge, received an adequate, convincing, and comprehensive *theological* explication. "Jurisdiction" is of course a key term in the papal lexicon, and a substantial ecumenical problem, but it is not, as Jean Tillard has reminded us, one that has ever been clearly and adequately defined, above all in practical terms.[34] Too often, rather, the term has been left undefined and into this vacuum all sorts of "maximalist" and "ultramontane" (and other) interpretations have been allowed to run rampant, as Tillard, Alberigo, and Pottmeyer have all argued.[35] Such a lack of theological clarity poses grave difficulties for ecumenical progress.[36] The question of jurisdiction very much requires an adequate explication in a commonly accepted way because, as Tillard and others have recognized, "the problem of universal jurisdiction . . . is the real stumbling block"[37] to Christian unity.

It seems more necessary than ever to propose some ways forward given a context today in which claims are made, challenges thrown down, history or precedent summarily and often fatuously invoked, and protests occasionally made—but very little insightful and comprehensive thought[38] given to the questions of what territoriality, jurisdiction, and the ancient canons[39] mean. In the world of the early twenty-first century, where peoples have long since moved en masse and where immigration from one country to another is a very common experience, ancient sees exist on paper but in reality are centred elsewhere (e.g., the various titulars of the patriarchate of Antioch live in Damascus or Beirut). Large numbers of Orthodox and Eastern Catholics live in traditionally Western (Anglican or Roman Catholic) territories and vice versa.[40] Cities, dioceses, provinces, patriarchates, and even the papacy itself are based in places whose pre-eminence was founded on the "principle of accommodation"[41] to ancient and now largely extinct imperial structures and vastly different urban centres.[42] In such a context, it is extremely difficult to speak, with any sense, about canonical territory exclusive to one Church or to attempt, in isolation, to conjure up for the Roman patriarchate "clear and credible boundaries" as some Orthodox have insisted.[43]

On what basis would one draw those boundaries today? Would it be current geopolitical or demographical realities? Would it consist of a reversion to earlier or even original demarcations?[44] Would boundaries be drawn up according to totally new criteria—and if so, what?[45] Who, in fact, commands the authority to draw those boundaries, and on what basis, now that Christians of all traditions are living side-by-side without an emperor and imperial structures common to all and available for borrowing? Virtually any city or country today in Western Europe, North America, and Australia is not just multicultural, but "multi-ecclesial" with different Eastern Catholic, Eastern Orthodox, Roman Catholic, Oriental Orthodox, and Protestant Christians living side by side. How does one decide questions of territory and jurisdiction when faced with such a situation?

To date, there has been much (especially Russian[46]) hectoring about these questions, but very little serious, comprehensive, and ecumenical scholarship done on these questions of "canonical territory" and "jurisdiction" in the context of modern geopolitical realities, and the uses and abuses of the ancient canons, often for nationalistic purposes.[47] Apart from the occasional, isolated, and incredible proposal to reconstruct the "pentarchy"[48] (even though the original never functioned very well, was designed in and for a world which has long since disappeared, and neither then nor today has ever been adequately justified in *theological* terms, as John Zizioulas and John Meyendorff[49] among others have observed), most people today seem to prefer that these canons be quietly ignored and the question of territoriality abandoned informally and *de facto* if not formally and *de jure*.[50]

These are questions of such complexity and immensity as to preclude resolution here, yet this issue is too significant to escape some discussion at this point. As an interim "answer" to these questions, consider the first of my four proposals for reconfiguring the papacy-patriarchate, viz., the creation of regional patriarchates within the Latin Church. These regional patriarchates would be simply the first modest but important step toward the reintroduction into the Latin Church of genuine regional units, breaking up the monolithic structure that currently exists and encouraging a new modus operandi for the Latin Church. A more diffused regional structure would encourage the Latin Church to understand in a deeper way her own particularity and territoriality. A more diffused regional structure would disabuse Latin ecclesiology of its unhelpful tendencies toward a falsely universalistic notion that other Churches may be regionally based or territorially circumscribed, but the Latin Church somehow transcends all territorial particularity to encompass the entire world. A more diffused regional structure would remind the Latin Church of her own nature as but one Church *sui iuris* in communion with many other Churches *sui iuris*.[51] A more diffused regional structure, encompassing its own patriarchates, finally, would show the Orthodox that the Latin Church is serious about unity, takes seriously the Eastern polity of patriarchs, and is ready to grapple in a substantial way with the vexed questions of jurisdiction and canonical territory.

To be sure, this is only a modest first step, and there are many complicated facets to these questions awaiting resolution. Ultimately these questions about jurisdiction and territoriality can only be properly and definitively resolved by an ecumenical council properly so called. Only there can Catholic and Orthodox bishops finally clarify these many issues and decide how they wish to move forward together. What follows are simply some suggestions that might provide a way forward until that council can be called.[52]

Regional Patriarchates

One way to deal with the questions of territory and jurisdiction in the Roman Church, and also at the same time to deal with the issue of the sheer overwhelming size of the Roman Church in numerical terms, is to create regional patriarchates within one overall Roman patriarchate. I propose therefore that within the Latin Church there be six continental patriarchates. Each patriarchate would be equal in status and have the same level of self-governance as the others, but would maintain a relationship with the Roman patriarchate, which would have additional responsibilities for the co-ordination of the overall life of the Latin Church much the same way the Armenian Catholicos-Patriarch of Etchmiadzin enjoys overall superintendence over the other catholicos and patriarchs in his Church.

I propose not national but regional patriarchates for four reasons. First, the ancient patriarchates have always been regionally based rather than strictly national (especially as that is understood in the terms of modernity's notion of the "nation-state"). My suggestion respects this ancient tradition but attempts to bring it up to date to reflect current geopolitical realities.

Second, nationalism is one of the greatest sins besetting far too many Eastern Christians—Catholic and Orthodox—and I am utterly loathe to see the possibility of it being used to form ecclesial structures in a Church that has generally managed to avoid its worst excesses.[53] Rightly has it been condemned (in its phyletistic guise) as heresy, even if that heresy still awaits extirpation in the overwhelming majority of Eastern Catholic and Orthodox Churches.[54]

Third, the sheer number of nations today would seem to preclude each having a patriarchate. To envisage nearly two hundred national patriarchs seems highly problematic for several reasons. Not all nations, e.g., are large and mature enough to support such a structure. (Would there be a patriarch for the tiny handful of Catholics living in, say, the Maldives or other "faraway countries of which we know nothing"?[55] Would a tiny handful of Catholics in overwhelmingly Muslim countries merit a patriarchate?) Patriarchates are usually only established in major centres long established and having a maturity and history to them as well as a substantial population. Many countries lack all these factors, and to persist in establishing patriarchates in tiny or very new countries would seem to disrespect the venerable nature of the institution. A continent, by contrast, is large enough to guarantee a substantial population base and would not be affected by the sometimes capricious political fortunes of countries, especially small ones.

Fourth and finally, establishing patriarchates on a largely continental basis returns us, in a fashion, to the use of the "principle of accommodation" of the early Church insofar as continents are, in a certain sense, "arbitrary" creations not of human politicians (whether secular or ecclesial) jockeying for national advantage but of the geophysical evolution of planetary structures, an evolution out of the control of human hands. The early Church, as Francis Dvornik demonstrated so clearly, did not content herself with setting up entirely new structures created *de novo* but instead accommodated herself to the extant imperial structures.[56] Even the very language of the empire ("diocese," "province," "metropolitan," etc.) was borrowed by the nascent Church.[57] The use of continents as the basis upon which to construct new patriarchates avoids several problems—nationalism, numbers, and the whole impossible business of trying to establish ecclesial-political agreement on commonly acceptable criteria on the basis of which some other circumscription would be used. Put more simply, continents are useful precisely insofar as they are not national creations, and one is not therefore confronted with the question of which countries or which cities should have pre-eminence, and why.

Patriarchal Territories: There would, then, be a patriarch of North America, one of South America, one of Europe, one of Africa, another of Asia, and a sixth of Australia (with responsibility for the southern Pacific region). Each of these would have jurisdiction over all the countries and territories of a given continent[58] and, moreover, over all Catholics of any Church *sui iuris* on that continent. This, it seems to me, is the most feasible way of proceeding, and no less a figure than Pope John Paul II himself would seem to support this notion as well. Two months after his election in 1978, he encouraged "the development of continental forms of cooperation."[59] In advance of the turn of the millennium, he convoked synods based on continental circumscriptions, and in the post-synodal document issued after one of these synods, he spoke approvingly of "the value of a communion . . . transcending individual Conferences of Bishops." He went on to note, "It would be helpful to specify more exactly the nature of these meetings, so that they may become a better expression of communion among all bishops."[60]

The noted canonist Myriam Wijlens has recently demonstrated that there are "supranational" organizations within the Latin Church bringing together local Churches, or at least their hierarchs or other representatives, in groupings larger than national episcopal conferences.[61] Some of these are based on continental groupings but others are based on linguistic or cultural ones.[62] There are, Wijlens notes, "at least 13 institutions of this kind," including some in Latin America, Africa, and Asia. Of these, "the oldest and probably most known one is CELAM, the Council (consejo) for the Bishops of Latin America." There are other types of these institutions, including those that "are rather large and include the local churches of a whole continent, such as the Council of the Episcopal Conferences of Europe (CCEE), the Federation of the Asian Bishops' Conferences (FABC) . . . , the Federation of Catholic Bishops' Conferences of Oceania, [and] the Symposium of the Episcopal Conferences of Africa and Madagascar."[63]

It would seem, then, that there are other ways to construct regional bodies apart from references to continents. Indeed, it is an important question as to whether continental patriarchates would be able to function and are the most sensible way of proceeding. Consider the vastness of Africa or Asia, for example, the relative poverty of many of their constituent countries, and the enormous number of very different cultures each encompasses. Africa and Asia encompass many countries speaking many languages. How realistic is it to expect that such territories would be able to function together as a coherent unit? I grant the force of these questions, and would reply as follows: *continental patri-archates are simply the first step in the evolution of Latin ecclesial struc-tures.* Once they are established, it would be possible to test their feasibility and to make adjustments accordingly. Perhaps at some future date, there would be the further creation of additional patriarch-ates based upon further geographical considerations—e.g., an "East Asia" and "West Asia" patriarchate—or upon other considerations (e.g., "French Africa" and "English Africa" patriarchates). Continental patri-archates, then, are merely an interim stage in the development of the Latin Church. This point must be kept in mind with all the provisions articulated below: none is to be taken as definitive and binding unto the ages of ages. Like the *CCEO,* the provisions are suggested as an *interim* step forward pending full unity between Catholics and Ortho-dox, at which time all these questions—especially of structure and jurisdiction—will again be revisited in, one hopes, a fully conciliar fashion.

Patriarchal See-City: Given that the patriarchates would be based on continents rather than countries, the question arises as to what the see-city of each patriarch should be. With the exception of two continents—Europe and Africa—there would seem to be no easy or clear answer. One could, for example, propose "floating" patriarchal see-cities, that is, the see-city of the patriarch would be whatever his see-city as a diocesan bishop is. A patriarch would remain a function-ing diocesan bishop even while patriarch.[64] Thus, e.g., if the bishop of Chicago were elected patriarch of North America, his see-city would be Chicago for as long as he remained patriarch. When his term ended and another—perhaps, say, the bishop of Halifax—were elected, the see-city of the patriarchate would accordingly shift. This proposal, however, is perhaps too abstract and attenuates the relationship be-tween a local Church (and her leadership) and the particular people of God in a particular place. Additionally, this proposal is clearly lacking in any historical precedent.

Instead of "floating" see-cities, one could proceed in (at least) two other ways. The first would be to make fresh use of the "principle of accommodation" to suggest that the largest or most important city of a continent would be the patriarchal see-city. Neither criteria, however, is without its limitations. In the case of North America, Mexico City is the largest—that is, most populous—city, but Washington, D.C. is arguably the most important insofar as it is the capital of the most powerful country on the continent. Clearly, for several reasons, the principle of accommodation alone will be an unhelpfully limited way to proceed.[65]

The second way would be to proceed based on claims of "apostolicity." This would work clearly in the case of at least two continents, viz., Europe (where Rome is the only obvious contender) and Africa (where Alexandria is equally the only obvious contender[66]). The application of this principle becomes perhaps somewhat trickier in the case of Asia, not least because one is confronted with the question of what constitutes Asia today. Is Turkey part of Asia? (That is a topic currently debated politically and theologically, but for the time being the convention would seem to concede that Turkey is not—yet—part of Europe in any formally recognized way, and it therefore remains a part of Asia.) Is Israel part of Asia? If we recall that the "Middle East" is not a continent per se but a very modern geopolitical term, then the answer would seem to be yes. On this basis, then, and applying the principle of apostolicity, one is confronted with *at least* three possible patriarchal see-cities in Asia: Antioch and Constantinople (in Turkey), and Jerusalem in Israel—and one cannot summarily dismiss the other apostolic claimants from the so-called non-Chalcedonian Churches, including the Church of the East.[67] Nonetheless, I would propose that Jerusalem be recognized as the patriarchal see-city for Asia because of its obvious and overwhelming apostolic foundations.[68] Where other cities can, with varying degrees of credibility, claim one (or, with Rome, two) apostles as founders, Jerusalem can claim to have had all the apostles there at least at some point for the most significant periods of the earliest years of Christian history.[69]

The principal of apostolicity is not without its limitations, and it seems clear that it was a later development, often used tendentiously when political circumstances changed. This principal runs into its clearest obstacle when it comes to the remaining three continents of North America, South America, and Australia, none of which ever had apostolic foundations for the simple reason that they are all "discoveries" of the middle to later second millennium. On what basis, then, could one choose a patriarchal see-city if apostolicity does not obtain? The apostles, Orthodox and Catholic (and some Anglican) Christians believe, chose successors, whom we today recognize as bishops. I would propose that one could extrapolate from the principal of apostolicity to argue that the appointment of a first bishop and the erection of the first diocese on a continent is sufficient to establish "apostolic" credentials for our purposes here. Thus, for the Catholic Church in North America, the most senior or "primatial" see is Québec, established in 1674; for South America the most senior see is Santo Domingo—established in 1511—in the Dominican Republic, the oldest European colony in the Western hemisphere; and for Australia the most senior "primatial" see is Sydney, established 1842.[70]

One could of course come up with different proposals for the erection of patriarchates and the selection of their see-cities. Further evolutions, including new patriarchates, or modification to those proposed here, remain possible, but it has been necessary to begin with a modest first step of proposing a Roman patriarchate itself and then five additional patriarchates as a way to overcome the problem of the size of the Latin Church and the serious problem of the collapse of patriarchal into papal roles.

Full Patriarchal Synod

As we have seen in great detail in the fourth chapter, patriarchs are always assisted by two synodal bodies—a larger "full" synod meeting infrequently and a much smaller residential or "permanent" synod meeting regularly to assist the patriarch in the ongoing administration of the patriarchate. I propose that each of the patriarchates have a full synod consisting of all sitting diocesan bishops of each continent holding office (that is, retired bishops would be permitted but not required to attend the synod, and they would not have a vote).[71] This synod, in ways each could determine, would be charged with, inter alia, regulating the liturgical life of that Church, and electing its own hierarchs through methods each could determine.[72]

Necessity of Synodality for the Life of the Church. The importance of synodality for the life of the Church cannot be stressed enough.[73] My proposal here is born of a desire to see this synodality manifested in the Latin Church so that she may realign herself more closely with her own history and theology, and, moreover, may allow her own recently redis-covered practices of synodality and "collegiality"[74] to be more fully manifested for her own good as well as for the good of the unity of the Church. A functioning legislative synod in each patriarchate of the Latin Church would allow the Latin Church to return to a practice that has historically marked all the apostolic Churches and is today ac-counted great weight not only among the Christian East but also among many ecclesial communities of the West, including especially the Anglican Communion. The fact that the Latin Church currently lacks such a fully functioning synod with real legislative powers is, ac-cording to the Roman Catholic theologian Michael Magee, "regrettable in the extreme,"[75] a view also echoed by numerous other Catholics in-cluding the retired Roman Catholic archbishop of San Francisco John Quinn, the late Melkite Patriarch Maximos IV, the historian and Jesuit Robert Taft, and the late Ukrainian Catholic Metropolitan Maxim Her-maniuk.[76] Stated positively, the Jesuit theologian and ecumenist Mi-chael Fahey and the current Melkite Patriarch Gregorios III have both suggested that the institution of real forms of synodality in the Roman Church today would be extremely helpful not merely for her ecu-menical relations but especially for her own internal ordering and gov-erning.[77]

History of Synods in the Latin Church. There is a very great deal of historical evidence of a genuine and functioning synod, with real and not merely "consultative" powers, in the Church of Rome from the ear-liest centuries until well into the second millennium.[78] Following the fifth canon of the first Council of Nicaea in 325, which prescribed that "synods shall be held at the following times: one before Lent . . . [and] the second after the season of autumn," Roman synods met with some bi-annual regularity and collaborated with their bishop until well into the second millennium. Even in the second millennium, the great cen-tralizing reformer Pope Gregory VII did not dare attempt many of his far-reaching changes without calling for and receiving support from synods, which were, as Eamon Duffy tells us, "genuine deliberative assemblies, in which dissident voices were allowed."[79] Kathleen Cushing's recent scholarship has argued that the reforms of the eleventh century, beginning with Gregory's predecessor and role model in some respects, Pope Leo IX, were carried about in significant measure precisely because they had synodal approval and force behind them. She notes that "there was an increasing appreciation by the eleventh-century papacy of the benefit of convening councils, especially in Rome, as a means by which the papacy could promote its reform agenda."[80] These were not ad hoc affairs convoked at papal whim but were felt to be mandated by the early ecumenical councils, a mandate the Church of Rome took seriously as evidenced by the fact that "by the pontificate of Gregory VII, the papacy was holding councils twice a year, attendance at which was obligatory for all summoned."[81] When those summoned gathered, they had, as Duffy notes and I. S. Robinson concurs, real authority to exercise and did so in a system of "checks and balances" very much like patriarchal synods, with bishops having the right to pass legislation but the pope at some periods seeming to possess a right to "veto" it by withholding his consent.[82]

Gradually, however, this synod was increasingly sidelined, replaced first by the newly created "cardinals" meeting in a synod-like "consistory,"[83] which took over many of the previous synod's responsibilities, and then, later still, by the new departments of the Curia, which took over other functions or created new ones for itself following increasingly departmental and bureaucratized methods quite removed from any sense or practice of synodality.[84]

There is, then, an abundance of both historical justification as well as pressing current need for fully functioning synods with legislative powers in the Latin Church as a whole. If the Latin Church is to be configured into regional patriarchates, then these synods are absolutely crucial. There is, as the previous chapter made clear, no patriarchate that functions except synodally. No patriarch exists or commands authority except in conjunction with his synod.

What would these Latin patriarchal synods seek to do? While the exact configurations of each patriarchal synod could be left to the individual patriarchates, synods—including both those that have histori-

cally existed in the Roman Church and those currently extant in
Orthodox Churches—have two major responsibilities. First, the full
synod is the electoral synod for choosing both a patriarch and all other
hierarchs. Second, the full synod also sets directions and makes decisions whose implementation is left to the patriarch in conjunction with
the permanent synod. These two broad areas of responsibility would,
then, also most likely pertain to the Latin patriarchal synods.

Permanent Patriarchal Synod

A full synod is not the body responsible for daily administration of a
given patriarchal Church. A full synod is generally too cumbersome
to make daily decisions and especially to execute them. A large body
like a full synod should therefore not undertake the quotidian "man-
agement" of the Church, but could only make key decisions that
would then be carried out by other hierarchs in the smaller, "permanent" synod. Patriarchates typically have permanent synods alongside
the "full" synod, and I propose the creation of such synods for each
of the continental patriarchates. The permanent synod would consist
of the patriarch and the presidents of all the episcopal conferences
under his jurisdiction.[85]

How these hierarchs are elected and for how long would be for each
patriarchate to determine. It seems important, however, to suggest that
the permanent synod be composed in the main of bishops who remain
functioning diocesan bishops rather than titular or "curial" bishops.[86] I
propose this so that these bishops are not unconnected from daily pastoral realities, and also so that we may avoid the problem—experienced
by Catholic and Orthodox hierarchs alike, though more acutely on the
part of the former—of those charged with the daily governance and
administration of the Church attempting to lord it over their brother
bishops, a problem that has notoriously bedevilled relations between
the Roman Curia and Latin bishops and, to a lesser extent, some Orthodox bishops at the hands of the hierarchs in the permanent synod.[87]

If these members of the permanent synod are to remain diocesan
bishops at the same time, the question naturally arises as to whether
their membership in the synod is going to take them away from their

dioceses for too long (thereby running the risk of episcopal absenteeism), or their residence in their dioceses is going to attenuate their
ability to assist the patriarch (thereby running the risk of the patriarch
assuming too many powers and becoming an isolated monarch-like
figure). It is important to strike a balance here. While bishops cannot
be away from home too often for practical and theological reasons,
neither can they fail to assist the patriarch as needed. I suggest a possible answer to this question of how to balance being away too often or
too little.

The permanent synod could "meet" very regularly without always
having to do so in person.[88] The advent of the computer, Internet,
satellite communications, video conferencing, and related technolo-
gies make it entirely plausible that sitting diocesan bishops could
regularly "gather" together for decision making in a permanent synod
without always having to leave home. These are all advances strongly
encouraged and supported by the Church for several decades now.
Successive papal and curial documents, building on the words of *Inter
Mirifica* of the Second Vatican Council, have advocated ever greater
confidence in, and widespread use of, various communications media
and technological advances both in general and then in the life of the
Church.[89] In "The Church and the Internet," the 2002 statement of
the Pontifical Council for Social Communications, the Internet and
related technology are lauded as "marvellous technical innovations"
(no. 1) and "gifts of God" (no. 2, quoting *Communio et Progressio*).
Catholics are exhorted to take maximum advantage of these gifts for
the good of the Church—"Hanging back timidly from fear of technology or for some other reason is not acceptable, in view of the very
many positive possibilities of the Internet" (no. 10). This document,
whose express purpose is to "consider the Internet's implications for
religion and especially for the Catholic Church," goes on generally to
say that "communication . . . is of the essence of the Church" (no. 3)
and, more particularly, that "the Church also needs to understand
and use the Internet as a tool of *internal* communications. This requires keeping clearly in view its special character as a direct, immediate, interactive, and *participatory* medium" (no. 6; my emphasis).
Even more directly, it is argued that the Internet "is an instrument

that can be put creatively to use for various aspects of administration and governance" including "such things as consulting experts, preparing meetings, and practicing collaboration in and among particular churches and religious institutes on local, national, and international levels" (no. 6).

History of Permanent Synods. A characteristic feature of patriarchates is the *synodus endemousa,* variously translated as the "residential" or "permanent" or "standing" synod, whose origins go all the way back to 394.[90] Almost all Orthodox Churches have a smaller "permanent synod" capable of meeting regularly and quickly with the patriarch (because usually "permanently" "standing" around the patriarch, the members typically reside in the patriarchal see-city or within easy reach of it), and then a larger "full" or "regular" or "holy" synod encompassing most if not all of the bishops of the Church, and meeting less regularly and quickly. The latter body typically elects the former.[91] This synod had its origin in the city of Constantinople and the relatively small number of bishops resident there in the imperial capital. Their residence made it very convenient for the patriarch to call upon them regularly for advice and decisions, and soon he was doing this often enough that these consultations became formalized and an official part of the ecclesial structures of the Constantinopolitan patriarchate. Proximity, convenience, and compact size were the attractive features of this synod.

College of Cardinals as a Form of Permanent Synod. Interestingly enough, a very similar body in the history of the Church of Rome has many of the same features—i.e., residency of a select and small number of senior hierarchs in or near Rome (in the so-called suburbicarian sees[92]) whose advice could quickly be sought, and who could, in turn, play the leading role in the election of the Roman bishop and in rendering him assistance in deciding matters of major importance for the Church of Rome and the Roman ecclesiastical province. Although—relative to the *synodos endemousa*—it has much later origins from the eleventh century onward, and although its origins are not usually conceived of in "synodal" terms, it is possible to conceive of the "College of Cardinals" (as it came to be known) as being, *de facto* if not *de jure,* a permanent, standing, quasi-synodal body offering assistance, counsel, and approval to the acts of the bishop of Rome in the governance of his Church.[93] As James Provost has summed up the matter, "during the twelfth century the curia received its first major reform after nearly a millennium of functioning in the manner *typical of a patriarchal see*. The regular meetings of Roman synods were replaced with the then-modern innovation of the . . . consistory."[94]

While the historical origins of the semantic and etymological meaning of "cardinal" and its ecclesiastical cognates are notoriously controverted, the history of the gathering of cardinals as a *collegium* is less so—even if theological disputes about the nature and authority of the college have been intense at periods in the history of the Church and remain less than satisfactorily resolved today.[95] The genesis of the college as such in the second millennium is bound up with one of the most far-reaching periods of ecclesiastical revolution ever seen in the history of the Roman Church. Broadly speaking, from the beginning of the eleventh to the late twelfth century, the Roman Church underwent numerous massive changes.[96] For our purposes here, four are especially noteworthy: the abandonment of a regular synod as an integral part of the polity of the Roman Church; the gradual replacement of the synod first by cardinals in "consistory"; then the sidelining of the consistory by the use of "general councils" of an increasingly advisory (rather than legislative) capacity; and finally the creation of individual offices, including those of papal "legates," and "bureaucratic" departments in the Roman Curia.[97] All this takes place in a context that is increasingly estranged from the Christian East and is increasingly inclined toward a monarchical view of *plenitudo potestatis*, unhindered by other claims from either fellow patriarchs or even other bishops.[98] In such a context, as Joseph Ratzinger recognized many years ago, the institution of the College of Cardinals comes to supplant the place of patriarchs:

> The cardinalate, an institution of the city of Rome, originally envisaged the deacons and parish priests of Rome as well as the bishops of the Roman province. The patriarchate, an institution of the universal Church, designates the bishops of the principal churches (the "primacies") and therefore the form by which the unity and interrelationship of wide areas of the Church was regulated. With the identification of the entire Church

with the local church of Rome, the cardinalate was seen as an office of the universal Church. The patriarchate became an honorary title bestowed by Rome. Since the thirteenth century a cardinal ranks above a patriarch: a local ecclesiastical honor stands above an ancient office of service to the whole Church.[99]

Leaving aside for now the question of the usurpation by cardinals of patriarchal roles, it is important to note that, for a time, the College of Cardinals was a quasi-synodal body having considerable authority in and for the good of the Roman Church. The college was founded and empowered both to elect the bishop of Rome (a right formally recognized in a decree of 1059 promulgated by the pope with his synod[100]) and to assist him in the ongoing governance of the Roman Church initially and, later, the rest of the Church in the West. These are the two most important functions of a patriarchal *synodos endemousa*.

The College of Cardinals emerged in its definitive form around the twelfth century, composed of three "orders" of bishops (seven), priests (twenty-eight), and deacons (eighteen), and possessed of its own institutions independent of the papal curia.[101] It is increasingly described— beginning c. 1065 with Peter Damian, the cardinal-bishop of Ostia and in many respects the first theologian of the cardinalate—as the "spiritual senate" of the Roman Church[102] and is accorded considerable powers in this period. According to I. S. Robinson, at times it clearly ranks as "an independent power within the Roman Church" (43) into which new members could be appointed not by the pope alone but only through an "election" by the existing members, who could propose names alongside those of the pope's candidates, which were not necessarily admitted merely because they were papal nominees (47). Those members had to be clearly attached to, a part of, or within easy reach of Rome; if they were not, or if they were sent or appointed to far-away sees, cardinals would sometimes resign as such to take up these distant appointments which would render them unable to provide "standing" assistance to the bishop of Rome (91).

There is considerable evidence that well into the second millennium the pope never acted without his synod[103] and, when that was sidelined by the College of Cardinals, he never acted without the latter's advice and consent as manifested through regular meetings of the "consistory."[104] I. S. Robinson reports that early in the twelfth century, a major crisis in Rome "compelled the pope himself to admit that a major papal decision could only be made with the cardinals' advice" (101–2). Thus cardinals, gathered in consistory, had substantial authority in areas of doctrine and discipline, overseeing new appointments, approving canonizations of saints, acting as courts for juridical review and appeal, and "defining the catholic faith" (108–10). By the middle of the twelfth century "decisions . . . were taken with the cardinals *in consistorio*" (115). For a time, then, cardinals gathered in consistory acted in ways that could be considered "synodal," and had genuine power and were not merely consultative "talking shops."[105]

The responsibilities of the college would change many times over the decades and centuries. At times it would be a large body with considerable powers; at other times it shrank to a tiny handful of members having very attenuated authority weakly exercised in heavily contested circumstances.[106] In broad terms, the college increasingly ceased to function in any "synodal" fashion even if it did continue occasionally to meet in an increasingly consultative consistory, which was itself more or less abolished by Pope Sixtus V in his decree *Immensa Dei* of 1588.[107] With the abolition of the consistory, Sixtus gave its responsibilities to the newly established congregations of the Roman Curia, which was now and increasingly a centralized, permanent "bureaucracy" around the bishop of Rome, beginning in the twelfth century but really coming to fruition for the first time in a major way under Pope Sixtus V (1585–1590). Subsequent reconfigurations of the Curia took place under numerous popes between the end of the sixteenth and twentieth centuries, the most recent being in 1988.[108] Gradually, then, throughout the second millennium synodal bodies in the Roman Church were eclipsed by curial officials, who increasingly took over responsibilities that had originally belonged to the synod of bishops and then the cardinals.[109]

By the time of the modern papacy, from the latter part of the nineteenth century onward,[110] the college remained small and dominated by Italians but would, as the twentieth century unfolded, grow in size and range of composition. Today the college is the most "international" in membership it has ever been, and, since the Second Vatican Council, has undergone several changes.[111] It currently occupies an uneasy place in contemporary Catholic ecclesiology, which even something so sober as the 1983 *Code of Canon Law* seems to recognize in repeatedly (and ambiguously) referring to the college as "special."[112] Canonically, the college is said to constitute "a special college which provides for the election of the Roman Pontiff according to the norm of special law. The cardinals assist the Roman Pontiff either collegially when they are convoked to deal with questions of major importance, or individually when they help the Roman Pontiff through the various offices they perform, especially in the daily care of the universal Church" (c. 349). Cardinals today may still gather in consistories (either "ordinary" or "extraordinary" according to canon 353) but only at the behest of the pope and only to do the work he charges them to do, which work is purely consultative: they have no legislative power at all unless it is given them on an ad hoc basis by the pope. They are to reside in Rome unless they are also diocesan bishops, in which case they are "to go to Rome whenever the Roman Pontiff calls them" (c. 356). Most cardinals,[113] regardless of residence, are given a "title to a suburbicarian church or a church in Rome" which they are to look after but over which they have "no power of governance" nor any ability to interfere in administrative matters, these being the prerogative of the bishop of Rome (c. 357).

Summary

I have proposed three ways of assisting the Latin Church in the development of her ecclesial structures. The first consists of establishing regional patriarchates, one for each of the six inhabited continents. This was proposed for three reasons: to assist the Latin Church to attain better internal governance, to deal with the question of territory and jurisdiction in a very complex globalized world, and to demonstrate to the Orthodox that Rome takes patriarchal polity seriously and wants to begin living it in newer and deeper ways than hitherto.

The second and third suggestions follow from this first one. No patriarchate properly so called exists that does not have a full synod and a permanent synod. I suggested therefore that these Latin patriarchates have such synods, the former consisting of all the diocesan bishops holding office in the patriarchal territory and the latter consisting of the presidents of the episcopal conferences in the patriarchal territory, together with the patriarch.

These patriarchates would then be able to take over almost all the functions that are currently performed for them by the Roman Curia. These patriarchates would thus have the responsibility for electing their own brother bishops (thus taking over most of the responsibility of the Congregation for Bishops), and for supervising their own clergy and religious and educational establishments (thus reducing the workload on the Roman Congregations for Clergy, Education, and Consecrated and Apostolic Life). The patriarchates would also supervise liturgy and sacramental practice in their territory, allowing for continued liturgical enculturation in their regions and reducing the demands made on the Roman Congregation for Divine Worship and the Discipline of the Sacraments. Patriarchates would take charge of the glorification of saints in their regions, relieving the Roman Congregation for the Causes of the Saints of many of its burdens. Patriarchates would act as appellate courts of the second instance, hearing appeals from various diocesan tribunals, but being themselves subject finally to the Roman Rota and Apostolic Signatura as the Latin Church's supreme courts. Finally, the patriarchates would exercise vigilance over doctrinal questions, thereby reducing the need for the Roman Congregation for the Doctrine of the Faith to be as interventionist as it has been in some recent cases in the Latin Church.

These continental patriarchates, then, would be the recipients of a substantial devolution of "papal" authority. The papacy has for too long undertaken an amalgam of responsibilities, some patriarchal, some papal, some purely local. The Latin continental patriarchates would take over those responsibilities once exercised by Latin synods in the past and currently exercised by Orthodox patriarchal synods. In this way, these patriarchates would relieve the Roman curial government of many of its overwhelming burdens and also give to the Latin Church a form of governance not merely recognized by the East, but above all useful to the Western Church.[114]

CHAPTER SIX

Papal Structures and Responsibilities

Resisting Predetermined Juridical Solutions

After having first differentiated patriarchal from papal functions and having set the papacy's relationship to the patriarchal Churches—East and West—into synodal relationship, I turn to what responsibilities would remain to the pope in his unique capacity as pope, that is, as first hierarch or "supreme pontiff" of the universal Church.[1] This list of responsibilities is necessarily the shortest because most of the responsibilities previously thought to be papal have now been seen to be properly patriarchal. This list is also necessarily the most general for two reasons at least. First, what is proposed has never really been tried or embodied before, and it seems important therefore not to be overly precise in specifying powers and procedures. Moreover, it seems important, as Olivier Clément has noted, to emphasize that "the one essential would be to pass from a situation where the hierarchical dovetailing of power structures has legal back-up to one where tensions are held in balance without predetermined juridical solutions."[2] I resist, therefore, the temptation to be overly specific in supplying "predetermined juridical solutions" in part because *Ut Unum Sint* does not, in its wisdom, supply them, seemingly leaving the door open to a wide and creative interpretation and application of what it does say about papal responsibilities in very general terms.

With these caveats in mind, then, it is appropriate now to reflect on those responsibilities that still remain as papal and personal, exercised by the pope himself over and above his roles as bishop of Rome and Roman patriarch. What are they?

Papal Responsibilities in *Ut Unum Sint*

Again and again *UUS* offers variations on the theme that the papal office has as its prime goal that of achieving and maintaining the *unity* of the Church. Section 94 describes the papal office as a "service of unity, rooted in the action of divine mercy."[3] Later in that section the pope is described as "the first servant of unity." Section 95 is perhaps the most direct: "Whatever relates to the unity of all Christian communities clearly forms part of the concerns of the primacy."

The encyclical goes on to briefly mention, without developing in any detail or specifying how they are to be lived, six papal responsibilities.[4] I think that this lack of detail was most likely deliberate so that new and creative solutions to the ecumenical problem of papal primacy could be produced. It is significant that these responsibilities are articulated in section 94, which precedes the request for ecumenical assistance in coming up with new ways of exercising the papacy. Taking the pope at his word, I look at what he thinks are papal responsibilities, and then, in logical sequence, conclude by suggesting a way in which they could be configured so that they would be acceptable to the Orthodox.

First, "the mission of the Bishop of Rome within the College of all the Pastors consists precisely in 'keeping watch' (*episkopein*), like a sentinel, so that, through the efforts of the Pastors, the true voice of Christ the Shepherd may be heard in all the particular Churches." Second, the pope is to "ensure the communion of all the Churches." Third, the pope exercises "vigilance over the handing down of the Word, the celebration of the Liturgy and the Sacraments, the Church's mission, discipline and the Christian life." Fourth, the pope has the responsibility to "recall the requirements of the common good of the Church, should anyone be tempted to overlook it in the pursuit of personal interests." Fifth, the pope has "the duty to admonish, to caution and to declare at times that this or that opinion being circulated is irreconcilable with the unity of faith. When circumstances require it, he speaks in the name of all the Pastors in communion with him." Sixth, the pope "can also—under very specific conditions clearly laid down by the First Vatican Council—declare *ex cathedra* that a certain doctrine belongs to the deposit of faith. By thus bearing witness to the truth, he serves unity."

What is crucial is the very next sentence, beginning section 95, and coming immediately after this "list":

> *All this however must always be done in communion.* When the Catholic Church affirms that the office of the Bishop of Rome corresponds to the will of Christ, she does not separate this office from the mission entrusted to *the whole body of Bishops,* who are also "vicars and ambassadors of Christ." The Bishop of Rome is a member of the "College," and the Bishops are his brothers in the ministry.[5]

This emphasis on the centrality of a relationship of communion between the bishop of Rome and the other bishops of the world accords very well with Orthodox arguments and approaches, as we saw in chapter two.[6] This relationship of communion between hierarchs has historically been manifested concretely in synods. Indeed, only in a relationship of synodality does primacy make any sense. None has made this relationship clearer nor argued it repeatedly with more force than John Zizioulas, whose thoughts are worth recalling here. Stated baldly, he argues that "the synodal system is a 'sine qua non conditio' for the catholicity of the Church" but "primacy is also a 'sine qua non conditio' for the catholicity of the Church."[7] More recently, he has elaborated these thoughts in another paper on the same topic, saying that "synods without primates never existed in the Orthodox Church, and this indicates clearly that if synodality is an ecclesiological, that is, dogmatic, necessity, so must be primacy. . . . The logic of synodality leads to primacy, and the logic of the ecumenical council to universal primacy."[8] The "logic" of both synodality and primacy only make sense in what he calls an "ecclesiology of communion" in which "the

Church consists of *full local churches* united into *One Church* without losing their ecclesial fullness, and that primacy at all levels is a necessary means to realize and guarantee this balance between the many and the one."[9]

Both the pope of Rome and the Orthodox Churches would seem, then, to be in agreement that papal responsibilities must always be lived in communion, that is synodally. Important grounds are given in *UUS* for arguing that papal responsibilities cannot be conceived or carried out in the "monarchical" terms as they were increasingly after the schism of the eleventh century[10] but must, rather, be carried out always and only "in communion" with all the bishops. In this light, then, I propose a new institution, primatial and synodal at the same time, to manifest this communion of the pope with other major hierarchs. This body I shall call a "permanent ecumenical synod." After describing its makeup and authority, I will then re-read the six responsibilities of *UUS* in light of this synod, arguing how each of them could be exercised anew.

A Permanent Ecumenical Synod

In a conversation in 1996, the Ukrainian Catholic theologian Andriy Chirovsky and the Orthodox theologian Thomas Hopko discussed the possibility of a papacy that would function in the spirit of Apostolic Canon 34,[11] that is, a pope functioning in synodal relationship with his brother bishops, each holding a check on the other. With that in mind, Hopko said that

> if ever the pope of Rome would agree to such a *synodos endemousa,* and limit himself to promulgating or vetoing its decisions, and that permanent body, composed of successors to the apostles would by definition include the heads of the autocephalous Churches, then I cannot see why the Orthodox would have any reservations.[12]

Building on this idea, I propose that any issues transcending patriarchal particularities and affecting the universal Church *as a whole,* and so requiring a unified response, would receive that response not by a pope acting in isolation but by a gathering of an ecumenical synod in which all the Eastern *and* Western patriarchs, under the presidency of the pope and patriarch of Rome and never without him, met together to decide the issue. Such synods would most likely be rare events given that patriarchs and their own synods would, in the overwhelming majority of cases, remain the autonomous appropriate bodies for resolving most issues. The synod would not exist as a body above patriarchs and their synods because it would include those self-same patriarchs. The synod, rather, would exist as a means for co-ordinating their common activities together and of maintaining the overall unity of the entire Church universal.

In keeping with the usual operations of patriarchal synods, this one would be called by the pope either on his own initiative or in response to a request from two or more patriarchs. It would be the papal prerogative to preside over the sessions and promulgate the decisions at a time and in a manner of his choosing, with the possibility of a veto (both temporary, by withholding promulgation of legislation for a time, and permanent, by returning the matter to the synod for fresh discussion) to be exercised in exceptional circumstances, and for demonstrably justifiable reasons.

What responsibilities would be exercised by this pope-in-synod? Consider the list of six responsibilities from *UUS*. The first and third responsibilities are very similar in nature and in the language used to describe them, and will therefore be treated together here. The first responsibility listed by *UUS* suggests that "the mission of the Bishop of Rome *within the College of all the Pastors* consists precisely in 'keeping watch' (*episkopein*), like a sentinel, so that, through the efforts of the Pastors, the true voice of Christ the Shepherd may be heard in all the particular Churches."[13] The third responsibility is for the pope to exercise "vigilance over the handing down of the Word, the celebration of the Liturgy and the Sacraments, the Church's mission, discipline and the Christian life." The language of supervision ("keeping watch," "vigilance") here is, especially in the first responsibility, already clearly articulated in what we could call "synodal" terms when it says the mission is to be exercised "within the college of all the Pastors." Thus the pope would have responsibility for general supervision over all the particular Churches to ensure that their liturgico-sacramental life, mission, and discipline all articulate the Word of God and manifest His voice to the world.

These responsibilities, as the very language suggests, should not be understood or exercised juridically but would consist of a "moral" and exhortative responsibility, a supervisory responsibility. In the event the papal "sentinel" or "watchman" found something wrong in one of the particular Churches, he would not generally intervene directly and immediately but would—as, again, the language implies—prompt and encourage "the efforts of the Pastors" in charge of the area. Only if those pastors were incapable of solving the matter at hand, and only if all other efforts, especially at the local and regional levels, had been exhausted, would the pope intervene to take action, reporting to and subsequently seeking the blessing of the ecumenical synod of patriarchs (if it were not in session or could not be quickly convoked) for his intervention, which would indeed have to be motivated by extremely serious and genuinely "extraordinary" circumstances to justify his intervention.

The second and fourth responsibilities are very similar also. The second is that the pope is to "ensure the communion of all the Churches." The fourth responsibility is to "recall the requirements of the common good of the Church, should anyone be tempted to overlook it in the pursuit of personal interests." There are at least three ways in which the pope could do this. First, it would be for the pope to bring together the ecumenical synod to settle disputes in matters of jurisdiction and "canonical territory"—for example, one patriarchate might contest the jurisdiction of another in a given area (as began in the 1990s in Estonia between Moscow and Constantinople), and both parties would have the dispute brought to a synodal review for a final, definitive settlement of the matter. Second, it would also be the responsibility of this synod to clearly and finally settle matters of overlapping jurisdiction anywhere in the world—e.g., North America. This synod would thus be charged with the task of determining how to implement the ancient practice of "one bishop to one city."[14] Third, this synod would be the place where, in emergency circumstances, crises in a patriarchal Church that could not be resolved by that Church would be brought for adjudication. For example, when a patriarchal synod was hopelessly deadlocked in its election of a new patriarch and requested the synod's assistance, the pope would gather the patriarchs to discuss the matter and decide on how to proceed. Fourth and finally, this synod would have the freedom to function as a court of final appeal beyond patriarchal jurisdictions. There would be no guarantee that the ecumenical synod would even hear a case: it would be its exclusive prerogative to determine whether the circumstances were so severe as to warrant such an extraordinary review of the matter or whether so proceeding would violate the autonomy of the patriarchate or otherwise harm the Church or relations between the patriarchal Churches. The synod would be free to simply refuse to hear the case thereby leaving the patriarchal jurisdiction's decision intact, to decide to hear the case itself, or to decide to turn the matter over to an appellate court of hierarchs constituted by it in a neighbouring region more intimately acquainted with the matter at hand and charged with issuing a definitive ruling on behalf of the synod.

The fifth and sixth responsibilities are clearly "doctrinal" in nature. In the fifth place the pope has "the duty to admonish, to caution and to declare at times that this or that opinion being circulated is irreconcilable with the unity of faith. When circumstances require it, he speaks in the name of all the Pastors in communion with him." Once more the language is instructive and expansive: an admonition, a caution, or a declaration of potential or real heterodoxy is the task of every bishop throughout the world, and the pope is claiming here nothing extraordinary and certainly nothing uniquely "papal." These are not "papal" responsibilities, then, so much as simply episcopal ones. It is important to note, moreover, that here too he says the pope should exercise this responsibility "in the name of all the pastors in communion with him." The admonition, caution, or declaration would not, then, be a monarchical or solitary act, but an act of communion with the other members of the ecumenical synod precisely for building up the communion of faith in all the Churches. This synod could clarify doctrinally disputed areas and promulgate decrees or encyclicals on new challenges to faith and morals that would arise in the future. These documents could be written *motu proprio* by the pope and then passed by the synod if they agreed with them; or they could arise from the synod itself, which, having expressed itself generally on the matter, would then charge the pope with the final writing and promulgation. On further doctrinal matters, the synod would also—and again only in exceptional circumstances—use its authority in matters of faith and morals to offer "fraternal correction" to one among their number who might be inclined toward heterodoxy.

Sixth, the pope, on behalf of the whole Church, "can also—under very specific conditions clearly laid down by the First Vatican Council— declare *ex cathedra* that a certain doctrine belongs to the deposit of faith. By thus bearing witness to the truth, he serves unity." Once more, the original language here would seem to be unobjectionable insofar as such a declaration would not arise from the pope alone but would be an act of speaking "in the name of all the Pastors in communion with him." Those pastors, then, would have to be consulted and to agree before the pope would in fact speak authoritatively.[15] Such a consultation is not merely an ecumenical "courtesy" but in fact a historical reality recognized by *Pastor Aeternus* itself:

> The Roman pontiffs, too, as the circumstances of the time or the state of affairs suggested, sometimes by summoning ecumenical councils or consulting the opinion of the Churches scattered throughout the world, sometimes by special synods, sometimes by taking advantage of other useful means afforded by divine providence, defined as doctrines to be held those things which, by God's help, they knew to be in keeping with Sacred Scripture and the apostolic traditions.[16]

Thus, before any future exercise of this charism, a consultation, beginning with the ecumenical synod, would take place before a wider consultation with the entire episcopate to discern whether it was opportune and necessary to invoke that charism for the upbuilding of the Church. If the synod and pope agreed together with the bishops that it was appropriate to manifest this charism, then the pope could conceivably invoke "that infallibility which the divine Redeemer willed His *Church* to enjoy in defining doctrine concerning faith or morals."[17]

Particular Papal Prerogatives

What remains now is to consider two questions: how would the Roman bishop-patriarch be elected, and what would he do on his own accord? What "individual" authority would he have?

Electoral Assembly for the Roman Pontiff

The reconfigurations discussed above have not until now dealt with one issue of importance, and that is the election of the man who would be concomitantly bishop of Rome, Roman patriarch, and universal pontiff and pope. The means by which popes have been chosen in the past has of course greatly varied and been an issue of no small controversy at times. Since the famous decree of 1059, papal elections have been generally, but not always, conducted by the College of Cardinals.

This method of election has not been without its problems over the years. Prescinding from especially protracted, difficult, or controverted elections—including such elections in which secular powers have attempted to interfere, the last of which was scarcely a century ago (in 1903, for the election of Pius X)—the most fundamental ecclesiological problem with the current practice of exclusive cardinalatial election of the bishop of Rome is that the local Church of Rome, including her parish clergy and lay faithful, has very little actual say in the election.[18] Moreover, the cardinals, in making their selection, concentrate exclusively on whether a given candidate will be a good pope and universal pastor, seemingly ignoring the candidate's qualifications to be a good bishop of Rome, the first and most important office without which no man can be pope or patriarch.[19] This is an understandable concern of the cardinal-electors in today's world, where the papacy, especially after Pope John Paul II, is such a massive global presence. Nonetheless, it is a serious ecclesiological and ecumenical problem insofar as the bishopric of Rome is *the* most important office from which all else flows.

If the current practice almost entirely ignores the local Church and instead concentrates on the Church universal, and is thus problematic in ecclesiological terms, this practice is also problematic in ecumenical terms as well, especially given the foregoing proposed reconfigurations, in which the papal and patriarchal offices will be clearly differentiated. In light of those proposed reconfigurations, it is important to conceive of new ways of electing the man who is simultaneously the bishop of Rome, Roman patriarch, and pope. I suggest the following, which finds some inspiration in the electoral assembly of the Armenian Church in particular, but more generally in those other patriarchates—including the Coptic and Russian—in which several "houses" or "bodies" participate, including a house of lay people.

To give explicit electoral recognition to the fact that he is the chief hierarch of the diocese as well as patriarchate of Rome, and also to give recognition (albeit secondary) to the fact that the Roman bishop and patriarch is also the pope around whom are united the other patriarchs and their local Churches, a new tri-cameral electoral assembly could be erected with the exclusive task of choosing the bishop of Rome. This assembly, motivated by the principle of Pope Celestine I (422–432) that "the one who is to be head over all should be elected by all," would have three "houses" or components, recognizing first and foremost the local Church and Diocese of Rome, then the Roman patriarchate, and finally the other Churches with which it would be in communion. Given that the local office of bishop of Rome is most important, the composition of this assembly would be such as to recognize this. I propose therefore that the first "house" of the assembly, representing the Church of Rome directly, would consist of 60 percent of the delegates (elected from among the clergy and laity by a diocesan synod or similar means of selection); the second "house," representing the patriarchate as a whole, would consist of 40 percent of the delegates; and the third house, consisting of the other patriarchs, would simply be in attendance upon the election, supervising it to ensure that everything is done in good order, but without voting. The other patriarchs would instead be endowed with the ability—which could only be used in absolutely dire emergency circumstances—to call a temporary halt to the proceedings, and to exhort and caution the assembly if, in their view, the election was proceeding in an especially divisive or difficult manner, or if one of the candidates posed grave problems by being, e.g., creditably and demonstrably accused of a grave offence against the faith and unity of the Church. If the election proceeded smoothly, and the patriarchal "house" found no objections, then the patriarchs would immediately communicate to their synods word of the election and seek together with their synods to grant to the one elected ecclesiastical communion, welcoming him into the "college of patriarchs" and acknowledging him as the new bishop and patriarch of Rome and universal pope.[20]

Unique Papal Responsibilities

With all the other responsibilities now outlined, it remains to ask: are there things that the pope as pope would do on his own accord, without necessarily having to consult with or wait for the consent or deliberation of the ecumenical synod? Would there be certain areas in which he would be free to act on his own if the good of the Church required it? Are there singular areas of individual papal authority that he and he alone would be free to invoke and exercise, and if so what are they and under what circumstances would they be invoked? In answer to that, I would suggest that there are three main areas.

First, the pope remains—as patriarchs do by virtue of their office— the chief administrative officer of his patriarchate and of the ecumenical synod. Thus he has responsibility for summoning the full, permanent, and ecumenical synods, for presiding over their sessions, and for promulgating their decisions at a time and in a manner of his choosing. Nobody else in the Church can do these things.

Second, the pope could and should retain his role as global spokesman for Christianity.[21] This is not an official role, of course, and it carries no canonical weight to it, and, moreover, it is a role that, as John Pollard, Owen Chadwick, and others have demonstrated, really only begins to be taken seriously from the late nineteenth century onward, when the pope ceases being monarch of the Papal States and instead becomes teacher of the nations, exercising his "monarchical" privileges in ways not dissimilar to when he had actual territory,[22] and, indeed, doing so now with even greater vigor.[23] Nonetheless, it is undeniable that the pope is the most widely known and respected religious figure in the world today, and this role should not be abandoned when so much evangelical good has come of it and could continue to come of it. The pope, as successor to the princes of the apostles Peter and Paul, those great evangelists of the early Church, has the "mission" of "bearing witness to and living out of the united witness of the apostles Peter and Paul, and in reminding other churches which accept the New Testament canon of their obligation to do the same."[24] In this light, he is at once a principal of Petrine "order" and Pauline "evangelism." He travels the world preaching the gospel (always, of course, at the invitation of the local Church). He seeks to bring Christians together. He co-ordinates the Christian response to such things as requests for dialogue between Christians and Muslims.

Third, the pope continues to retain his sovereignty as head of the Vatican City-State. This role, of course, is not ecclesiological at all, and at first glance may seem secondary (at best) to his role as universal pontiff. Since 1929 the pope has reigned as sovereign of the Vatican City-State.[25] In this capacity, he is absolute monarch over a tiny landlocked territory in Rome as well as extra-territorial properties in central Italy.[26] He exercises diplomatic relations with nearly 200 countries—the results of the 1929 Lateran Treaty with Italy, which was updated in 1984.[27] The Vatican City-State is the smallest and most unique state in the world, a fact that occasionally generates comment from sources that are sometimes skeptical, sometimes envious, and sometimes even hostile—but almost always ignored.[28] When the question about its status is raised, the Vatican itself has consistently responded that "the pope is sovereign not because he rules over Vatican City; he rules over Vatican City because he is sovereign."[29]

I suggest that these ecclesiological problems do need to be looked at—especially the role of nuncios inserting themselves into local hierarchies and episcopal appointments—but that it is important to maintain the pope's independent status because of the obvious advantages it has conferred on the Catholic Church. It is precisely this lack of territorial independence that has bedeviled so many Eastern Churches, enslaving them to tsarist or communist (among the East-Slavs) or Muslim (among the Middle Eastern Orthodox) regimes, or otherwise smothering their apostolic witness under nationalist or ideological guise. Precisely because the pope is a citizen of no territory except his own, a ruler independent of all other secular rules, he is able to transcend ethno-nationalist narrowness and avoid political entanglements and the compromises to the gospel they so often bring. He is able to remind Christians that no Church can be beholden to an ethnic, nationalist, or political regime. He is able to act as a voice advocating the *libertas Ecclesiae* precisely in those countries (e.g., China) where it is still not fully manifested. He is able to be a free and complete witness to the Kingdom of God and the Church of Christ, in which there is neither male nor female, Greek nor Jew, slave nor freeman.

Summary

I have, with some caution, proposed four major and several derivative changes to the operation of the papacy in order that it might be more fully the instrument of unity it wishes to be and was designed by God to be. Thus I proposed that the papacy needs to clearly differentiate its responsibilities from those that are properly patriarchal, a differentiation that has been often called for in the past several decades but never sufficiently articulated in a detailed fashion. To remedy that problem, I then proposed, as interim measures for the good of the Latin Church pending full unity with the Orthodox, the establishment of six continental patriarchates; the establishment of a full synod within each of those; and the establishment of a permanent synod within each patriarchate. The history of the Roman Church was reviewed to show that many patriarchal functions have taken place throughout her history, even when not recognized as such; that synods have a venerable history of regular meeting in the Roman Church; and that the College of Cardinals has functioned, *de facto* if not *de jure*, as a permanent synod.

With these "patriarchal" functions thus articulated, I turned to the remaining question of what functions would remain to the pope *qua* pope, that is, the universal pontiff who builds bridges between Churches and among the faithful of the world. Here I noted that the pope as pope should remain head of Vatican City-State, should remain global spokesman for Christianity, and should be elected by a new assembly to take account of his role as local bishop, patriarch, and universal pontiff. But the major change proposed here was that of the permanent ecumenical synod, first discussed by Andriy Chirovsky and Thomas Hopko, as the means through which all the patriarchs together, under the presidency of the pope, could take responsibility for the unity of the one, holy, Catholic, apostolic, and Orthodox Church of Christ.

Afterword

What Has Been Done and What Remains?

The changes just outlined above came in response to a request originally posed in 1995 by Pope John Paul II in *Ut Unum Sint*. Since then we have seen many (largely Protestant) responses to his historic request, and we have seen much recent progress in the Orthodox-Catholic dialogue, though much work remains to be done. Things needing further study include, in no especial order:

• A comprehensive and detailed study of *all* the patriarchates in the world today—their functioning and their history. This book has dealt with only ten. The other patriarchates need to be studied, including the "minor" Latin "patriarchates" and other very ancient Churches, such as the Church of Cyprus, which has long enjoyed a quasi-patriarchal style of governance and level of autonomy.

• A dispassionate study, free from nationalistic tendentiousness, of the highly controverted issue of "canonical territory."[1] This, and related issues of "jurisdiction" and the applicability of the canon "one bishop to one city," all need very sober, serious examination unclouded by historical sentimentalism or denominational triumphalism.

• An examination of the recent "episcopal assemblies" of the Orthodox Churches in North America, Western Europe, and elsewhere.

These are strikingly new and potentially revolutionary in their import but have as yet received no serious analysis whatsoever.

• Further serious historical research into the first millennium, which continues to be stressed in the Ravenna and Crete documents of the official international Orthodox-Catholic dialogue.

All this, of course, is for future studies. Let us conclude the present work by returning once more to what John Zizioulas rightly said in 1999: the "primacy of the Bishop of Rome has to be theologically justified or else can be ignored altogether."[2] As we conclude this study, let us finish by looking briefly at the theological justification for the papacy, and by asking, of my proposals, "But will they work?" Both questions turn out to be closely connected and the answer to them is the same.

While history, tradition, and practicality are important reasons for the ongoing existence of the papacy, the most important one remains theological. At risk of a Pseudo-Dionysian[3] kind of over-identification between divine realities on the one hand, and ecclesial ones on the other, let me nonetheless come to my central thesis: *the papacy's theological justification is Trinitarian in nature, that is, the papacy must be capable of witnessing to and upholding the unity and diversity of the Churches as part of the one Church of Christ.*[4] The theological justification for the papacy remains the same for that office as for the Church at large: not just to be an icon of the unity of the Trinity, but in fact to embody that unity, that communion of Persons, and to call all Christians toward greater unity, that is, toward a deeper participation in the very life of God. As Constantine Scouteris has put it, "Church unity is not understood as autonomous, as exclusive in itself, but rather as a continuous, vital, and dynamic participation in the united divine life."[5] Unity, then, is not an extrinsic or external quality to the Church, useful sociologically perhaps for the cohesion or successful operation of the organization. Unity, rather, is a very part of the being of the Church properly so called precisely because the Church is God's own Body in the world. The Church, as Origen, reflecting patristic ecclesiology, says, is "filled with the Holy Trinity."[6] The Church and all hierarchical and other offices within her, including the papacy, exist to draw people toward a participation in the unity of the triune God and to manifest that unity to the world.

Only in and through the Trinity can the divisions of our sinful human nature be overcome. Only in response to our prayers to the Father, through the Son, in the power of the Holy Spirit, will the divisions of the Church be healed. Only by means of participation in the very life of God, by becoming more and more like God through *theosis,* are we able to become what we already are—a communion of persons made such by the communion of Persons of the Father, Son, and Holy Spirit.[7]

To the extent that we are capable of understanding the very life of God, we know that He is not just one, but also, as Saint John the Theologian tells us, "God is love."[8] Following that great Johannine "disciple" and patristic figure, Ignatius of Antioch, we may say that "the Church itself is love (*agape*)"[9] and that this love, this "kenotic love . . . is at the foundation of all the ministries of the Church."[10] The kenotic love of Christ is free and fearless, grasping at nothing, withholding nothing, but giving everything, pouring forth ceaselessly and limitlessly.[11] Such kenotic self-emptying is also the task and challenge of every Christian, but it is especially the task of the bishops of the Church—including the bishop of Rome—as Afanasiev argues: "[A]s the highest hierarchical ministry it [the episcopacy] is the highest model of love and the most complete imitation of Christ's self-sacrificing love. This is the culmination point of all ministries, their beginning and end being in love."[12]

In answer, then, to the questions of the theological justification of the papacy, and also whether the proposals here would "work" at all or are hopelessly unrealistic and unworkable, I reply that both the justification for, and the necessary *modus operandi* of, the papacy are the same: to live Christ's self-sacrificing love in the Church and for the world, and to that extent embody the very life of the Triune God in whom we live and move and have our being. The pope could indeed again be an acceptable figure of unity to the Orthodox but only if they and he together constantly strive to live kenotically, seeking not their own glory or still less their own power, but only "the power based on love and flowing from love."[13]

Introduction

1. John Meyendorff, "Vatican II: Definitions or Search for Unity?" *St. Vladimir's Seminary Quarterly* 7 (1963): 166.

2. Paul VI, "Address to the Secretariat for Promoting Christian Unity," 28 April 1967, in *Doing the Truth in Charity: Statements of Pope Paul VI, Popes John Paul I, John Paul II, and the Secretariat for Promoting Christian Unity 1964–1980,* ed. Thomas F. Stransky and John B. Sheerin (New York: Paulist Press, 1982), 273; French original, *AAS* 59 (1967): 493–98. Cf. John Paul II: "as I acknowledged on the important occasion of a visit to the World Council of Churches in Geneva on 12 June 1984, the Catholic Church's conviction that in the ministry of the Bishop of Rome she has preserved, in fidelity to the Apostolic Tradition and the faith of the Fathers, the visible sign and guarantor of unity, constitutes a difficulty for most other Christians, whose memory is marked by certain painful recollections. To the extent that we are responsible for these, I join my Predecessor Paul VI in asking forgiveness" (*Ut Unum Sint,* English edition [Vatican City: Vatican Polyglot Press, 1995], §88).

3. Emmanuel Lanne, "To What Extent Is Roman Primacy Unacceptable to the Eastern Churches?" in *Papal Ministry in the Church,* ed. Hans Küng (New York: Herder and Herder, 1971).

4. George A. Maloney, "Papal Primacy and Reunion," *Diakonia* 14 (1979): 185. Maloney ended his life in the Orthodox Church.

5. Valamo Statement, "The Sacrament of Order in the Sacramental Structure of the Church," *One in Christ* 24 (1988): 377.

6. Walter Kasper, *That They May All Be One: The Call to Unity Today* (London: Burnes & Oates, 2004), 19; cf. pp. 6, 61.

7. My translation. Olivier Clément, Epigraph, *Rome autrement: Un orthodox face á la papauté* (Paris: Desclée de Brouwer, 1997): "le problème de la papauté est certainement le plus difficile qui se pose aujourd'hui dans le di-

alogue oecuménique, et plus particulièrement entre catholicisme et ortho-doxie." See my review of the English translation, "Letter from the East: Olivier Clément's *You Are Peter: An Orthodox Theologian's Reflection on the Exercise of Papal Primacy," First Things* 147 (November 2004): 46–50.

8. John Zizioulas, "Primacy in the Church: An Orthodox Approach," in *Petrine Ministry and the Unity of the Church: "Toward a Patient and Fraternal Dialogue"*, ed. James F. Puglisi (Collegeville, MN: Liturgical Press, 1999), 116.

9. Vsevolod Majdansky, "What about the Roman Primacy?" in his *We Are All Brothers* (Fairfax, VA: Eastern Christian Publications, 1999), 223.

10. Details of the history of the JIC together with some initial reflections and plans by and about the JIC are available in John Erickson and John Borelli, eds., *The Quest for Unity: Orthodox and Catholics in Dialogue* (Crestwood, NY: St. Vladimir's Seminary Press, 1996). The "Joint Declaration" of Ecumenical Patriarch Dimitrios and Pope John Paul II of 30 November 1979 announcing the official establishment of the dialogue and its membership is available at the Vatican website http://www.vatican.va under John Paul & Dimitrios. The JIC's first statement, "The Mystery of the Church and of the Eucharist in the Light of the Mystery of the Holy Trinity," otherwise less clumsily known as the Munich statement, is available at http://www.vatican.va under Joint Commission 6 July 1982.

11. See E. Lanne and M. van Parys, "Le dialogue catholique-orthodoxe à Baltimore-Emmitsburg," *Irénikon* 3–4 (2000): 405–18.

12. Catholic World News linked to the communiqué: http://portal-credo .ru/site/?act=news&id=47488; this is also available on the official website of the Ecumenical Patriarchate: http://www.patriarchate.org.

13. See "Moscow Patriarchate's Representative Urges Vatican Not to Impose the Patriarch of Constantinople as an 'Eastern Pope' on the Orthodox World," *Europaica Bulletin* 106 (4 October 2006).

14. With the January 2009 election of Patriarch Kyril, Hilarion became an archbishop and head of the Russian Church's external affairs department, vaulting him to even greater ecumenical prominence as seen, e.g., in recent private meetings with Pope Benedict XVI. For details on their meeting, see "Will the 'Third Rome' Reunite with the 'First Rome'?" at http://www.zenit .org/article-26932?l=english. Hilarion has also been instrumental in unprecedented co-operation between Moscow and Rome as seen in his writing an introduction to a singular Moscow-published collection of Pope Benedict's talks about the future of Europe. The Russian patriarchate published this book in Italian and Russian in 2009. For further details, see Sandro Magister, "For Rome and Moscow, It's Spring Again," at http://www.chiesa.espresso .republica.it in the chronological archives for 11 December 2009.

15. I treat this question in my "Orthodoxy, Catholicism, and Primacy: A Plea for a New Common Approach," *Ecumenical Trends* 37 (April 2008): 5–8.

16. "Bishop Hilarion Voices His Protest to Cardinal Kasper against Procedure at the Orthodox-Catholic Dialogue," *Europaica Bulletin* 106 (4 October 2006).

17. "Moscow Patriarchate's Representative Urges Vatican Not to Impose." For more on different understandings of the Ecumenical Patriarch, see such studies as Maximos of Sardes, *The Oecumenical Patriarchate in the Orthodox Church* (Thessaloniki: Patriarchal Institute for Patristic Studies, 1976); John Meyendorff, "The Ecumenical Patriarch, Seen in the Light of Orthodox Ecclesiology and History," *Greek Orthodox Theological Review* 24 (1979): 227–44; and Lewis J. Patsavos, *Primacy and Conciliarity: Studies in the Primacy of the See of Constantinople and the Synodal Structure of the Orthodox Church* (Brookline, MA: Holy Cross Orthodox Press, 1995).

18. The official text of the statement may be found on the Ecumenical Patriarchate's website and on the Vatican's at http://www.vatican.va under Ravenna 13 October 2007. For discussion of it, see the North American Orthodox-Catholic Theological Commission's October 2009 study, at once grateful but also, in parts, critical: http://www.usccb.org under Ravenna Response. The major issue the North American document recognizes is one that has long been a lacuna in both Catholic and Orthodox ecclesiology: viz., the place of the local parish. The North American group—reflecting recent scandals in both Catholic and Orthodox dioceses in the United States especially—also raises the question of episcopal accountability, particularly to lay people over financial matters. Finally, it very commendably says that Ravenna is lovely theory, but very short on practical application. I deal with some parts of the statement in "Ravenna and Beyond: The Question of the Roman Papacy and the Orthodox Churches in the Literature 1962–2006," *One in Christ* 41 [2008]: 99–138. The question of Constantinople inevitably raises for Orthodoxy related questions about regional primacy, regional jurisdictional unity, and the fact that the situation, especially within North America, is an ecclesiological mess. The Orthodox have begun grappling with the overlapping jurisdictions on that continent through a series of meetings in Switzerland, the most recent being in June 2009, which built on an October 2008 meeting of all the heads of the Orthodox Churches. In June 2009, a series of regional "episcopal assemblies" was proposed to deal with the problem of the "Orthodox diaspora." For details on the nature of these assemblies and the regulations by which they are proposed to function, see "Chambesy Documents" at Greek Orthodox Archdiocese of America website http://www.goarch.org/archdiocese. For further discussion of these proposals, see below, in chs. 4 and 5.

19. Details of the Cyprus meeting may be found at http://www.zenit.org/article-27320?l=english.

20. See Cindy Wooden, "As Some Protest, Catholic-Orthodox Dialogue Discusses Role of Papacy," at the Catholic News Service website http://www.catholicnews.com under "As Some Protest."

21. See Benedict XVI, "Message to Bartholomew for the Feast of St. Andrew," at http://www.catholicculture.org under Message to Bartholomew.

22. The best example of such scholarship to date is Susan Wessel's superlative study, *Leo the Great and the Spiritual Rebuilding of a Universal Rome* (Leiden: Brill, 2008). Wessel has rendered ecumenists and historians a very considerable service in showing that Pope Leo (440–461), at once hailed in the East for his famous *Tome* at Chalcedon but also rendered suspect by his refusal to accept that council's canon 28, was not, in rejecting the canon's "privileges" for Constantinople, jealous of Constantinople as some kind of political-patriarchal *parvenu* and was, further, *not* concerned with expanding papal reach into the East. He opposed canon 28 because he thought it reflected an intolerable "politicization" of the patriarchal *taxis*—a too-flagrant ecclesial application, that is, of the "principle of accommodation" to extant imperial jurisdictions. Leo, by contrast, was adamant that patriarchal sees should be justified on the basis of "apostolicity," a theory which, until Leo, almost nobody anywhere thought significant given how commonplace "apostolic" sees were in the East—but, conveniently for Leo, not in the West. Wessel shows that he was—as a quintessential Roman—concerned with the *tranquillitas ordinis* without which the Church *in the West* would continue to suffer, as it had in his day, with the Visigothic Alaric's sacking of Rome in 410 (and the impending collapse of the empire in the West at the end of that century, after Leo's death in 461). To strengthen and unify the Church in the West in the face of socio-political collapse, Leo had waged a hard-fought battle for papal "privileges," which word Chalcedon also used in canon 28, thereby leading to a conflict of understandings between Constantinople and Rome, and the East and West more widely. (Leo also had other objections to this canon, including the fact it was passed after his legates, for reasons still unclear to scholars, had left the session.) According to Wessel's scholarship, this misunderstanding was baseless: "the privileges that Rome claimed were not an attempt to subject the patriarchal sees to Roman domination" (285). Moreover, Constantinople's attempt to claim "privileges" for itself was simply a desire to have "'a comparable authority over metropolitan sees.' . . . It was not, in other words, competition with Rome, but rather practical considerations that governed Constantinople's plan to formalize its exercise of jurisdiction in the region" (306).

23. George Weigel, *Witness to Hope: The Biography of Pope John Paul II* (New York: HarperCollins, 1999).

24. John Paul II, *Ut Unum Sint,* §§95–96. This encyclical—and the writings in general of Pope John Paul II—are remarkable both for their arguments and also, not insignificantly, for their style: the royal "we" has been abandoned; the florid language and exalted titles are vastly scaled back; and one no longer encounters ringing denunciations of other Christians as "heretics" and "schismatics" whose only task is to "return" to Roman obedience.

25. See, e.g., Carl E. Braaten and Robert W. Jenson, eds. *Church Unity and the Papal Office: An Ecumenical Dialogue on John Paul II's Encyclical* Ut Unum Sint (Grand Rapids, MI: Eerdmans, 2001). See also the essays—by theologians of the Lutheran, Methodist, Anglican, Baptist, and Pentecostal traditions—in James F. Puglisi, ed., *Petrine Ministry and the Unity of the Church: "Toward a Patient and Fraternal Dialogue"* (Collegeville, MN: Liturgical Press, 1999).

26. David Hart would write: "As an Orthodox Christian definitely in the ecumenical 'left wing' of my church, I cannot speak for all my co-confessionalists; but I can record my own shame that so few Orthodox hierarchs have even recognized the remarkable gesture made by John Paul II in *Ut Unum Sint* (1995), in openly soliciting advice on how to understand his office (even indeed the limits of its jurisdiction), or been moved to respond with anything like comparable Christian charity" ("The Future of the Papacy: A Symposium," *First Things* 111 [March 2001]: 34). Edward Idris Cardinal Cassidy, then-head of the PCPCU, would write in 2001 that "responses from the Orthodox churches have been rather few and, given the importance of the primacy for the Roman Catholic–Orthodox theological dialogue, rather disappointing" (in *Church Unity and the Papal Office: An Ecumenical Dialogue on John Paul II's Encyclical* Ut Unum Sint, ed. Carl E. Braaten and Robert W. Jenson [Grand Rapids, MI: Eerdmans, 2001], 17–18).

27. Michael Magee, *The Patriarchal Institution in the Church: Ecclesiological Perspectives in the Light of the Second Vatican Council* (Rome: Herder, 2006), 175–76.

28. Thomas Norris, "The Development of Doctrine: 'A Remarkable Philosophical Phenomenon,'" *Communio* 22 (1995): 486.

29. Cf. the PCPCU, which has said that "a mutually acceptable *ministry of unity* cannot be defined one-sidedly and a priori by the Catholic Church or by the Bishop of Rome" ("Petrine Ministry," *Information Service* 1–2, no. 109 [2002]: 30).

30. My translation. Yves Congar, *Vraie et Fausse Réforme dans l'Eglise* (Paris: Cerf, 1950), 335–36: "la grande loi d'un réformisme catholique sera donc de commencer par un retour aux principes du catholicisme. Il faudra

d'abord interroger la tradition, se replonger en elle: étant bien entendu que 'tradition' ne signifie pas 'routine' non même proprement 'passé'." I am indebted to Professor Catherine Clifford for pressing me to read more of Congar, particularly this work.

31. Magee, *Patriarchal Institution in the Church*, 444.

32. As does, e.g., John Panagopoulos, "*Ut Unum Sint*: Remarks on the New Papal Encyclical from an Orthodox Perspective," in *Ecology and Poverty*, ed. Leonardo Boff and Virgil Elizondo (London: SCM Press, 1995), 137–40.

33. On this, see, inter alia, Vatican I's *Pastor Aeternus* (Denz. 1821) and also Vatican II's *Lumen Gentium*, esp. §§18–22. See also the 1992 *Catechism of the Catholic Church*: "The Lord made Simon alone, whom he named Peter, the 'rock' of his Church. He gave him the keys of his Church and instituted him shepherd of the whole flock. 'The office of binding and loosing which was given to Peter was also assigned to the college of apostles united to its head.' This pastoral office of Peter and the other apostles belongs to the Church's very foundation and is continued by the bishops under the primacy of the Pope" (881). The next paragraph continues: "The Pope, Bishop of Rome and Peter's successor, 'is the perpetual and visible source and foundation of the unity both of the bishops and of the whole company of the faithful'" (882).

34. The "institutional memory" of the Curia is formidable indeed if one accepts the thesis that its origins lie in the bureaucracy, first, of the City of Rome, then that of the Roman Empire, and only latterly that of the Roman Church. For more on this whole question, see Peter Huizing and Knut Walf, eds., *The Roman Curia and the Communion of Churches* (New York: Seabury Press, 1979) (= *Concilium* 127 [1979]).

35. Kasper, *That They May All Be One*, 90. Kasper elsewhere, and much earlier, articulated some of the changes the papacy has undergone and those that could still occur: see his "Ce qui demeure et ce qui change dans le ministère de Pierre," *Concilium* 108 (1975): 29–41.

36. I have analyzed this decision and the subsequent reasons given for it by the PCPCU. See my "On the Patriarchate of the West," *Ecumenical Trends* 35 (June 2006): 1–7.

Chapter One.   *Ut Unum Sint* in Context

1. Pope John XXIII's *Humanae Salutis* of Christmas 1961 formally convoked the council and made clear the ecumenical hopes of the council. On the history of the Secretariat, see Herbert Vorgrimler, ed., *Commentary on the Documents of Vatican II*, vol. 2 (Montreal: Palm; Freiburg: Herder,

1967–69), 1–6, and Joseph Komonchak, "The Secretariat for Promoting Christian Unity and the Preparation of Vatican II," *Centro Pro Unione Bulletin* 50 (1996): 11–17. See also Giuseppe Alberigo and Joseph Komonchak, eds., *History of Vatican II,* vol. 1, *Announcing and Preparing Vatican Council II* (Maryknoll, NY and Louvain: Orbis and Peeters, 1995), 167–356. For more personal reflections by two men who would eventually head up the Secretariat, see Augustin Cardinal Bea, *Ecumenism in Focus* (London: Geoffrey Chapman, 1969), 3–60, and Edward Idris Cardinal Cassidy, *Ecumenism and Interreligious Dialogue* (New York: Paulist Press, 2005), 3–7.

2. The intricacies of the formulation of this text, its revision and discussion, and ultimately the votes taken upon it are told in painstaking detail by Giuseppe Alberigo et al., eds., *History of Vatican II,* vol. 3, *The Mature Council* (Maryknoll, NY and Louvain: Orbis and Peeters, 2000), 257–345.

3. Kasper, *That They May All Be One,* 7.

4. For in-depth analysis of *UR* in the period of its promulgation, see Lorenz Cardinal Jaeger, *A Stand on Ecumenism: The Council's Decree,* trans. Hilda Graef (London: Geoffrey Chapman, 1965); Gregory Baum, *The Quest for Christian Unity* (London and New York: Sheed and Ward, 1963); Bernard Leeming, *The Vatican Council and Christian Unity* (London: Darton, Longman, and Todd, 1966); and Michael Adams, *Vatican II on Ecumenism* (Dublin and Chicago: Scepter Books, 1966). Kasper underscored the "binding" manner (*That They May All Be One,* 6), and in (*UUS* (§3) John Paul II emphasizes the same: "At the Second Vatican Council, the Catholic Church committed herself *irrevocably* to following the path of the ecumenical venture."

5. For the major highlights of postconciliar ecumenism, see Cassidy, *Ecumenism and Interreligious Dialogue,* 22–103. For a retrospective analysis on where and how *Unitatis Redintegratio* influenced various documents and developments in the postconciliar period, see Edward Idris Cassidy, "Vatican II and Catholic Principles on Ecumenism," *Centro Pro Unione Bulletin* 50 (1996): 3–10.

6. See my "On the 'Healing of Memories:' An Analysis of the Concept in Papal Documents in Light of Modern Psychotherapy and Recent Ecumenical Statements," *Eastern Churches Journal* 11 (2004): 59–88.

7. Three years later, the substance of this appeal would be repeated in slightly different words to, significantly, an audience of Eastern Catholic patriarchs. In 1998, John Paul II referred to the rights and duties of the Eastern patriarchs which must be safeguarded as a part of the "divinely revealed" nature of the Church while also "adapted somewhat to present-day conditions." See "Address of the Holy Father Pope John Paul II to Eastern Catholic Patriarchs," 28 September 1998, available at the Vatican website http://www.vatican.va under John Paul II and Eastern Catholic Patriarchs.

8. George Weigel, "The Church's Teaching Authority and the Call for Democracy in North Atlantic Catholicism," in *Church Unity and the Papal Office: An Ecumenical Dialogue on John Paul II's Encyclical* Ut Unum Sint, ed. Carl E. Braaten and Robert W. Jenson (Grand Rapids, MI: Eerdmans, 2001), 142.

9. It is curious to note that the pope called for a dialogue on the papacy and ended up not so much engaged in that dialogue as in reading responses from others—a more one-sided, even abstract process than the word "dialogue" would seem to suggest.

10. This is based on an interview in the Italian daily *Avvenire* and reported in a document, "Notes on *Ut Unum Sint* and the Orthodox Response," faxed from Cardinal Cassidy's office.

11. PCPCU, *Information Service* 1–2, no. 109 (2002), 31 (my emphasis).

12. There is an interview with the Ecumenical Patriarch in Switzerland in December 1995 following the publication of the encyclical, but it is not clear in what capacity he was speaking nor what weight, if any, to give his thoughts in the face of considerable *intra*-Orthodox criticism of his remarks. The interview is in Olivier Clément, *Conversations with Ecumenical Patriarch Bartholomew I,* trans. Paul Meyendorff (Crestwood, NY: St. Vladimir's Seminary Press, 1997). For some of the criticisms, see John Erickson's "First among Equals: Papal Primacy in an Orthodox Perspective," *Ecumenical Trends* 27, no. 2 (February 1998): 1–9. Clément himself, in a subsequent book, criticized Bartholomew's remarks as being "somewhat reductive and polemical." See *You Are Peter: An Orthodox Theologian's Reflection on the Exercise of Papal Primacy,* trans. M. S. Laird (New York: New City Press, 2003), 87.

13. Cf. Anthony Ugolnik, "The Art of Belonging," *Religion and the Intellectual Life* 1 (1984): 113–27, and "Tradition as Freedom from the Past: Eastern Orthodoxy and the Western Mind," *Journal of Ecumenical Studies* 21 (1984): 278–94.

14. John Meyendorff has some characteristically insightful things to say about the influence of nationalism on Orthodox ecclesiology and its attitudes toward Catholicism; see his "Ecclesiastical Regionalism: Structures for Communion or Cover for Separatism? Issues of Dialogue with Roman Catholicism," *St. Vladimir's Theological Quarterly* 24 (1980): 162–65 especially.

15. Father Don Boland, an official of the PCPCU, in discussion with me noted that "*no Orthodox Churches submitted an official response to the invitation, because they agreed that it should be something done collectively, and they have not yet had the opportunity to do so*" (private e-mail, 19 December 2003, my emphasis).

16. See, inter alia, Erich Bryner, "Stumbling-Blocks to Ecumenism," *Religion, State & Society* 26 (1998): 83–88. Some expressions of anti-ecumenical

sentiments from various Orthodox figures can be found at http://www
.isidore-of-seville.com/orthodoxy_and_catholicism/5.html. See also http://
www.orthodoxinfo.com/ecumenism/default.aspx.

17. Hart, "The Future of the Papacy: A Symposium," 34. One thinks, for
example, of the protests and slogans liberally employed against the visit of
John Paul II to Greece in 2001. See John Allen, "Orthodox Christians Wary of
Papal Visits," *National Catholic Reporter,* 13 April 2001, and also Allen's
"Mourning Bells to Chime for Pope's Visit," *National Catholic Reporter,* 5 May
2001; both are archived at the *National Catholic Reporter* website, http://www
.natcath.org/NCR.

18. For a good introduction and overview of the issues, see Robert F. Taft,
"The Problem of 'Uniatism' and the 'Healing of Memories:' Anamnesis, Not
Amnesia," *Logos: A Journal of Eastern Christian Studies* 41–42 (2000–01):
155–96 and idem., "Reflections on 'Uniatism' in the Light of Some Recent
Books," *Orientalia Christiana Periodica* 65 (1999): 153–84.

19. On the attempted destruction of the Ukrainian Catholic Church, see
B. R. Bociurkiw, *The Ukrainian Greek Catholic Church and the Soviet State
(1939–1950)* (Edmonton and Toronto: Canadian Institute of Ukrainian Studies
Press, 1996); Ivan Bilas, "The Moscow Patriarchate, the Penal Organs of the
USSR, and the Attempted Destruction of the Ukrainian Greco-Catholic
Church during the 1940s," *Logos: A Journal of Eastern Christian Studies* 38
(1997): 41–92; and Serge Keleher, *Passion and Resurrection: The Greek Catho-
lic Church in Soviet Ukraine 1939–1989* (Lviv: Stauropegion, 1993).

20. See Joseph Loya, "Interchurch Relations in Post-Perestroika Eastern
Europe: A Short History of an Ecumenical Meltdown," *Religion in Eastern
Europe* 25 (2005).

21. John H. Erickson, "A Retreat from Ecumenism in Post-Communist
Russia and Eastern Europe?" *Ecumenical Trends* 30 (2001): 129–38.

22. See Vladimir Fedorov, "Barriers to Ecumenism: An Orthodox View
from Russia," *Religion, State & Society* 26 (1998): 129–43.

23. On the Russian Orthodox generally for this period, see Zoe Knox,
"Postsoviet Challenges to the Moscow Patriarchate, 1991–2001," *Religion, State
& Society* 32 (2004): 87–113, and Andrew Evans, "Forced Miracles: The Russian
Orthodox Church and Postsoviet International Relations," *Religion, State &
Society* 30 (2002): 33–43. On renewed Catholic structures, see Daniel Schlafly,
"Roman Catholicism in Today's Russia: The Troubled Heritage," *Journal of
Church and State* 39 (1997): 681–96 and "Roman Catholicism in Post-Soviet
Russia: Searching for Acceptance," *Religion in Eastern Europe* 21 (2001).

24. The story of this bungling is told by George Weigel in *Witness to Hope,*
638–41.

25. John H. Erickson, "A New Crisis in Catholic-Orthodox Dialogue," *Ecumenism* 107 (1992): 22–24.

26. "Message of the Heads of Orthodox Churches," *Ecumenism* 107 (1992): 35.

27. Gerd Stricker, "Fear of Proselytism: The Russian Orthodox Church Sets Itself against Catholicism," *Religion, State & Society* 26 (1998): 165.

28. Rembert Weakland, "Inside the Orthodox Psyche," *Tablet* 254 (28 October 2001).

29. On which see the balanced article of Stricker, "Fear of Proselytism," 155–65. See also Fedorov, "Barriers to Ecumenism," in the same issue, 129–43.

30. See Patriarch Alexi, "Statement Reacts to Vatican Establishment of Four Russian Dioceses," *Origins* 31 (2002): 618–20. Aside from the fact that the complaints in this statement had not changed in a decade, it is almost impossible to take seriously a statement that contains such howlers as "the establishment of a *church province*, a *metropolitanate*, . . . is atypical even of Catholic countries where there are no church provinces or dioceses governed actually by a metropolitan" (p. 619). These statements reveal massive, and likely deliberate, ignorance about the long-standing structure of the Catholic Church, where provinces and metropolitanates are very much the norm.

31. Stricker, "Fear of Proselytism," 163.

32. Russian suspicion of Catholicism has very long roots. See Dennis J. Dunn, *The Catholic Church and Russia: Popes, Patriarchs, Tsars and Commissars* (Aldershot: Ashgate, 2004), especially chapter 1, and Sergei Filatov and Lyudmila Vorontsova, "Catholic and Anti-Catholic Traditions in Russia," *Religion, State & Society* 28 (2000): 69–84. This anti-Catholicism must not be thought of as a relic of the past: Gregory Zyablitsev makes it clear that it may be found today even among members of the Russian hierarchy; see his "The Ecumenical Problem in the Russian Orthodox Church in Relation to the 1994 Synod," *Concilium* 32 (1996): 101–9. In addition, for greater context, see also Aleksandr Verkhovsky, "The Role of the Russian Orthodox Church in Nationalist, Xenophobic and Antiwestern Tendencies in Russia Today: Not Nationalism, But Fundamentalism," *Religion, State & Society* 30 (2002): 333–45; and Zoe Knox, "Russian Orthodoxy, Russian Nationalism, and Patriarch Aleksii II," *Nationalities Papers* 33 (2005): 533–45.

Chapter Two.   Orthodox Positions on the Papacy

1. There were, of course, important earlier reflections on the papacy such as Vladimir Soloviev's celebrated but often tendentiously misunderstood *La*

Russie et l'église universelle (Paris: A. Savine, 1889) that will not be considered directly here. The focus of this work is on the period following the Second Vatican Council and especially on responses to *Ut Unum Sint*. Many earlier Orthodox arguments or concerns about the papacy are recapitulated in the writings of the authors reviewed below.

2. Erickson, "First among Equals," 4.

3. I have excluded works of an obvious superficial character or gratuitously polemical nature, typically published (or often self-published on the internet) by presses manifestly hostile to ecumenism and Catholicism (e.g., Uncut Mountain Press, www.uncutmountain.com). In this category I include such error-riddled tracts as Michael Whelton, *Two Paths: Papal Monarchy—Collegial Tradition: Rome's Claims of Papal Supremacy in the Light of the Orthodox Church* (Salisbury, MA: Regina Orthodox Press, 2001) or his more recent *Popes and Patriarchs: An Orthodox Perspective on Roman Catholic Claims* (Ben Lomond, CA: Conciliar Press, 2006). (I have dealt with *Popes and Patriarchs* in a review in *Canadian Journal of Orthodox Christianity* 2, no. 1 [2007].) I also exclude John Karmiris, "The Schism of the Roman Church" (available at http://www.myriobiblos.gr/texts/english/roman_church.htm) and similar papers found at a variety of Orthodox websites, many of them having no authority and not a few out of communion with canonical Orthodoxy.

4. As a consequence I will not be treating the views of such as John Romanides (1927–2001), who wrote almost nothing sensible about the papal office per se, and wrote nothing at all in response to *UUS*.

5. On Peter see Joachim Gnilka, "The Ministry of Peter—New Testament Foundations," in *The Petrine Ministry: Catholics and Orthodox in Dialogue,* ed. Walter Kasper (New York: Newman Press, 2006), 24–36; Metropolitan Emilianos Timiadis, "'Tu Es Petrus': An Orthodox Approach," *Patristic and Byzantine Review* 2 (1983): 5–26. More generally, see Michael Winter, *Saint Peter and the Popes* (Baltimore: Helicon Press, 1960) and Terrence V. Smith, *Petrine Controversies in Early Christianity: Attitudes towards Peter in Christian Writings of the First Two Centuries* (Tübingen: J. C. B. Mohr, 1985). For Matthew 16, see generally *Peter in the New Testament: A Collaborative Assessment by Protestant and Roman Catholic Scholars,* ed. Raymond Brown et al. (Minneapolis: Augsburg, 1973), and Veselin Kesich, "Peter's Primacy in the New Testament and the Early Tradition," in *The Primacy of Peter: Essays in Ecclesiology and the Early Church,* ed. John Meyendorff (Crestwood, NY: St. Vladimir's Seminary Press, 1992), 35–66. On the bishop of Rome in the early Church, see Nicholas Koulomzine, "Peter's Place in the Primitive Church," in *The Primacy of Peter,* ed. Meyendorff, 11–34, and Vittorio Peri, "The Role of the Bishop of Rome in

the Ecumenical Councils," in *The Petrine Ministry,* ed. Kasper, 123–58. For the view of the Fathers, see Jean-Claude Larchet, "The Question of the Roman Primacy in the Thought of Saint Maximus the Confessor," in *The Petrine Ministry,* ed. Kasper, 188–209, and the Roman Catholic scholar Vittorino Grossi, "Patristic Testimonies on Peter, Bishop of the Church of Rome: Aspects of a Historical-Theological Reading," in the same volume, 83–122. A good overview of later Byzantine theologians is provided in Milton Anastos, *Aspects of the Mind of Byzantium: Political Theory, Theology, and Ecclesiastical Relations with the See of Rome* (London: Ashgate, 2001).

6. For much of the documentation surrounding these meetings, see E. J. Stormon, ed., *Towards the Healing of Schism: The Sees of Rome and Constantinople: Public Statements & Correspondence between the Holy See and the Ecumenical Patriarchate 1958–84* (New York: Paulist Press, 1987).

7. John Meyendorff, ed., *The Primacy of Peter: Essays in Ecclesiology and the Early Church* (Crestwood, NY: St. Vladimir's Seminary Press, 1992). This is a reprint of the original 1963 English text.

8. Meyendorff does this in other places with more acute historical detail. See especially his *Imperial Unity and Christian Divisions: The Church 45–680* (Crestwood, NY: St. Vladimir's Seminary Press, 1989).

9. John Meyendorff, "St. Peter in Byzantine Theology," in *Primacy of Peter,* 68. Cf. Donald M. Nicol, "The Byzantine View of Papal Sovereignty," in *The Church and Sovereignty c. 590–1918: Essays in Honour of Michael Wilks,* ed. Diana Wood (Oxford: Blackwell, 1991), 173–85.

10. John Meyendorff, *Catholicity and the Church* (Crestwood, NY: St. Vladimir's Seminary Press, 1983), 142.

11. John Meyendorff, "The Ecumenical Patriarchate Yesterday and Today," in his *The Byzantine Legacy in the Orthodox Church* (Crestwood, NY: St. Vladimir's Seminary Press, 1982), 254.

12. Nicholas Afanasiev, "The Church Which Presides in Love," in *The Primacy of Peter,* ed. Meyendorff, 91–143.

13. Alexander Schmemann, "The Idea of Primacy in Orthodox Ecclesiology," in *The Primacy of Peter,* ed. Meyendorff, 145–71.

14. Kallistos Ware, "Primacy, Collegiality and the People of God," in *Orthodoxy: Life and Freedom,* ed. A. J. Philippou (Oxford: Oxford University Press, 1973). This lecture was reprinted in a variety of places.

15. Kallistos Ware, *The Orthodox Church* (London: Penguin, 1993), 27.

16. Stylianos Harkianakis, "Can a Petrine Office Be Meaningful in the Church? A Greek Orthodox Reply," in *Papal Ministry in the Church,* ed. Hans Küng (New York: Herder and Herder, 1971).

17. Paul Evdokimov, "Can a Petrine Office Be Meaningful in the Church? A Russian Orthodox Reply," in *Papal Ministry in the Church,* ed. Hans Küng (New York: Herder and Herder, 1971), 122–26.

18. Robert Stephanopoulos, "Christian Unity and the Petrine Ministry: Remarks of an Orthodox Christian," *Journal of Ecumenical Studies* 11 (1974): 309–14.

19. Emmanuel Clapsis, "The Papal Primacy," *Greek Orthodox Theological Review* 32 (1987): 115–30.

20. For some of the results of these dialogues on this question, see Colin Davey, "Statements on Primacy and Universal Primacy by Representatives of the Orthodox Churches," *One in Christ* 35 (1999): 378–82. See also Brian E. Daley, S.J., "Headship and Communion: American Orthodox-Catholic Dialogue on Synodality and Primacy in the Church," *Pro Ecclesia* 5 (1996): 55–72.

21. The documents of the JIC are helpfully located in one volume, Erickson and Borelli, *The Quest for Unity.*

22. Clapsis, "Papal Primacy," 127.

23. A theme echoed by others, most of whom are reviewed here. But see also in this regard Chrysostom Frank, "Orthodox-Catholic Relations," *Pro Ecclesia* 7 (1998): 72, for another reiteration of the importance of distinguishing Rome's many roles, including the patriarchal.

24. Vsevolod Majdansky, "Response to Bishop Basil (Losten): 'Patriarch and Pope: Different Levels of Roman Authority,'" *Logos: A Journal of Eastern Christian Studies* 35 (1994): 255. Archbishop Vsevolod fell asleep in the Lord in December 2007.

25. Majdansky, *We Are All Brothers,* 177.

26. Majdansky, "Response to Bishop Basil," 244–45.

27. Vsevolod Majdansky, "One, Holy, Catholic and Apostolic Church," in *Orientale Lumen VII Conference 2003 Proceedings* (Fairfax, VA: Eastern Christian Publications, 2004), 97.

28. Majdansky, *We Are All Brothers,* 245.

29. Antonios Kireopoulos, "Papal Authority and the Ministry of Primacy," *Greek Orthodox Theological Review* 42 (1997): 45–62. The timing of this article is highly curious: it was, he tells us in a footnote, "first presented at the Orthodox Theological Society of America meeting in June 1995," that is, only days— at most weeks—after Pope John Paul II promulgated *Ut Unum Sint* on 25 May 1995. In many respects one cannot expect Kireopoulos to have taken account of the encyclical for the initial presentation of the paper, coming as the two did so nearly coterminous. However, one would have expected Kireopoulos to expand his original piece and make mention of the encyclical when the paper appeared in print in 1997. This does not seem to be the case.

30. Ibid., 50. More frankly still, Kireopoulos admits that "despite our objections to universal ecclesiology, the reasons are obvious why Orthodox should take note of this criticism" (about a powerless "primacy of love and service"), viz., because of their own "disheartening reality of parallel jurisdictions" (59).

31. Puglisi, ed., *Petrine Ministry and the Unity of the Church.*

32. Mesrob K. Krikorian, "The Primacy of the Successor of the Apostle St. Peter from the Point of View of the Oriental Orthodox Churches," in Puglisi, *Petrine Ministry and the Unity of the Church,* 83–98.

33. Dumitru Popescu, "Papal Primacy in Eastern and Western Patristic Theology: Its Interpretation in the Light of Contemporary Culture," in Puglisi, *Petrine Ministry and the Unity of the Church,* 99–113. Another Romanian Orthodox theologian, Dumitru Staniloae, does not—surprisingly—seem to have written much at all about the papacy even in his major ecclesiological works, including *Theology and the Church,* trans. Robert Barringer (Crestwood, NY: St. Vladimir's Seminary Press, 1980).

34. Popescu, "Papal Primacy in Eastern and Western Patristic Theology," 104.

35. For critical discussions of Zizioulas's thought, especially in ecclesiology, see the many essays gathered in Douglas H. Knight, ed., *The Theology of John Zizioulas: Personhood and the Church* (Burlington, VT: Ashgate, 2007). For much of the Trinitarian background to Zizioulas's anthropology and ecclesiology, see the new collection of essays, John Zizioulas, *Communion and Otherness: Further Studies in Personhood and the Church,* ed. Paul McPartlan (London: T&T Clark, 2006).

36. Zizioulas, "Primacy in the Church: An Orthodox Approach," 115–25.

37. After Brian Daly's landmark article, it is inexcusable to ever again use the phrase "primacy of honour" in the typically careless fashion one so commonly finds it. See his "Position and Patronage in the Early Church: The Original Meaning of 'Primacy of Honour,'" *Journal of Theological Studies* 44 (1993): 529–53.

38. John Zizioulas, "Recent Discussions on Primacy in Orthodox Theology," in *The Petrine Ministry,* ed. Kasper, 231–48.

39. Nicholas Lossky, "Conciliarity-Primacy in a Russian Orthodox Perspective," in *Petrine Ministry and the Unity of the Church: "Toward a Patient and Fraternal Dialogue",* ed. James Puglisi (Collegeville, MN: Liturgical Press, 1999), 127–35, at 127.

40. Clément's book, important and unique though it is, is not without certain flaws, which I discuss in "Letter from the East," 46–50.

41. Clément, *You Are Peter,* 57. Cf. his "The Pope, the Council and the Emperor during the Period of the Seven Ecumenical Councils," *Sourozh: A Journal of Orthodox Life and Thought* 42 (November 1990): 1–15.

42. Clément, *You Are Peter,* 59.

43. Erickson, "First among Equals," 1–9.

44. Ibid., 5, quoting Meyendorff.

45. Panagopoulos, "*Ut Unum Sint:* Remarks from an Orthodox Perspective," 137–40.

46. Vigen Guroian, "A Communion of Love and the Primacy of Peter: Reflections from the Armenian Church," in *Ecumenism Today,* ed. Francesca Murphy et al. (Burlington, VT: Ashgate, 2008), 139–50.

47. This kenotic note is also sounded in an earlier work by Paul Verghese, who argues that "the Papacy itself will regain its true glory only when it voluntarily relinquishes its special claims to be the Vicar of Christ in a manner substantially different from that in which all bishops are sacramental presecenses of the One Good Shepherd." See his "Aggiornamento and the Unity of All: An Eastern Orthodox View of the Vatican Council," *Ecumenical Review* 15 (1963): 381.

48. David Bentley Hart, "The Myth of Schism," in *Ecumenism Today,* ed. Francesca Murphy et al. (Burlington, VT: Ashgate, 2008), 95–106.

49. Thomas Hopko, "Roman Presidency and Christian Unity in Our Time," a paper given at the Woodstock Forum in September 2005 and available on Hopko's personal page at St. Vladimir's Seminary: http://www.svots .edu/Faculty/Thomas-Hopko/Articles/Roman-Presidency-and-Christian -Unity.html.

50. Hopko lists several doctrinal changes he insists upon (e.g., deleting the *filioque;* insisting on a Palamite understanding of uncreated divine energies; and denying the existence of "Purgatory" as Catholic theology has traditionally understood it) as well as liturgical reforms (e.g., mandatory baptisms by immersion only; Holy Communion always under both kinds; widespread parochial celebration of "Vespers, Compline, Matins and the Hours in the churches"; the restoration of "the practice of having the priestly celebrant in the Latin liturgy face the altar with the faithful"; and, finally, the possible "enforcing [of] the ancient ascetical and penitential practice of forbidding the celebration of Holy Eucharist . . . on weekdays of Great Lent") (7). Hopko alone of all recent Orthodox theologians has drawn up such a comprehensive list, and it is hard to know what to make of it, not least because he himself has not hitherto been inclined to be so demanding and inflationary in his rhetoric. He does not at all seem representative of the rest of "mainstream" Orthodox theologians dealing with Orthodox-Catholic unity, where one finds no such

lists. Most disturbing of all is the lack of logic in Hopko's paper: he demands the pope be stripped of almost all his powers, but equally Hopko demands that the pope use those powers—and others Hopko erroneously claims the pope possesses!—to enforce or forbid certain things that no pope has ever attempted to enforce or forbid. Is the pope to use those powers one last time to enforce and forbid everything Hopko demands and then forswear the use of those powers ever after? Is he to use them one last time and then be stripped of them—and if so, by whom?

51. Theodore Stylianopoulos, "Concerning the Biblical Foundation of Primacy," in *The Petrine Ministry: Catholics and Orthodox in Dialogue,* ed. Walter Kasper (New York: Newman Press, 2006), 37. I have reviewed this book elsewhere. See my review in *Studia Canonica* 40 (2006): 269–72.

52. Stylianopoulos, "Concerning the Biblical Foundation of Primacy," 44.

53. V. Nicolae Durã, "The 'Petrine Primacy': The Role of the Bishop of Rome according to the Canonical Legislation of the Ecumenical Councils of the First Millennium—An Ecclesiological-Canonical Evaluation," in *The Petrine Ministry: Catholics and Orthodox in Dialogue,* ed. Walter Kasper (New York: Newman Press, 2006), 159–87.

54. Vlasios Pheidas, "Papal Primacy and Patriarchal Pentarchy in the Orthodox Tradition," in *The Petrine Ministry: Catholics and Orthodox in Dialogue,* ed. Walter Kasper (New York: Newman Press, 2006), 65–82.

55. Hilarion Alfeyev, *Orthodox Witness Today* (Geneva: WCC Press, 2006).

56. See canon 43 of the 1990 *Code of Canons of the Eastern Churches* (henceforth: *Codex Canonum Ecclesiarum Orientalium* = *CCEO*) and cf. canon 331 in the 1983 Latin *Code of Canon Law.* For an analysis of the *CCEO's* papal canons, see Andrew Onuferko, "The New Code of Canons of the Eastern Churches: Ecclesiological Presuppositions," *Logos: A Journal of Eastern Christian Studies* 35 (1994): 133–72.

57. Kallistos Ware, "Primacy, Collegiality and the People of God," 4. Cf. Majdansky, *We Are All Brothers,* 241–44.

58. Clapsis, "The Papal Primacy," 127.

Chapter Three.   A Renewed Roman Patriarchate

1. The story was picked up by several electronic news outlets. See, for example, Cindy Wooden, "Vatican removes title 'patriarch of the West' after pope's name," at the Catholic News Service website http://www.catholicnews .com under "Vatican removes title."

2. An editorial in *Irénikon* has rightly detected that the PCPCU explanation "manifeste un certain embarrass." This decision the editorialist regards with some ecumenical skepticism, noting also that "*L'Annuaire pontifical* ne jouit d'aucune autorité magistérielle. En fait, seuls les *Acta Apostolicae Sedis* engagent formellement l'autorité du Saint-Siège. De plus, ce n'est pas parce que le titre de 'patriarche d'Occident' n'apparaît plus sur l'Annuaire pontifical qu'il serait devenu obsolete en ecclésiologie catholique." See "Éditorial," *Irénikon* 74 (2006): 201.

3. See Daniel Stramara, "'Patriarch of the West' and the Importance of the Title *Patriarch*," *Ecumenical Trends* 35 (November 2006): 7–10. Stramara is blunt in his assessment, calling the decision to delete the title "highly significant" and suggesting it "inadvertently negatively impacts ecumenical dialogue" (7). As I did in my earlier article, "On the Patriarchate of the West," 1–7, Stramara notes that if the problem was with "of the West" then the title could have been clarified to "of Rome" (8). Stramara raises the question of whether a pope can legitimately "dissolve an ancient patriarchate" and concludes not only that he cannot, but that he should not—"the title Patriarch of Rome should be reclaimed as soon as possible, for the ancient and God-sanctioned patriarchate of Rome cannot be abolished" (9).

4. I am using the English translation, checked against the Italian and French, provided by Zenit, which itself said it was using the translation of the Vatican Information Service. See http://www.zenit.org/english/visualizza.phtml?sid=86437. See also the English version in *Origins* 36 (2006): 94–95. The Italian and French originals, as I argue in "On the Patriarchate of the West," remain crucial and the English translation is highly problematic on at least one important point.

5. The papal office is a complex conglomeration: the 2004 *Annuario Pontificio* notes that John Paul II is (in order) "Vescovo di Roma, Vicario di Gesù Cristo, Successore del Principe degli Apostoli, Sommo Pontefice della Chiesa Universale, Patriarca dell'Occidente, Primate d'Italia, Arcivescovo e Metropolita della Provincia Romana, Sovrano dello Stato della Città del Vaticano, Servo Dei Servi di Dio." At the foot of the page, it also records the date on which his papacy began, calling it the solemn inauguration of his "ministero di Pastore universale della Chiesa," thus adding if not another title then at least a variant on the title of "supreme pontiff of the universal Church."

6. The canonist John Faris agrees. See his "The Latin Church *Sui Iuris*," *Jurist* 62 (2002): 282 n9.

7. The official website of this Church is http://www.bulgarian-orthodox-church.eu. The chief hierarch of the Romanian Orthodox Church is styled "Teoctist, Archbishop of Bucharest, Metropolitan of Muntenia and Dobrud-

gea, Locum Tenens of Caesarea of Cappadochia and Patriarch of the Romanian Orthodox Church" (the official website is http://www.patriarhia.ro). The chief hierarch of the Serbian Orthodox follows a similar style to the Romanian: see http://www.serbianorthodoxchurch.com.

8. Some of this history is told in Klaus Schatz, *Papal Primacy: From Its Origins to the Present,* trans. John Otto and Linda Maloney (Collegeville, MN: Liturgical Press, 1996), 1–73. For earlier works, see Francis Dvornik, *Byzantium and the Roman Primacy* (New York: Fordham University Press, 1966); and Pierre Batiffol, *Cathedra Petri: Etudes d'Histoire ancienne de l'Eglise* (Paris: Cerf, 1938).

9. The argument in favor of episcopal conferences is not advanced as categorically in the original document as in the English: the Italian original says of these structures merely that they are "l'ordinamento canonico *adeguato* alle necessità di oggi" while the French original notes that they are simply "*approprié* aux necessities actuelles" (my emphasis).

10. Silvestrini suggested—before the PCPCU clarification was issued—that the decision was a "sign of ecumenical sensitivity" on the part of Pope Benedict who apparently felt that the existence of the title was an incentive to some people toward negative comparisons between the unending, limitless nature of the western patriarchate and the clearly geographically circumscribed jurisdictions of traditional Orthodox (and, perforce, Eastern Catholic) patriarchates. "It seems to me the pope wanted to eliminate this type of comparison and that his gesture is meant to stimulate the ecumenical journey," Cardinal Silvestrini said. See Wooden, "Vatican removes title."

11. Alfeyev's comments were posted in French and then English, see http://orthodoxeurope.org/page/14/89.aspx#4 and repeated by some other news agencies.

12. Ibid.

13. The letter is Protocol 1343 (Dispatch no. 173) and is posted on the official website of the Greek Church: http://www.ecclesia.gr.

14. Ibid. The archbishop's letter was answered in short order: on 12 April 2006, Pope Benedict replied with a short and formulaic note assuring Christodoulos that the pope had "given careful consideration to the observations contained in your letter" and that he had asked "Cardinal Walter Kasper . . . to make contact with you to explain this decision in more detail." Benedict's letter was posted on the website of the Church of Greece, but has not, to my knowledge, been otherwise published by the Vatican. See the letter at www.ecclesia.gr/English/archbishop/letters/benedictus.html.

15. The "Announcement of the Chief Secretary of the Holy and Sacred Synod Regarding the Denouncement by Pope Benedict XVI of Rome of the

Title 'Patriarch of the West'" was available on the official website of the Ecumenical Patriarch.

16. This statement, one must suggest charitably if firmly, could not have been well edited if it could make the claim that the title "Patriarch of the West" is the "*only*" one going back the farthest and enjoying the greatest Orthodox recognition. Surely both Orthodox and Catholics agree that what is a far more ancient, far more important title, with far greater ecumenical recognition both historically and currently, is "Bishop of Rome," that title without which all the others are void.

17. One needs to read this argument about the centrality of geography with the awareness that its strictures are not always practiced by the Orthodox. Cf. Meyendorff's "Ecclesiastical Regionalism."

18. To the argument that this decision was a matter internal to the Latin Church, which needs to consult nobody about her own affairs, I reply with the obvious *sed contra* of the extraordinary consultation undertaken by Rome in 2004 when the vexed question of a patriarchate for Ukrainian Catholics was being bandied about. The PCPCU, in the person of its president, Cardinal Kasper, undertook personal consultation with virtually every major Orthodox hierarch in the world, and on the basis of the extremely negative reaction of the Orthodox, Rome decided against granting patriarchal status to the Ukrainian Greco-Catholic Church. If Rome was willing to consult in this instance, how much more she should have done so with a vastly more influential and important decision pertaining to the very nature of the papacy as such.

19. One Catholic theologian not included here is Adriano Garuti, author of *Papa Patriarca d'Occidente? Studio storico dottrinale* (Bologne: Edizioni Francescane, 1990), who attempts to deny any significance, historical or theological, to the title "Patriarch of the West," a title he would have suppressed as a threat to universal papal jurisdiction. Garuti's scholarship has been almost unanimously condemned by very learned theologians, canonists, ecumenists, and senior hierarchs. All the scholars whose reviews I have read have said that this book is exceedingly tendentious, badly argued, one-sided, historically and theologically inaccurate, and by no means representative of Catholic theology and history, or still less of official magisterial positions. As I argued in my review of Garuti's *The Primacy of the Bishop of Rome and the Ecumenical Dialogues* (San Francisco: Ignatius Press, 2004) in "Primacy Time," *Touchstone* 18 (June 2005): 44–45, Garuti likes to slyly give the impression that he speaks for the Congregation of the Doctrine of the Faith, of which he was for many years an official. I have seen no reviews of this book that are even remotely positive and read no theologian who has been convinced by Garuti's thesis.

See, e.g., André de Halleux's review in *Revue Theologique de Louvain* 23 (1992): 208–11, in which he dismisses Garuti's flimsy case and flatly retorts, "Il y a donc raison de maintenir la distinction traditionnelle d'un niveau patriarchal dans la primauté juridictionnelle de l'évêque de Rome" (p. 211). See also George Nedungatt, "Patriarchal Ministry in the Church of the Third Millennium," *Jurist* 61 (2001): 10, where Nedungatt provides contrary evidence to Garuti, whom Nedungatt dismissively mocks as "seemingly more Catholic than the pope." Perhaps most authoritatively, Walter Cardinal Kasper has dismissed Garuti's arguments as nothing more than "a personal historical thesis, one which is vigorously disputed by reputable historians" (*That They May All Be One*, 82). Finally, see Magee's exceedingly polite, exactingly careful, detailed and therefore devastating demolition of Garuti in his *Patriarchal Institution in the Church*, 427–48. Nobody else has given such careful treatment of Garuti, and Magee is especially helpful in showing how Garuti is not in fact reflecting a traditional Latin ecclesiology at all (nor Western ecclesiastical history) and how his arguments go against the Second Vatican Council, which Garuti distorts in many ways. Garuti was forced to respond to the early criticisms of his book in "Ancora a Proposito del Papa Patriarca d'Occidente," *Antonianum* 70 (1995): 31–45, a response that disingenuously ducks the most severe criticisms and safely fastens onto other derivative and secondary issues, thereby tacitly conceding the case of his critics.

20. Joseph Ratzinger, "Primacy and Episcopacy," *Theology Digest* 26 (1971): 201.

21. Ibid. Cf. Ignace Dick, who argued that "nothing prevents Rome from establishing true patriarchates in China, India, or in . . . Africa" (*What Is the Christian Orient?* trans. C. Gerard Guertin [Westminster, MD: Newman Press, 1967], 20).

22. Joseph Ratzinger, "Primato ed Episcopato," *Il Nuovo Popolo di Dio: Questioni Ecclesiologiche* (Brescia: Queriniana, 1992 [1969]). I am relying on the translation of this text used by Magee in his *Patriarchal Institution in the Church*, 387–96.

23. Joseph Ratzinger, "Konkrete Formen bischöflicher Kollegialität," in *Ende der Gegenreformation? Das Konzil: Dokumente und Deutung*, ed. J. C. Hampe (Berlin: Kreuz Verlag, 1964), 156; translated and quoted in Magee, *Patriarchal Institution in the Church*, 391.

24. Ibid.

25. Ratzinger, "Primato ed Episcopato," 153; in Magee, 392.

26. Ibid., 155–56; in Magee, 393. There is something of an unconscious contradiction here insofar as Ratzinger says that the East's recognizing papal "power to interpret in a binding way the revelation wrought by Christ, and

submitting . . . to this interpretation when it is made in a definitive way" would "not need to change anything at all in the latter's concrete ecclesial life." Such "submission" to such "definitive" and "binding" papal declarations is precisely what the Orthodox find objectionable.

27. One other important Roman Catholic thinker writing shortly after Ratzinger was Louis Bouyer (*L'Eglise de Dieu* [Paris: Cerf, 1970]). Bouyer does not spend much time on the question of patriarchates, but he does echo Ratzinger in noting the "abnormal development of the Roman patriarchate in the West, which (in the eyes of the East as well) compromised the papacy by confusing it with freakish turgidity," leading to very "harmful consequences" for the life of the Church universal and her unity (*The Church of God,* trans. C. U. Quinn [Chicago: Franciscan Herald Press, 1982], 453).

28. *God and the World: A Conversation with Peter Seewald* (San Francisco: Ignatius Press, 2002), 384. Here Ratzinger acknowledges that perhaps his earlier work overestimated the place and importance of patriarchates, and that today episcopal conferences may be more appropriate means to accomplish what he earlier thought patriarchates would or could do in the Western Church.

29. See Yves Congar, "Le Pape, Patriarche d'Occident," the first chapter in his *Eglise et Papauté* (Paris: Cerf, 1994), 11–30; citations at 11.

30. My translation, ibid., 19: "la notion même de patriarcat n'a guère été comprise, ni donc honorée, par Rome."

31. My translation, ibid., 29: "est-il possible, est-il raisonnable, est-il réaliste d'imaginer la structure de l'Eglise réunie sous la forme d'une collégialité concrétisée dans une collégialité de patriarcats?" Congar has some characteristically insightful things to say about papal titles, tracing the history of each of the main ones in the relevant literature. When it comes to the title "Patriarch of the West," Congar notes that "Le pape s'intitule toujours patriarche d'Occident. Ce n'est pas un titre papal comme tel." Moreover, of all the titles noted above, "'Souverain Pontife' est devenu le titre le plus fréquemment employé dans l'usage moderne pour designer le pape" (Yves Congar, "Titres donnés au Pape," *Concilium* 108 [1975]: 57, 63).

32. J.-M. R. Tillard, *Church of Churches: The Ecclesiology of Communion,* trans. R. C. De Peaux (Collegeville, MN: Liturgical Press, 1992), 269–70.

33. J. Michael Miller, *The Divine Right of the Papacy in Recent Ecumenical Theology* (Rome: Gregorian University Press, 1980) and his *The Shepherd and the Rock: Origins, Development and Mission of the Papacy* (Huntington, IN: Our Sunday Visitor, 1995).

34. E.g., "Owing to the polemical character of so many writings, it is necessary to use carefully both Catholic and Orthodox sources, avoiding the extreme positions of each tradition" (Miller, *The Shepherd and the Rock,* 115).

35. Christopher O'Donnell, "Patriarchs," in *Ecclesia: A Theological Encyclopedia of the Church* (Collegeville, MN: Liturgical Press, 1996), 352.

36. Hermann Pottmeyer, *Towards a Papacy in Communion: Perspectives from Vatican Councils I & II* (New York: Crossroad, 1998).

37. On this question of the formation of triadic structures, see the important work of the canonist Myriam Wijlens, discussed below. See also Ton van Eijk, "The Structure of the Church Dyadic or Triadic?" and Jan Jacobs, "Beyond Polarity: On the Relation between Locality and Universality in the Roman Catholic Church," both in *Of All Times and All Places: Protestants and Catholics on the Church Local and Universal,* ed. Leo J. Koffman and Henk Witte (Meinema, Netherlands: Zoetermeer, 2001).

38. Frederick Bliss, *Catholic and Ecumenical: History and Hope* (Franklin, WI: Sheed and Ward, 1999), 9.

39. Nedungatt, "Patriarchal Ministry in the Church."

40. Nedungatt specifically mentions Adriano Garuti's *Papa Patriarca D'Occidente?*

41. Nedungatt goes on to argue that such a distinction is also necessary for better *internal* functioning of the Roman Church herself.

42. Myriam Wijlens, "The Intermediate Level in the Roman Catholic Church: An Organizational or Ecclesiological Category?" in *Of All Times and All Places: Protestants and Catholics on the Church Local and Universal,* ed. Leo J. Koffman and Henk Witte (Meinema, Netherlands: Zoetermeer, 2001), 95–130. See also her more recent work, "Cooperation of Bishops on a Supranational or Continental Level: A New Institution on the Intermediate Level?" in *Synod and Synodality: Theology, History, Canon Law and Ecumenism in New Contact,* ed. Alberto Melloni and Silvia Scatena (Münster: Lit Verlag, 2005), 33–60.

43. Wijlens, "The Intermediate Level in the Roman Catholic Church," 122.

44. Waclaw Hryniewicz, "The Cost of Unity: The Papal Primacy in Recent Orthodox Reflection," *Journal of Eastern Christian Studies* 55 (2003): 17.

45. Kasper, *That They May All Be One,* 86. In June 2003, the annual "Orientale Lumen Conference," held in Washington, D.C., was organized on the theme "Patriarchates: Ancient Model for Future Church Unity?" The results of this conference were published in 2004. See Roma Hayda, ed., *Orientale Lumen VII Conference 2003 Proceedings* (Fairfax, VA: Eastern Christian Publications, 2004).

46. Gregorios III, "Patriarches d'Orient et d'Occident: similarités et différences. Comment Rome pourrait fonctionner comme l'un d'entre eux?" *Logos: A Journal of Eastern Christian Studies* 46 (2005): 16–17 (my translation): "Le principe patriarcal, modèle équilibré d'unité et de synodalité, d'autonomie

locale et de système de communion intégré, reste un idéal qui doit toujours nous inspirer et nous aider à trouver des solutions ecclésiologiques pour les nouvelles situations que doit affronter l'Église au XXIᵉ siècle."

47. My translation, ibid., 28: "le modèle centralisateur propre au fonction-nement *ad intra* de l'Église Latine ne peut être appliqué aux relations entre les Églises patriarcales ou *sui juris*."

48. My translation, ibid., 29: "autour de la personne du Pape" of an "assem-blée des Patriarches Catholique Orientaux qui aurait pour rôle d'être une sorte de 'sénat de la papauté' pour un certain nombre de sujets."

49. My translation, ibid., 32: "On pourrait ensuite imaginer une sorte de 'super-Patriarcat' qui rassemblerait les différentes Églises patriarcales issues de la communion Romaine."

50. My translation, ibid., 32–33: "D'autre part, une plus grande décentrali-sation de l'Église Romaine, qui pourrait s'inspirer de la structure patriarcale, permettrait de mieux circonscrire le domaine d'exercice du ministère pétri-nien et, par là, de le rendre plus acceptables aux autres chrétiens. Il ne s'agit nullement de notre part d'une volonté d'imposer un modèle ecclésiologique oriental. Mais nous voulons imaginer une ecclésiologie pour le XXIᵉ siècle qui ne soit ni Orientale ni Occidentale mais réellement catholique: communion d'Églises autonomes, synodalité à la fois inter reliée et rassemblée par un centre d'unité, collégialité qui soit, sur cette terre tellement éprouvée, un reflet vivant de la divine Trinité. "

51. Michel Dymyd, "Les enjeux de l'abandon du titre de 'patriarch d'Occi-dent'," *Istina* 51 (2006): 30–32.

52. My translation. Antoine Lévy, "Au service de l'évêque de Rome: Collège patriarchal et unité de l'Eglise," *Istina* 51 (2006): 49 n34: "Nous proposons d'inverser la logique profonde des conciles d'union (Lyon 1274, Florence 1439). . . . Au lieu d'unir les patriarcats orientaux aux siege romain, tout en préservant les privilèges de ces patriarcats, nous proposons de rétablir la com-munion entre les patriarcats orientaux et le siege romain, tout en préservant les privileges de l'évêque de Rome. . . . Au lieu d'une assimilation sous condi-tion des patriarcats à l'Église de Rome, nous suggérons le rétablissement d'un veritable organism collegial entre les divers patriarcats qui récapitulent l'Église universelle. . . . En d'autres termes, si l'évêque de Rome veut que son charism spécifique en faveur de la communion des Églises soit reconnu par les autres patriarches, il doit lui-même, préalablement, retrouver son identité de pa-triarche d'Occident. Il sera ainsi membre du collège patriarchal à part égale avec ceux qui, comme lui, représentent leur Église *tamquam pater et caput*."

53. Gisbert Greshake, "Die Stellung des *Protos* in der Sicht der römisch-katholischen dogmatischen Theologie," *Kanon* 9 (1989): 17–50. I am relying on

Magee's extensive translation of and commentary on this article in *Patriarchal Institution in the Church.*

54. Magee, *Patriarchal Institution in the Church,* 416.

55. Greshake, in Magee, 421.

56. Greshake, in Magee, 420.

57. Greshake, in Magee, 421.

58. A. Raphael Lombardi, *The Restoration of the Role of the Patriarch of the West* (Fairfax, VA: Eastern Christian Publications, 2006). Lombardi's attempt is almost entirely unconvincing because inadequately researched and argued. He essentially confines himself to merely summarizing three sources: Adriano Garuti, Thomas Kane, and the *New Catholic Encyclopedia,* and promises far more than he is able or was willing to deliver. Vast sections of the book consist in nothing more than translations of Garuti's *Il Papa Patriarca D'Occidente?* which are then summarized in English in long quotations. This is problematic for several reasons, most especially because Lombardi nowhere acknowledges, let alone considers, the near-unanimous and extremely damning criticism Garuti has received for this book and others.

59. Geoffrey Robinson, *Confronting Power and Sex in the Catholic Church: Reclaiming the Spirit of Jesus* (Mulgrave, Victoria, Australia: John Garratt, 2007). Robinson, appointed in 1984, retired in 2004, well in advance of the canonical age limit (he was only sixty-seven at the time of retirement), because his experience dealing with sexual abuse as well as the mauling he received from the Curia had exhausted him (20–22).

60. Ibid., 144–45, 265–67. Robinson's third level is a rather vague and somewhat incoherent "mind of the whole Church" and how this is differentiated from the first and second levels is not entirely clear. Most of his proposals pertain to the running of a diocese and selection of parish clergy, and so are not directly relevant here.

61. He coins this neologism because of feminist sensitivities (see p. 274).

62. Why an election must be succeeded or seconded by papal appointment is not clear in Robinson's proposal.

63. Robinson is making an argument I have made elsewhere in reference to the appointment of bishops: why can Eastern Catholics be entrusted with the synodical election of their hierarchs but Roman Catholics are somehow felt unworthy or ineligible for this "privilege?" For more on this, see my "Look to Tradition: The Case for Electing Bishops," *Commonweal* 134 (23 March 2007): 15–18.

64. Robinson, *Confronting Power and Sex in the Catholic Church,* 275 (my emphasis).

65. Emphasis in original.

66. Finally, Robinson briefly proposes two further changes of interest. The first is to find a mechanism to allow for wider participation in papal elections on the basis of the principle that "he who governs all must be elected by all." He suggests rather weakly that nations elect representatives to an electoral college, still called the "College of Cardinals" but coming into existence only for an election, and that these cardinals then choose the pope. Finally, he proposes that the local churches have a role in the election of their own bishop, but that the bishop of Rome retain a role in actually making the appointment. See ibid., 278–82.

67. "It is not at all easy to determine what precise role the Roman Church played in the first three centuries of the Christian era within a *distinct grouping* of local Churches" (Magee, *Patriarchal Institution in the Church,* 115) (emphasis in original).

68. Ignace Dick has argued that "Rome has the title of Patriarchate of the West, but she seldom used it" and the patriarchal role was often "confused with the power of the pope as vicar of the Church." Further confusion stems from the fact that "the ecclesiastical West lacked cohesion. Rome exercised effective patriarchal power only in Italy" (Dick, *What is the Christian Orient?* 9, 13).

69. Magee, *Patriarchal Institution in the Church,* 100–4.

70. Richard Bavoillot-Laussade, "Tiara," in *The Papacy: An Encyclopedia,* ed. Philippe Levillain (London: Routledge, 2002), 3:1488–92.

71. Magee, *Patriarchal Institution in the Church,* 516.

72. Interestingly and importantly, not only Catholic and Orthodox theologians have studied the problem of Rome as a patriarchate. For a Protestant perspective, cf. the work of the Groupe des Dombes, which has also suggested that a resurrection of the office of patriarch, together with a clarification about the currently confused and overlapping roles which the bishop of Rome plays, will be very important for Catholic-Protestant unity. For more on this, see their 1985 statement, "Le ministère de communion dans l'Eglise universelle," in *Pour la communion des Eglises: L'apport du Groupe des Dombes 1937–1987* (Paris: Le Centurion, 1988), especially 173.

73. As Michael Magee notes, most authors who treat this at all tend, after lamenting the lack of differentiation, to "plunge immediately thereafter into the altogether different question of whether the Western Patriarchate should be divided" (*Patriarchal Institution in the Church,* 413).

74. The history of this code is told in several places, including Frederick McManus, "The Code of Canons of the Eastern Catholic Churches," *Jurist* 53 (1993): 22–61; and Thomas Green, "Reflections on the Eastern Code Revision Process," *Jurist* 51 (1991): 18–37; see also Michael Fahey, "A Note on the 'Code

of Canons of the Eastern Churches' and Orthodox/Catholic Reunion," *Jurist* 56 (1996): 456–64.

75. Curiously, some Orthodox have disdained the whole concept of codification, notwithstanding the fact that their much-promised "great and holy synod," in the works for the last fifty years (at least) had this on its agenda. See the article of the now Ecumenical Patriarch Bartholomew, "A Common Code for the Orthodox Churches," *Kanon* 1 (1973): 45–53, and Nicholas Afanasiev's "Canons and Canonical Consciousness" (published in *Put'* in 1933 in Russian and translated into English at http://www.orthodoxresearchinstitute.org/articles/canon_law/afanasiev_canonical_consciousness.htm), which wants to have it both ways, arguing that "it is obvious . . . that the agenda of a future Council must include the question of the codification of canons" while in the same paragraph failing to understand how such a codification can take place and thus denouncing it: "The compilation of such a Codex is not likely to meet the present needs of the Orthodox Church nor is it likely to become a reality. A general Orthodox compilation of laws would be an innovation which would not reflect the spirit of the Orthodox Church. A unification of canonical legislation assumes such a state of uniformity in the canonical structures of Church life of Autocephalous Churches which the Orthodox world does not know."

76. For analysis see Francis J. Marini, *The Power of the Patriarch— Patriarchal Jurisdiction on the Verge of the Third Millennium* (Brooklyn: St. Maron Publications, 1998) and for a more in-depth discussion about many of these canons, and especially their history, see Marini, *The Catholic View of Patriarchal Jurisdiction and Its Relation to Future Church Unity* (Fairfax, VA: Eastern Christian Publications, 2003). See also John D. Faris, *Eastern Catholic Churches: Constitution and Governance* (Brooklyn: St. Maron Publications, 1992), 211–357. In addition, see Paul Alappatt, *The Election of the Patriarch in the Eastern Catholic Canonical Tradition: A Historical-Juridical Study* (Rome: PIO, 1997).

77. See "Preface to the Latin Edition," in Canon Law Society of America, *Code of Canons of the Eastern Churches* (Washington, DC: Canon Law Society of America, 1990), xxix–xli.

78. Ibid., 3; my emphasis.

79. The noted canonist Ivan Žužek draws out some of these controverted questions and how the commission had to rule, sometimes satisfactorily and at other times less so. See his article "The Patriarchal Structure According to the Oriental Code," in *The Code of Canons of the Oriental Churches: An Introduction*, ed. Clarence Gallagher (Rome: Mar Thoma Yogam—St. Thomas Christian Fellowship, 1991), especially 38–50.

80. John Paul II, Apostolic Constitution, *Sacri Canones* in *Code of Canons of the Eastern Churches,* xxiii.

81. This is even more forcefully stated in a public address of 25 October 1990, where Pope John Paul II affirmed that "there is no norm in the Code which does not favor the path of unity among all Christians, and there are clear norms for Catholic Oriental Churches regarding how to promote this unity" (cited in *The Code of Canons of the Oriental Churches: An Introduction,* ed. Clarence Gallagher [Rome: Mar Thoma Yogam—St. Thomas Christian Fellowship, 1991], 17).

82. Fahey, "Note on the 'Code of Canons of the Eastern Churches'," 464.

83. It also builds on, and in many cases corrects or ignores, earlier canonical legislation, including especially the four documents (all issued *motu proprio*) of Pope Pius XII: *Crebrae Allatae* (on marriage law; issued 22 Feb 1949); *Sollicitudinem Nostram* (on procedural law; issued 6 Jan 1950); *Postquam Apostolicis Litteris* (on religious and temporal goods; issued 9 Feb 1952); and *Cleri Sanctitati* (on persons; issued 2 June 1957).

84. Alexander Schmemann, "A Response," in *The Documents of Vatican II: Introductions and Commentaries by Catholic Bishops and Experts; Responses by Protestant and Orthodox Scholars,* ed. Walter M. Abbot, trans. Joseph Gallagher (Piscataway, NJ: New Century, 1966). This "tainted" ecclesiology is also heavily criticized by Patrick Viscuso, "Orthodox-Catholic Unity and the Revised Code of Eastern Canon Law," *Journal of Ecumenical Studies* 27 (1990): 108–15.

85. See, e.g., the criticisms of Victor Pospishill, who was disputing the nature and direction of the CCEO even in draft stage: "The Constitutional Development of the Eastern Catholic Churches in the Light of the Re-Codification of Their Canon Law," *Kanon* 5 (1978): 36–71. See also Onuferko, "The New Code of Canons of the Eastern Churches," 153–62 especially. Ihor Kutash, in the same issue, in his "Response to Fr. Andrew Onuferko, 'The New Code of Canons of the Eastern Churches'" (pp. 169–72), argues that Catholic canon law has "no place for other than honourary Patriarchates in the Church since the Pope of Rome becomes the only true Patriarch."

86. This is an almost verbatim repeating of canons 331–34 of the Latin *Code of Canon Law.*

87. "Supreme authority" is a dangerously ambiguous phrase insofar as it seems, in practice at least, to allow the functionaries of the Roman Curia to participate vicariously in the authority of the pope.

88. Žužek, "Patriarchal Structure According to the Oriental Code," 49.

89. Ibid., 50.

Chapter Four.   Patriarchates

1. Nedungatt, "Patriarchal Ministry in the Church of the Third Millennium," 19.

2. Magee, *Patriarchal Institution in the Church*, 150.

3. John Erickson, "Common Comprehension of Christians Concerning Autonomy and Central Power in the Church in View of Orthodox Theology," *Kanon* 3–5 (1975–78): 101. Erickson quotes a letter of Patriarch Philotheos Kokkinos in 1370 to certain Russian princes in which the patriarch opens by claiming that "Since God has appointed Our Humility as leader of all Christians found anywhere," the patriarch therefore enjoys the right to appoint bishops over "all other areas of the earth . . . so that each, in the country and place appointed him, enjoys territorial rights, and episcopal see, and all the rights of Our Humility" (111).

4. Patsavos, "Synodal Structure of the Orthodox Church," 74.

5. My translation. Patriarch Gregorios III, "Patriarches d'Orient et d'Occident: similarités et differences," 15–16: "Les usages ecclésiologiques de l'Orient Chrétien ne sont pas apparus un beau jour dans leur intégralité, comme Athéna sortie toute armée de la cuisse de Jupiter [*sic*]. Ils ont eux-mêmes été l'objet d'une genèse et d'un processus de développement complexe. D'autre part, ils sont loin d'être aussi uniformes que ne le laisse supposer l'expression: *ethos* ecclésiologique Orthodoxe.' . . . [L]es pratiques de l'Orient chrétien ont elles-mêmes varié selon les temps et les lieux."

6. Nicholas Ferencz, *American Orthodoxy and Parish Congregationalism* (Piscataway, NJ: Gorgias Press, 2006), 47. This "holy synod" was more than a synod insofar as its "oberprocuror" was a layman heading up a department of state that happened to include bishops.

7. Cf. Schmemann, "Idea of Primacy in Orthodox Ecclesiology," 49–50 especially.

8. The obvious rejoinder to this line of argument is that a strongly centralized papacy has been the *cause* of some of the confusion and disorder in the Church today. Consider one issue central to the contemporary papacy and certainly central to Orthodox-Catholic discussions about the papacy: the appointment of bishops. As other scholars, such as John Pollard, Joseph O'Callaghan, Peter Norton, and Eamon Duffy, have all recently demonstrated, and as I have also argued elsewhere on more than one occasion (see, inter alia, my "Look to Tradition: The Case for Electing Bishops," 15–18), the Roman monopoly on the appointment of bishops—in addition to being a staggering

canonical "coup" engineered in Rome only in the early years of the twentieth century and so lacking any historical validity—has not always served the Church well. For example: in the Diocese of Palm Beach, Florida not one but *two* bishops *in succession,* both of whom sailed through Rome's fabled system of scrutiny, were forced to resign because of homosexual offences with minors. In March 2002, Bishop Anthony O'Connell resigned after it came to light that he had engaged in sexual improprieties with a seminarian a quarter-century earlier. O'Connell's resignation came a scant four years after his immediate predecessor, Bishop Keith Symons, was *also* forced to resign because he had sexually abused five young men. I am not saying that another method of episcopal selection is guaranteed to be better, but I am attempting to debunk the idea that breaking the Roman monopoly on appointments would result in worse appointments and more disorder in the Church.

9. John Meyendorff hints at this in his "Rome and Orthodoxy: Authority or Truth," in *A Pope for All Christians: An Inquiry into the Role of Peter in the Modern Church,* ed. Peter J. McCord (New York: Paulist Press, 1976), especially 144–45.

10. Patrick Reardon, "One, Holy, Catholic and Apostolic Church," http://www.beliefnet.com/story/44/story_4478_1.html.

11. Quoted by Olivier Clément, *You Are Peter,* 92.

12. Lewis Patsavos comes the closest to filling this lacuna with his "Synodal Structure of the Orthodox Church," a study that does not deal with all the Orthodox Churches and is now out of date.

13. E.g., Ron Roberson, *The Eastern Christian Churches: A Brief Survey,* 6th ed. (Rome: PIO, 1999); Ware, *The Orthodox Church;* John Binns, *An Introduction to the Christian Orthodox Churches* (Cambridge: Cambridge University Press, 2002).

14. The best example of this is Kostas E. Tsiropoulos, ed., *The Splendour of Orthodoxy: 2000 Years of History, Monuments, Art,* vol. 2, *Patriarchates and Autocephalous Churches* (Athens: Ekdotike Athenon, 2000). See also John Meyendorff, "Ecclesiastical Organization in the History of Orthodoxy," *St. Vladimir's Seminary Quarterly* 4 (1960): 2–22.

15. For perhaps obvious reasons, almost all these studies focus on the Church of Constantinople: see, e.g., Maximos, *Oecumenical Patriarchate;* Meyendorff, "The Ecumenical Patriarch, Seen in the Light of Orthodox Ecclesiology and History"; Patsavos, *Primacy and Conciliarity.*

16. See, e.g., Daniel D. Benjamin, *The Patriarchs of the Church of the East: Dinkha III not IV,* trans. from Assyrian into English by Youel A. Baaba (Piscataway, NJ: Gorgias Press, 2006); and Michael Burgess, *The Eastern Orthodox Churches: Concise Histories with Chronological Checklists of Their Primates*

(London and Jefferson, NC: McFarland, 2005). I have discussed these books at length in my "Eastern Ecclesial Polity: A Review Essay," *Logos: A Journal of Eastern Christian Studies* 48 (2007).

17. E.g., Ferencz, *American Orthodoxy and Parish Congregationalism.* I have discussed this book in my "Eastern Ecclesial Polity."

18. I will not be examining the other Orthodox Churches whose chief hierarch is not a patriarch or catholicos. In addition, I have confined myself to the patriarchates named in the text for three reasons: first these patriarchates are among the oldest and govern the largest and most important Orthodox Churches in the world. Second, to include every patriarchate in the world would make this book unwieldy. Third, I *have* examined the other patriarchates and concluded that there is either insufficient evidence or no accessible published material on the basis of which to say anything meaningful about them.

19. Metropolitan Maximos has written that this official title "brings him close to the status of the Pope of Rome." See Maximos, *Oecumenical Patriarchate,* 250.

20. For an overview of the historical development of the Ecumenical Patriarchate, see Vasil Stavrides, "A Concise History of the Ecumenical Patriarchate," *Greek Orthodox Theological Review* 45 (2000): 57–153. See also Vlasios Pheidas, "The Oecumenical Patriarchate of Constantinople," in *The Splendour of Orthodoxy: 2000 Years of History, Monuments, Art,* vol. 2, *Patriarchates and Autocephalous Churches,* ed. Kostas E. Tsiropoulos (Athens: Ekdotike Athenon, 2000), 30–46.

21. Vasil Istavridis, "The Authority of the Ecumenical Patriarch in the Life of the Orthodox Church," *Greek Orthodox Theological Review* 35 (1990): 16.

22. The imperial structures were used by the Church in structuring her own affairs in the first several centuries of her life. This "principle of accommodation" has been famously discussed in detail by Dvornik in *Byzantium and the Roman Primacy,* 27–39.

23. The Greek and Latin are alongside the English in Norman Tanner, ed., *Decrees of the Ecumenical Councils,* 2 vols. (London: Sheed & Ward and Washington, DC: Georgetown University Press, 1990), 1:32. The meaning of the phrase "privileges of honor" has never achieved universal consensus and understanding, and is still debated today by scholars and historians. In practice and for most of the time, it seems safe to say, as Metropolitan Maximos has, that the privileges "were not a simple honorary distinction in the hierarchical order, but involved genuine power in reciprocal relationship with the prerogatives of the other bishops" (*Oecumenical Patriarchate,* 115; see also 327). Cf. Brian Daley, "Position and Patronage in the Early Church: The

Original Meaning of 'Primacy of Honour,'" *Journal of Theological Studies* 44 (1993): 529–53.

24. Adrian Fortescue, "Introduction," in *The Patriarchs of Constantinople,* ed. Claude Delaval Cobham (Cambridge: Cambridge University Press, 1911), 25 and 27.

25. These rising and falling fortunes are told in a variety of places, but see in particular Vasil Istavridis, "The Ecumenical Patriarchate," *Greek Orthodox Theological Review* 14 (1969): 198–225; Deno J. Geanakoplos, *A Short History of the Ecumenical Patriarchate of Constantinople (330–1990)* (Brookline, MA: Holy Cross Orthodox Press, 1990). Ecclesiastical fortunes often fluctuate in conjunction with the political, and J. M. Hussey is especially good in delineating these interconnections in the imperial period: *The Orthodox Church in the Byzantine Empire* (Oxford: Clarendon Press, 1986), esp. 297–331. For later developments, see Theodore Papadopoulos, *The History of the Greek Church and People under Turkish Domination* (New York: AMS Press, 1973), 25–105. Finally, for developments in the twentieth century, see Basil Giannakakis, *International Status of the Ecumenical Patriarchate* (Cambridge, MA: n.p., 1959). See Geoffrey Korz, "Papal Hopes and Orthodox Popes: Did the Turks Get Something Right?" *Orthodox Canada: A Journal of Orthodox Christianity on the 'Net* 2 (2007): at http://www.orthodoxcanada.com/journal/2007-04-09 .html.

26. Peter L'Huillier, "The Origins, Development and Significance of the Administrative Institutions of the Orthodox Church: Patriarchates, Autonomous Churches and Autocephalous Churches," in *The Splendour of Orthodoxy: 2000 Years of History, Monuments, Art,* vol. 2, *Patriarchates and Autocephalous Churches,* ed. Kostas E. Tsiropoulos (Athens: Ekdotike Athenon, 2000), 26.

27. See, e.g., Donald M. Nicol, who has argued that "some of the last patriarchs of Constantinople before the Turkish conquest in 1453 indeed arrogated to themselves a form of universal authority over the Orthodox Church not unlike that of the popes" ("Byzantine View of Papal Sovereignty," 177).

28. "Archbishopric of Constantinople," at http://www.patriarchate.org.

29. On which see Whit Mason, "Constantinople's Last Hurrah: Turkey and the Ecumenical Patriarchate," *World Policy Journal* 18 (2001): 55–64. See also Timothy (Kallistos) Ware, *Eustratios Argenti: A Study of the Greek Church under Turkish Rule* (Oxford: Oxford University Press, 1964).

30. Elsewhere on the website, we are told that "the Greek Orthodox Church of America was founded as an Archdiocese of the Ecumenical Throne in 1922. As such, the Archdiocese of America is an eparchy of the Ecumenical Patriarch." For more on the territorial claims, see the document "Territorial

Jurisdiction According to Orthodox Canon Law: The Phenomenon of Ethno-phyletism in Recent Years," http://www.patriarchate.org.

31. Interestingly, the one area not mentioned, for perhaps obvious political reasons, is Mount Athos.

32. "The Immediate Jurisdiction of the Ecumenical Patriarchate," http://www.patriarchate.org.

33. Ferencz, *American Orthodoxy and Parish Congregationalism,* 86, 89. See the official text of the charter in "Chambesy Documents" at Greek Orthodox Archdiocese of America website http://www.goarch.org/archdiocese.

34. Thus the official "Decision," in no. 2.b.

35. Official "Decision," no. 1.b.

36. Further details about their operations may be found in the "Rules of Operation."

37. Thus article 5 of the "Rules of Operation."

38. The Russians, not surprisingly, continue to dispute the nature of the Ecumenical Patriarch's authority.

39. The list that follows should be compared to the sixteen "rights and duties" enumerated in Istavridis, "Authority of the Ecumenical Patriarch," 17–18.

40. "A Brief Historical Note about the Ecumenical Patriarchate," §2: http://www.patriarchate.org.

41. Ethno-phyletism remains a live issue today. See the scathing comments of the Armenian Orthodox theologian Vigen Guroian, "The Crisis of Orthodox Ecclesiology," in *The Ecumenical Future,* ed. Carl E. Braaten and Robert W. Jenson (Grand Rapids, MI: Eerdmans, 2004), 162–75. For a helpful analysis that links phyletism with questions of ecclesiology, see Philip Walters, "Notes on Autocephaly and Phyletism," *Religion, State & Society* 30 (2002): 357–64.

42. Much of the history of the Ecumenical Patriarchate's involvement in early ecumenical endeavors is told in Constantin G. Patelos, ed., *The Orthodox Church in the Ecumenical Movement: Documents and Statements 1902–1975* (Geneva: WCC Press, 1978).

43. It is far from being clearly and unanimously established among Orthodox canonists, theologians, and hierarchs whether Constantinople has this right, and, especially, whether it *alone* has this right. The Russian Orthodox Church has been advancing the argument that a "mother" Church has the right of bestowing autocephaly on a "daughter" without recourse to Constantinople. The Russians did this in fact in 1970 in making the Orthodox Church of America autocephalous, a fact still unrecognized by Constantinople, which denies any validity to the principle upon which Moscow acted. There is a considerable literature on this problem. For some of the early history, see John

Erickson, "Autocephaly in Orthodox Canonical Literature to the Thirteenth Century," *St. Vladimir's Theological Quarterly* 15 (1971): 28–41; for some later history, see his "The 'Autocephalous Church'," in *The Challenge of Our Past: Studies in Orthodox Canon Law and Church History* (Crestwood, NY: St. Vladimir's Seminary Press, 1991), 91–113. For a good general overview, see Peter L'Huillier, "Accession to Autocephaly," *St. Vladimir's Theological Quarterly* 37 (1993): 267–304. See also L'Huillier's "Problems Concerning Autocephaly," *Greek Orthodox Theological Review* 24 (1979): 165–91 and the response following by John Boojamra (191–99). Additionally, see Panagiotis Trembelas, *The Autocephaly of the Metropolia in America,* trans. Robert Stephanopoulos (Brookline, MA: Holy Cross Orthodox Press, 1973). Much of the literature focuses on individual churches since the circumstances vary so widely as to make generalizations hazardous. For treatment of the Church in Montenegro, see Panteleimon Rodopoulos, "Autocephaly in the Orthodox Church and the Manner in Which It Is Declared: The Orthodox Church in Montenegro," *Greek Orthodox Theological Review* 42 (1997): 213–21. For the Church in Georgia, see Michael Tarchnisvili, "The Origin and Development of the Ecclesiastical Autocephaly of Georgia," *Greek Orthodox Theological Review* 46 (2001): 89–111. See also Paul Werth, "Georgian Autocephaly and the Ethnic Fragmentation of Orthodoxy," *Acta Slavica Iaponica* 23 (2006): 74–100. For the Orthodox Church of America, see Alexander Bogolepov, *Toward an American Orthodox Church: The Establishment of an Autocephalous Orthodox Church* (Crestwood, NY: St. Vladimir's Seminary Press, 2001 [1963]). In addition, see the many articles and documents in *St. Vladimir's Theological Quarterly* 15 (1971): 3–80. Critical documents about Moscow's decision to grant autocephaly to the Orthodox Church of America are helpfully gathered in *Russian Autocephaly and Orthodoxy in America* (New York: Orthodox Observer Press, 1972). Also on the question of the dispute between Moscow and Constantinople, see Kallistos Ware, "Autocephaly Crisis: Deadlock between Constantinople and Moscow," *Eastern Churches Journal* 3 (1971): 311–15. For the Church in Czechoslovakia, see Josef Fejsak, "The Orthodox Church in Czechoslovakia: The Path to Autocephaly," *Journal of the Moscow Patriarchate* 12 (1981): 46–49. For the Church in Macedonia, see Stevan K. Pavlowitch, "The Church of Macedonia: 'Limited Autocephaly' or Schism?" *Sobornost* 9 (1987): 42–59. For some understanding of the complex situation in Ukraine, with several so-called Orthodox Churches declaring themselves autocephalous or seeking recognition as such from canonical Orthodox Churches, see Nikolai Mitrokhin, "Aspects of the Religious Situation in Ukraine," *Religion, State & Society* 29 (2001): 173–96 and Geraldine Fagan and Aleksandr Shchipkov, "'Rome Is Not Our Father But Neither Is Moscow Our Mother:' Will There Be a Local

Ukrainian Orthodox Church?" *Religion, State & Society* 29 (2001): 197–205. Finally, for some insight into the mess in Estonia in 1996, with Moscow and Constantinople excommunicating each other for a time over, inter alia, who could grant autocephaly, see Alexander F. C. Webster, "Split Decision: The Orthodox Clash over Estonia," *Christian Century* 113 (5 June 1996): 614–21.

44. "Bartholomew, Archbishop of Constantinople, New Rome and Ecumenical Patriarch," http://www.patriarchate.org.

45. Ibid. For more on the relationships between the Ecumenical Patriarchate and the other patriarchs, see Maximos, *Oecumenical Patriarchate,* 278–300.

46. Pheidas, "The Oecumenical Patriarchate of Constantinople," 46. There have been periods in which the synod was totally ignored, undermined, or composed in such a way as to allow the patriarch to run roughshod over the entire Church, exercising powers many scholars consider monarchical or papal and therefore erroneous. See Meyendorff, "The Ecumenical Patriarch Seen in the Light of Orthodox Ecclesiology and History," 233.

47. "The Holy and Sacred Synod," http://www.patriarchate.org.

48. Roberson, *Eastern Christian Churches.*

49. Part of the explanation for this exclusion of lay people may be the fact that the patriarchate is in an ongoing fight for survival in the face of pressure and persecution from the Turkish government, and the former may fear that any lay involvement might open the door more widely to this interference.

50. Patsavos, "Synodal Structure of the Orthodox Church," 76.

51. Patsavos, "Primacy of the See of Constantinople in Theory and Practice," 250.

52. Though dated, see John Mason Neale, *The Patriarchate of Alexandria* (London: J. Masters, 1847). Neale's book has recently been brought back into print by Gorgias Press.

53. On this see N. H. Baynes, "Alexandria and Constantinople: A Study in Ecclesiastical Diplomacy," *Byzantine Studies and Other Essays* (London: Greenwood Press, 1955), 97–116. See also Glanville Downey, "The Claim of Antioch to Ecclesiastical Jurisdiction over Cyprus," *Proceedings of the American Philosophical Society* 102 (1958): 224–28.

54. Canon 6: "The ancient customs of Egypt, Libya and Pentapolis shall be maintained, according to which the bishop of Alexandria has authority over all these places since a similar custom exists with reference to the bishop of Rome. Similarly in Antioch and the other provinces the prerogatives of the churches are to be preserved."

55. Baynes, "Alexandria and Constantinople," 101. Stephen Davis has recently written that "the lack of information about the first two centuries of Egyptian church leadership has caused historians much consternation" (*The*

Early Coptic Papacy: The Egyptian Church and Its Leadership in Late Antiquity
[Cairo and New York: American University of Cairo Press, 2004], 16).

56. Metropolitan Makarios Tillyrides, "History of the Patriarchate," http://
www.patriarchateofalexandria.com.

57. See Leo Donald Davis, *The First Seven Ecumenical Councils (325–787):
Their History and Theology* (Collegeville, MN: Liturgical Press, 1983), 170–206
and especially 194ff.

58. Euthymios Soulogiannis, "The Patriarchate of Alexandria," in *The
Splendour of Orthodoxy: 2000 Years of History, Monuments, Art,* vol. 2, *Patriarchates and Autocephalous Churches,* ed. Kostas E. Tsiropoulos (Athens: Ekdotike Athenon, 2000), 114.

59. Ibid., 126.

60. Ibid., 120.

61. Ron Roberson, "The Patriarchate of Alexandria," http://www.cnewa
.org/ecc-bodypg-us.aspx?eccpageID=14&IndexView=toc.

62. Patsavos, "Synodal Structure of the Orthodox Church," 77, 78.

63. For a general introduction, see Janet Timbie, "Coptic Christianity," in
The Blackwell Companion to Eastern Christianity, ed. Ken Parry (Oxford:
Blackwell, 2007), 94–116.

64. See "The Pope: Patriarch" at the official website: http://www
.copticchurch.net/topics/thecopticchurch/sacraments/7_priesthood.html.

65. Adel Azer Bestawros, "The Concept of the Protos 'Patriarch' in the
Coptic Orthodox Church," *Kanon* 3 (1975): 135.

66. "Coptic Orthodox Church of Alexandria," http://en.wikipedia.org/
wiki/Coptic_Orthodox_Church.

67. Mesrob Krikorian, "Conflict of Laws and Respective Rules within the
Community of the Oriental Churches," *Kanon* 3 (1975): 58.

68. "The Pope: Patriarch" at the official website.

69. Bestawros, "Concept of the Protos 'Patriarch'," 136–37.

70. Ibid.

71. Ibid., 132. The different methods used—the authors enumerate nine—
in selecting a patriarch are told by S. M. Saad and N. M. Saad, "Electing Coptic Patriarchs: A Diversity of Traditions," *Bulletin of Saint Shenouda the Archimandrite Coptic Society* 6 (2001): 20–32. In the 117 cases they review, a general
election is the most commonly used method, followed by election by the pres-
byters of Alexandria alone and then a casting of lots.

72. On the history of lay involvement, see Adel Azer Bestawros, "The
Organization and History of the Patriarchal/Laical Councils in the Coptic
Orthodox Church of Egypt," 39–50. On the selection of the patriarch, see
Bestawros, "Concept of the Protos 'Patriarch'," 49–50. This use of a lot to de-

cide the patriarchal election demonstrates a great deal of trust in the Holy Spirit and a willingness not to be anxious to control everything. Such trust is something important that the Roman Church in particular could learn to emulate. After all the voting and "human politicking" are over, the Holy Spirit is given a free hand to pick the new patriarch.

73. Thus the section "Historical Information" of the official website: http://www.antiochpat.org. It is not clear which parts of Turkey are included. Other sources are either equally unclear or entirely silent (Ron Roberson's *Eastern Christian Churches* omits entirely any mention of Turkey as part of Antioch's jurisdiction). Antiochian jurisdiction over today's Turkey is the result of the shifting of these geopolitical boundaries and borders many times over the centuries. Antioch originally had jurisdiction over what is today the extreme southeastern parts of Turkey. On this, see the very helpful map of the patriarchates in Eamon Duffy, *Saints and Sinners: A History of the Popes* (New Haven, CT: Yale University Press, 1997).

74. In February 2009, the synod in Antioch abruptly announced that the diocesan bishops installed in the Church in North America were reduced to "auxiliary" status, subordinate to the Metropolitan Philip of North America. This has generated considerable controversy and debate as to the purpose and meaning of this gesture, which does seem ecclesiologically anomalous at best—though, as noted earlier, there is no one model of patriarchal structures enjoined upon all churches, so such a move as this, while irregular, is nonetheless permissible. Much of the history and timeline is told here: http://ocanews.org/news/TroubleinAntioch3.9.09.html.

75. It is not clear in the literature whether this jurisdiction extends to the entire country as such, or only to the parishes of the patriarchate within that country. In at least one country, Turkey, it seems safe to say that it extends only to the patriarchate's parishes given that Turkey is the home, of course, of the Ecumenical Patriarchate.

76. Patsavos, "Synodal Structure of the Orthodox Church," 78.

77. The website notes that all bishops attend, but that "overseas" bishops do not vote.

78. Patsavos, "Synodal Structure of the Orthodox Church," 79.

79. Roberson, "The Patriarchate of Antioch," in his *Eastern Christian Churches*. See also "Church of Antioch," http://orthodoxwiki.org/index.php?title=Church_of_Antioch;

80. Roberson, "Patriarchate of Antioch"; Patsavos, "Synodal Structure of the Orthodox Church," 79.

81. For background, see Heleen Murre–van den Berg, "Syriac Christianity," in *The Blackwell Companion to Eastern Christianity,* ed. Ken Parry (Oxford:

Blackwell, 2007), 249–68. In 1971 and again in 1984 significant statements on Christology were agreed to by the Syriac Orthodox Church and the Roman Catholic Church. Traditionally known as "Syrian," this Church opted in 2000 to change its name to "Syriac" in order, as Ron Roberson tells us, "to avoid confusion with Syrian nationality. This decision applied only to the English language and was to be adopted generally over the course of time. In practice, however, the use of the term 'Syriac' is mostly limited to North America" (Roberson, "The Syrian [*sic*] Orthodox Church of Antioch," http://www.cnewa.org/ecc-bodypg-us.aspx?eccpageID=8&IndexView=toc).

82. Some of the history of this Church is told in "The Syrian Orthodox Church of Antioch at a Glance" on the official website: http://syriacchristianity.org.

83. Ibid.

84. These are described as having been approved by the synod of bishops in September 1998, and were recently made available in English at the official website of the Church in the United States: http://www.soc-wus.org.

85. "The Syrian Orthodox Church of Antioch at a Glance."

86. The four subsections of article 104 detail this extraordinary situation involving the patriarch and his deposition.

87. Elsewhere in the Constitution, these "patriarchal assistants" and "patriarchal vicars" are described as being bishops having the rank of metropolitan: see articles 95–97. The Syrian Church also recognizes the possibility of "titular" metropolitans (article 89).

88. See Harry Hagopian, "The Armenian Church in the Holy Land," in *Eastern Christianity: Studies in Modern History, Religion and Politics,* ed. Anthony O'Mahony (London: Melisende, 2004), 215–68.

89. "The title of Patriarch or Primate gives a prerogative of honour, but in the Latin Church does not carry with it any power of governance" according to canon 438 of the 1983 *Code of Canon Law.*

90. Recall here the great controversy that erupted in October 1841 over the Church of England's scheme to set up an Anglican bishopric in Jerusalem where the incumbent would be a joint nominee of Anglican England and Lutheran Prussia. See David Newsome, *The Parting of Friends: The Wilberforces and Henry Manning* (Grand Rapids, MI: Eerdmans, 1993 [1966]), 289. Newman famously denounced the Jerusalem bishopric in biting terms but would later call it "one of the greatest mercies . . . [that] brought me on to the beginning of the end" of his Anglican days. See Ian Ker, *John Henry Newman: A Biography* (Oxford: Clarendon Press, 1988), 236. See also, e.g., Kjartan Anderson, "Pilgrims, Property, and Politics: The Russian Orthodox Church in Jerusalem," in *Eastern Christianity: Studies in Modern History, Religion and Politics,*

ed. Anthony O'Mahony (London: Melisende, 2004), 388–430, and in the same volume, Louis Wehbe, "The Maronites of the Holy Land: A Historical Overview," 431–51. The Melkite Greek Catholic Patriarch also includes "Jerusalem" in his title.

91. Sotiris Roussos, "Patriarchs, Notables and Diplomats: The Greek Orthodox Patriarchate of Jerusalem in the Modern Period," in *Eastern Christianity: Studies in Modern History, Religion and Politics,* ed. Anthony O'Mahony (London: Melisende, 2004), 372–87, and Roberson, *Eastern Christian Churches.*

92. The official website for these communities in the U.S. is http://jerusalempatriarchate.org. These parishes came under the jurisdiction of Jerusalem after splits in and problems with the Antiochene Orthodox Church in North America. Some of this history is told at http://www.pokrov.org/controversial/aeom.html.

93. Patsavos, "Synodal Structure of the Orthodox Church," 80.

94. Ibid., 81.

95. By way of general background, see Basil Lourié, "Russian Christianity," in *The Blackwell Companion to Eastern Christianity,* ed. Ken Parry (Oxford: Blackwell, 2007), 207–30. See also Roberson, *Eastern Christian Churches,* 68; cf. Timothy (Kallistos) Ware, *The Orthodox Church* (London: Penguin Books, 1997), 6. On pre-eminence claims, see, inter alia, Serge Keleher, "Orthodox Rivalry in the Twentieth Century: Moscow versus Constantinople," *Religion, State & Society* 25 (1997): 125–37.

96. On Church-state relations up to World War II, see Dimitry Pospielovsky, *The Orthodox Church in the History of Russia* (Crestwood, NY: St. Vladimir's Seminary Press, 1998). For a postwar survey, see Zoe Knox, "The Symphonic Ideal: The Moscow Patriarchate's Post-Soviet Leadership," *Europe-Asia Studies* 55 (2003): 575–96.

97. See especially Vatro Murvar, "Russian Religious Structures: A Study in Persistent Church Subservience," *Journal for the Scientific Study of Religion* 7 (1968): 1–22. But cf. an important new study by John Mack, "Peter the Great and the Ecclesiastical Regulation: Secularization or Reformation" *St. Vladimir's Theological Quarterly* 49 (2005): 243–69. Mack argues that "the picture usually painted is that of an aggressive state (i.e., the autocrat) subduing a passive church. The purpose of this article is to suggest an alternative image: that of a 'new' religious system arising out of a swirling sea of chaotic change" (247). A similar "revisionist" approach to this question is taken by Gregory Freeze, "Handmaiden of the State? The Church in Imperial Russia Reconsidered," *Journal of Ecclesiastical History* 36 (1985): 82–102. Much of the scholarly history of the persecution of the Russian Church is helpfully synthesized in

Michael Bourdeaux and Alexandru Popescu, "The Orthodox Church and Communism," in *The Cambridge History of Eastern Christianity,* ed. Michael Angold (Cambridge: Cambridge University Press, 2006), 558–75. See also William Stroyen, *Communist Russia and the Russian Orthodox Church 1943–1962* (Washington, DC: Catholic University of America Press, 1967).

98. See, for example, Keith Armes, "Chekists in Cassocks: The Orthodox Church and the KGB," *Demokratizatsiya: The Journal of Post-Soviet Democratization* 1 (1994): 72–83.

99. Alexander Bogolepov, "The Statutes of the Russian Orthodox Church of 1945," *St. Vladimir's Seminary Quarterly* 2 (1958): 23–39

100. On its establishment see Boris Gudziak, "The Creation of the Moscow Patriarchate," *Logos: A Journal of Eastern Christian Studies* 37 (1996): 219–71; on the abolishment, see James Cracraft, *The Church Reform of Peter the Great* (Stanford, CA: Stanford University Press, 1971). The debates about restoring the patriarchate are told in fascinating detail by Catherine Evtuhov, "The Church in the Russian Revolution: Arguments for and against Restoring the Patriarchate at the Church Council of 1917–1918," *Slavic Review* 50 (1991): 497–511. As for the council itself, see Hyacinthe Destivelle, *Le Concile de Moscou (1917–1918): La création des institutions conciliaires de l'Église orthodoxe russe* (Paris: Cerf, 2005).

101. Evtuhov, "The Church in the Russian Revolution," 509–11. As Evtuhov demonstrates, some wanted a mere *primus inter pares,* others wanted a super-patriarch, and most also wanted—regardless of the ecclesial configuration—an "ethnarch" and strong sociopolitical leader amidst the revolutionary chaos. The council was apparently bombarded with telegrams from parishes across Russia with the demand "Give us a father!"

102. One metropolitan was said to have told the government "The Church is full of . . . holy hatred for the enemy" (Pospielovsky, *The Russian Church under the Soviet Regime,* 1:208). This sobor was designed as a "showcase," and invitations were sent to all Orthodox leaders in the world to demonstrate that there was no religious persecution in the Soviet Union. See Stroyen, *Communist Russia and the Russian Orthodox Church,* 42.

103. Pospielovsky says that the whole sobor was "highly deceptive" and the statute "clearly incompatible" with the 1917 decisions as well as Orthodox ecclesiology in general (*The Russian Church under the Soviet Regime,* 1.215).

104. Bogolepov, "The Statutes of the Russian Orthodox Church of 1945," 25–26.

105. Chapter XVIII of the new statutes gives the dates of their alteration. The statues and information about them are taken from the official website of the Moscow Patriarchate, http://www.mospat.ru/en/.

106. Other authors have denounced the remaining powers of the patriarch not as "monarchical" but as "oligarchic," "authoritarian," "autocratic," and reflective of "spiritual Stalinism." These and other denunciations are from Sergei Hackel, "Managerial Patterns in a Patriarchal Church," *Sobornost* 23 (2001): 7–22.

107. In Russian, the title is "Patriarch of Moscow and All Rus'," which is necessary, it would seem, to be able to continue to claim jurisdiction over Estonia, Belarus, and Ukraine.

108. For background, see Mircea Pacurariu, "Romanian Christianity," in *The Blackwell Companion to Eastern Christianity,* ed. Ken Parry (Oxford: Blackwell, 2007), 186–206. Some of the history of Romanian Christianity is told in Mircea Pacurariu, "The Patriarchate of Rumania: History and Spiritual Tradition," in *The Splendour of Orthodoxy: 2000 Years of History, Monuments, Art,* vol. 2, *Patriarchates and Autocephalous Churches,* ed. Kostas E. Tsiropoulos (Athens: Ekdotike Athenon, 2000), 298–321.

109. I say "ostensibly" because Church-State relations are still far from straightforward, if Michael Mates is to be believed. See his "Politics, Property Restitution, and Ecumenism in the Romanian Orthodox Church," *Logos: A Journal of Eastern Christian Studies* 46 (2005): 73–94. See further in this regard Gavril Flora, Gerogina Szilagyi, and Victor Roudometof, "Religion and National Identity in Post-Communist Romania," *Journal of Southern Europe & the Balkans* 7 (2005): 35–55. Finally, see Lavina Stan and Lucian Turcescu, "The Romanian Orthodox Church and Post-communist Democratisation," *Europe-Asia Studies* 52 (2000): 1467–88, who have developed these reflections at much greater length in their new book, *Religion and Politics in Post-Communist Romania* (Oxford: Oxford University Press, 2007).

110. "Romanian Orthodox Church: History," from the official website: http://www.patriarhia.ro/Stiri/2006/074.html.

111. "Short History of the Romanian Orthodox Church," http://www.patriarhia.ro/eng/history.htm. See also "The Romanian Orthodox Church," http://www.crestinism-ortodox.ro/html_en/index.html.

112. Nicolae V. Durã, "The Protos in the Romanian Orthodox Church According to Its Modern Legislation," *Kanon* 3 (1975): 144.

113. My translation from the official website: http://www.patriarhia.ro/Organizare/organizare.html.

114. "Short History of the Romanian Orthodox Church," II.

115. "The Romanian Orthodox Church," §2.

116. "The Romanian Orthodox Church: The Dioceses and Members of the Holy Synod."

117. "Short History of the Romanian Orthodox Church," II.

118. "Romanian Orthodox Church: History."

119. "The Romanian Orthodox Church," §2.

120. This assembly elected a new patriarch, Daniel, in September 2007 after the previous patriarch died on 30 July 2007. See www.patriarhia.ro for the details.

121. I am greatly indebted to the Reverend Father Nicholas Apostola of Worcester, MA, a Romanian Orthodox priest and theologian who sits on the North American Orthodox-Catholic dialogue, for supplying this information to me via e-mail.

122. John Rinne, "The Role of the Laity in the Administration of the Orthodox Patriarchates of Serbia, Rumania, and Bulgaria," *Kanon* 3 (1975): 147.

123. For background, see Ivan Zhelev Dimitrov, "Bulgarian Christianity," in *The Blackwell Companion to Eastern Christianity,* ed. Ken Parry (Oxford: Blackwell, 2007), 47–72.

124. Todor Sabev, "The Patriarchate of Bulgaria," in *The Splendour of Orthodoxy: 2000 Years of History, Monuments, Art,* vol. 2, *Patriarchates and Autocephalous Churches,* ed. Kostas E. Tsiropoulos (Athens: Ekdotike Athenon, 2000), 324–25.

125. Ibid., 326–28.

126. Ron Roberson, "The Orthodox Church of Bulgaria," http://www .cnewa.org/ecc-bodypg-us.aspx?eccpageID=20&IndexView=toc.

127. See Peter Kanev, "Religion in Bulgaria after 1989: Historical and Socio-Cultural Aspects," *South-East Europe Review* 1 (2002): 75–96, for a general overview of the religious situation of Bulgaria in the post-communist period.

128. This schism has been covered by Janice Broun in a series of articles: "The Schism in the Bulgarian Orthodox Church," *Religion, State & Society* 21 (1993): 207–20; "The Schism in the Bulgarian Orthodox Church, Part 2: Under the Socialist Government," *Religion, State & Society* 28 (2000): 263–89; "The Schism in the Bulgarian Orthodox Church, Part 3," *Religion, State & Society* 30 (2002): 365–94; and "The Bulgarian Orthodox Church: The Continuing Schism and the Religious, Social and Political Environment," *Religion, State & Society* 32 (2004): 209–45.

129. "Statute of the Bulgarian Orthodox Church," no. 2, from the official website of the Church: http://bulch.tripod.com/boc/order.htm.

130. Sabev, "The Patriarchate of Bulgaria," 329.

131. "Statute of the Bulgarian Orthodox Church," no. 3.

132. Sabev, "Patriarchate of Bulgaria," 329.

133. Ibid., and "Statute of the Bulgarian Orthodox Church," no. 5.

134. For more on the question of lay involvement, see Rinne, "Role of the Laity in the Administration of the Orthodox Patriarchates of Serbia, Rumania, and Bulgaria," 151ff.

135. By way of general background, see Vrej Nerses Nersessian, "Armenian Christianity," in *The Blackwell Companion to Eastern Christianity*, ed. Ken Parry (Oxford: Blackwell, 2007), 23–46. For general introductions to the Armenian Church see Diocese of the Armenian Church of America, *The Armenian Church: A Brief Outline* (New York, 1973); Papken Catholicos Gulesserian, *The Armenian Church*, trans. Terenig Vartabed Poladian (New York: AMS Press, 1970 [1939]); and Malachia Ormanian, *The Church of Armenia: Her History, Doctrine, Rule, Discipline, Liturgy, Literature, and Existing Condition*, ed. Terenig Poladian, trans. G. M. Gregory (London: A. R. Mowbray, 1912). See also Hratch Tchilingirian, "The Armenian Apostolic Orthodox Church," http://hyeforum.com/index.php?showtopic=5432.

136. "The history of the Armenian Apostolic Orthodox Church is intimately intertwined with the history of the Armenian people" says Hratch Tchilingirian in "The Catholicos and the Hierarchical Sees of the Armenian Church," in *Eastern Christianity: Studies in Modern History, Religion and Politics*, ed. Anthony O'Mahony (London: Melisende, 2004), 140. For more history of the Church and her structures, see especially Garabed Amadouni, "L'autocéphalie du Katholikat arménien," in *I Patriarcati Orientali Nel Primo Millennio* (Rome: PIO, 1968), 137–78 (= *Orientalia Christiana Analecta* 181). For more recent developments and changes, see Yeznik Petrossian, "The Development of the Law of the Armenian Apostolic Church during the 19th and 20th Century," *Kanon* 18 (1991): 45–55.

137. Cf. Pope John Paul II, "Apostolic Letter for the 1700th Anniversary of the Baptism of the Armenian People," 2 February 2001: http://www.vatican.va/holy_father/john_paul_ii/apost_letters/documents/hf_jp-ii_apl_20010217_battesimo-armenia_en.html.

138. Tchilingirian, "Catholicos and Hierarchial Sees of the Armenian Church," 140. These close relationships, of course, have not always had happy outcomes for the Church. See Charles A. Frazee, "The Christian Church in Cilician Armenia: Its Relations with Rome and Constantinople to 1198," *Church History* 45 (1976): 166–84; and Edward Alexander, "The Armenian Church in Soviet Policy," *Russian Review* 14 (1955): 357–62.

139. Aram I, "The Armenian Church beyond Its 1700th Anniversary," *Ecumenical Review* 54 (2002): 88.

140. Tchilingirian, "Catholicos and Hierarchical Sees of the Armenian Church," 142, quoting Tiran Archbishop Nersoyan, "The Administration and

Governing of the Armenian Church," in *Armenian Church Historical Studies,* ed. Nerses Vrej (New York: St. Vartan Press, 1996), 271. The early history of the establishment and differentiation of these sees, together with the varying levels of authority and autocephaly, is told in Amadouni, "L'autocéphalie du Katholikat arménien."

141. Tchilingirian, in "Catholicos and Hierarchical Sees of the Armenian Church," 140.

142. On the ecumenical vocation of the Armenian Church, see generally Peter M. Cooke, "The Armenian Church—A Guiding Light on the Ecumenical Highway?" *One in Christ* 37 (2002): 75–88; and Karekin I, "Ecumenical Trends in the Armenian Church," *Ecumenical Review* 51 (1999): 31–39. For earlier treatments, see David Bundy, "Armenian Relations with the Papacy after the Mongol Invasions," *Patristic and Byzantine Review* 5 (1986): 19–32

143. Cooke, "The Armenian Church—A Guiding Light," 75.

144. At one time, there was a third catholicosate, that of Aghauank (Gantsasar) in Karabagh, which existed from 552 to 1815 but was collapsed into a diocese of Etchmiadzin "in the early 19th century" (Tchilingirian, "Catholicos and Hierarchical Sees of the Armenian Church," 147).

145. Ibid., 141.

146. Ibid., 148–51.

147. See ibid., 141, especially n4. See the official website of the Catholicosate of Cilicia: http://www.armenianorthodoxchurch.org where we are told that "the existence of two Catholicosates within the Armenian Church, namely the Catholicosate of Etchmiadzin (the Catholicosate of All Armenians), Etchmiadzin-Armenia, and the Catholicosate of the Great House of Cilicia, Antelias-Lebanon, is due to historical circumstances" having chiefly to do with the tenth-century devastation of Armenia by Seljuks, which forced many Armenians to settle in Cilicia, where the Catholicosate soon reestablished itself.

148. See "A Migrating Catholicosate" at the official website of the Catholicosate of Cilicia and "Peregrinations of Patriarchs," in Ormanian, *Church of Armenia,* 37.

149. Ormanian, *Church of Armenia,* 80–85.

150. Tchilingirian, "Catholicos and Hierarchical Sees of the Armenian Church," 146.

151. Hagopian, "The Armenian Church in the Holy Land," 224. Hagopian advances the claim that the "history of the establishment of the Armenian Patriarchate in Jerusalem goes as far back [as] 637 AD." I am not inclined to trust Hagopian's rather ambiguous claim both because he does not provide much evidence and because his claim conflicts with the official his-

tory, which I accept here as authoritative. For the history, structure, and territory, see the offical website of the Jerusalem patriarchate http://www .armenian-patriarchate.org.

152. The specific territories under Jerusalem's jurisdiction has changed over time. On this latter point, see Gulesserian, *The Armenian Church*, 58. On the role of Jerusalem's "brotherhood" see Tchilingirian, "Catholicos and Hierarchical Sees of the Armenian Church," 153.

153. Tchilingirian, "Catholicos and Hierarchical Sees of the Armenian Church," 147.

154. Gulesserian, *The Armenian Church*, 52.

155. Tchilingirian, "Catholicos and Hierarchical Sees of the Armenian Church," 155–56.

156. A catholicos is "a Greek term signifying 'Universal Leader of the Church,'" and as such "ranks higher than Patriarchs, Archbishops and Bishops in the Armenian Church." See "Catholicos of All Armenians," http://www .armenianchurch.org.

157. "History," at http://www.armenianorthodoxchurch.org.

158. "After the split of 1441, Gregory and his successors continued to reside in Sis, and in order not to cause confusion, they took the name 'Catholicos of Cilicia'" (Gulesserian, *The Armenian Church*, 51).

159. For the United States see "Prelacy History" at the official website of the Eastern Prelacy in the United States, http://www.armenianprelacy.org and for Canada see the official website of the Church in Canada, http://www .armenianprelacy.ca under "Structure." Also see "Dioceses" at http://www .armenianorthodoxchurch.org.

160. Sometimes this is given as "Catholicos of All Armenia" though most often it is listed as "All Armenians." The point is not insignificant: "All Armenia" describes jurisdiction over just the geophysical nation-state of Armenia whereas "All Armenians" became prevalent after the fifteenth century "to indicate . . . jurisdiction over new dioceses created in Armenian colonies spread outside Armenia" (Tchilingirian, "Catholicos and Hierarchical Sees of the Armenian Church," 142). For the establishment of the see, see http://www .armeniapedia.org/index.php?title=Mother_See_of_Holy_Etchmiadzin. See also Gulesserian, *The Armenian Church*, 47.

161. "Catholicos of All Armenians," http://www.armenianchurch.org.

162. "The Patriarchate," www.holyland.org.

163. "Mother See of Holy Etchmiadzin," http://www.armenianchurch.org.

164. There have been disputes between Cilicia and Etchmiadzin over the centuries and these are today not fully resolved. During the Cold War, Cilicia,

outside immediate Soviet control, was thought to be anti-Soviet while Etch-miadzin, inside the Soviet sphere, was accused of being pro-Soviet. See Tchi-lingirian, "Catholicos and Hierarchical Sees of the Armenian Church," 150.

165. Gulesserian, *The Armenian Church,* 47. See also Ormanian, *Church of Armenia,* 77.

166. "Current Structure," http://www.armenianchurch.org.

167. Diocese of the Armenian Church of America, *The Armenian Church,* 21.

168. Gulesserian, *The Armenian Church,* 47.

169. "Patriarchal Sees," at www.armenianchurch.org.

170. "Catholicos of All Armenians," at ibid.

171. Tchilingirian, "Catholicos and Hierarchical Sees of the Armenian Church," 143.

172. See "National Ecclesiastical Assembly" at www.armenianchurch.org. See also Krikor Maksoudian, *Chosen of God: The Election of the Catholicos of All Armenians* (New York: St. Vartan Press, 1995.), which contains recent stat-utes in force governing elections, including the 1995 election of the catholicos. According to the official website the inclusion of laity was deliberate: "Admin-istratively, great care has been taken to be inclusive of a wide cross-section of the faithful. Both clergy and lay are involved in today's administrative struc-ture of the Church." See "Current Structure" at www.armenianchurch.org. For more on this question of lay involvement, especially historically, see Tiran Nersoyan, "Laity in the Administration of the Armenian Church," *Kanon* 3 (1975): 96–119. Nersoyan traces the rising and falling fortunes of lay involve-ment in the Church, noting, in general terms, that "the participation of the laity in the election of bishops and patriarch-catholicoi was generally estab-lished in the tradition of the Armenian Church since ancient times (103) and that "the involvement of the laity in the administration of the Church is im-portant and beneficial" for the Armenian Church, which "invites and wel-comes the participation of laymen" (119). This is confirmed in nearly every other source on the history and structure of the Armenian Church.

173. "Catholicos of All Armenians" at www.armenianchurch.org.

174. Tchilingirian, "Catholicos and Hierarchical Sees of the Armenian Church," 143.

175. "Current Structure" at www.armenianchurch.org.

176. Tchilingirian, "Catholicos and Hierarchical Sees of the Armenian Church," 145.

177. Ibid., especially n17.

178. Archbishop Nersoyan, "Problems and Exercise of Primacy in the Ar-menian Church," quoted in ibid., 145–46.

179. "National Ecclesiastical Assembly" at www.armenianchurch.org. I emphasize the word "suggestions" here because, as Tchilingirian ("Catholicos and Hierarchical Sees of the Armenian Church," 157) explains it, the bishops are supposed to be the "highest spiritual authority . . . [but] for decades, successive catholicoi, due to political circumstances and personal leadership styles, have single-handedly dictated and administered the affairs of the Armenian Church, all along reducing the authority and ecclesiastical function of the College of Bishops to mere formality. At best, the college has been a 'consultative' rather than an 'authoritative' body."

180. Aram I, "The Armenian Church beyond Its 1700th Anniversary," 88. Aram does not shy away from acknowledging that this prominence of the laity has sometimes generated problems or at least a certain tension. He notes that it is an unresolved source of tension in the Church today as to whether the "episcopal synod" is the "locus of collegial authority" and has primacy in the Church or "the people's assembly [is] the highest authority" (88–89).

181. Tchilingirian, "Catholicos and Hierarchical Sees of the Armenian Church," 144.

182. It is quite possible that one of the reasons for the success of the Armenian Church in maintaining her ecclesial unity is shared nationality and ethnicity on the part of her members. Armenia is always famously described as the "first Christian nation," and in Armenia perhaps more than anywhere else, "religion" and "nationality" have been deeply intertwined in a people who have lacked the formal apparatus of a state for most of their existence. As Archbishop Nersoyan has written, "in times when political rule in Armenia was divided or even fragmented, the authority of the primate has been enhanced as a symbol and mainstay of the principle of unity of a culturally cohesive people" (*Armenian Church Historical Studies: Matters of Doctrine and Administration* [New York: St. Vartan Press, 1996], 212). He goes on to note that "the Catholicos was recognized to be primate of all ethnic Armenians . . . rather than the primate only of a defined geographical territory" (224). So great has been the union between ecclesiality and nationality or ethnicity that Vrej Nerses Nersessian, an Armenian priest and curator for the British Library in London, reports the rather startling fact that during the Second World War Catholicos Geworg VI Tchorek'tchian (1945–1954) was able to take up a "collection of funds in the diaspora in 1944 [that] was successful enough to help form the 'David of Sasun' and 'General Baghramyan' tank divisions for the Soviet army fighting the Nazi invasion." Shortly thereafter the catholicos was able to reopen his printing press and seminary, and more than 200 priests who had been imprisoned by the Soviets as political prisoners were freed ("Armenian Christianity," 42). (This closely mirrors liberties awarded, for a time, to

the Russian Orthodox Church following similar services rendered to the Soviet state during the "Great Patriotic War" against the Nazi invasion of June 1941.) This close identification of religion and ethnicity or nationality is not welcomed by everyone, including Vigen Guroian, who was born, educated, and has spent his entire life in the United States and is today the most prominent of all theologians of Armenian extraction in North America. He has vigorously denounced Armenian nationalism in several places, including his essay "Religion and Armenian National Identity: Nationalism Old and New," *Religion in Eastern Europe* (1994) at the university website http://www.georgefox.edu under the author's name. See also his "Nationalism, a Non-Liberal Assessment," in his *Rallying the Really Human Things: The Moral Imagination in Politics, Literature, and Everyday Life* (Wilmington, DE: ISI Books, 2005), 201–10. Guroian's assessment, however, should be set alongside the work of the sociologist Peter Rutland, whose study "Democracy and Nationalism in Armenia," *Europe-Asia Studies* 46 (1994): 839–61, argues that "religion has not been a driving force in modern Armenian nationalism in the same way it has in, say, Poland—despite the fact that the Armenians have the oldest independent church in Christendom. The Armenian church was an important vehicle for the preservation of national identity over the centuries, but was not a strong advocate of an independent Armenian nation-state. Armenian society today is fairly secular" (840). For a recent work that takes a balanced approach to this question, see Daniel Payne, "Nationalism and the Local Church: The Source of Ecclesiastical Conflict in the Orthodox Commonwealth," *Nationalities Papers* 35 (2007): 831–52. Finally and more generally, for further studies on nationalism in many different parts of the Orthodox world, see Victor Roudometof, Alexander Agadjanian, and Jerry Pankhurst, eds., *Eastern Orthodoxy in a Global Age: Tradition Faces the Twenty-First Century* (New York: Rowman and Littlefield, 2005).

183. Hratch Tchilingirian has collected the data for the 1995 election of Karekin I as catholicos of Etchmiadzin, noting that the electoral assembly was composed of "430 delegates from 32 countries (74 percent lay and 26 percent clergy), representing over 8.5 million Armenians . . . around the world. . . . In 1999, the same Assembly, made up of 455 delegates from 43 countries, elected Catholicos Karekin II of All Armenians" ("Catholicos and Hierarchical Sees of the Armenian Church," 144 n12).

184. Peter Steinfels observed, "The idea of electing bishops renders most conservatives and virtually all the hierarchy and Vatican officialdom apoplectic" (quoted in Joseph F. O'Callaghan, *Electing Our Bishops: How the Catholic Church Should Choose Its Leaders* [Lanham, MD: Rowman and Littlefield, 2007], 143).

185. Robert F. Taft, "Eastern Presuppositions and Western Liturgical Renewal," *Antiphon* 5 (2000): 10–22.

186. As Magee says at the end of his long study, "As the Church looks forward, such insights from outside the Latin Church ought to be regarded as contributing to a still more catholic understanding of the multi-faceted figure of the Bishop of Rome" (*Patriarchal Institution in the Church*, 517).

Chapter Five.   Patriarchates within the Latin Church

1. Meyendorff, "Ecclesiastical Regionalism," 155.

2. Perhaps the only proposal that escapes this danger, at least in part, is John Quinn's work, *The Reform of the Papacy: The Costly Call to Christian Unity*, 2nd ed. (New York: Crossroad, 2007), but his treatment is rather brief and inadequate at points and does not address in any serious way the actual erection of regional structures such as patriarchates within the Latin Church.

3. Despite repeated and extensive searches, I have been unable to find an exact reference for this quotation, or further bibliographic information supporting it. It seems to have become one of those shibboleths, often cited in Catholic-Orthodox discussions, whose origins remain unclear.

4. Hryniewicz, "The Cost of Unity," 5, 10.

5. Ibid., 15 and 17. I have attempted to suggest one very practical manifestation of "kenosis in action" in my article "*Kenosis vs. La Bella Figura*," *Canadian Journal of Orthodox Christianity* 2 (Fall 2007): 94–106.

6. Congar, *Vraie et Fausse Réforme*, 125–207. On the inadequacy of "moral" reform in particular, see Quinn's essay "The Exercise of the Primacy and the Costly Call to Unity," in *The Exercise of the Primacy: Continuing the Dialogue*, ed. Phyllis Zagano and Terrence W. Tilley (New York: Crossroad, 1998), 7–12 especially. See more generally his *Reform of the Papacy*.

7. Walter Kasper, "Petrine Ministry and Synodality," *Jurist* 66 (2006): 299.

8. Ibid., 309.

9. "The Primacy of the Successor of Peter in the Mystery of the Church: Reflections of the Congregation for the Doctrine of the Faith," no. 12.

10. Clément, *You are Peter*, 57.

11. Magee, *Patriarchal Institution in the Church*, 413–14.

12. My translation. Congar, *Vraie et Fausse Réforme*, 335.

13. It is generally accepted that the crisis in authority in the Catholic Church began following the Second Vatican Council and especially following the publication, in July 1968, of *Humanae Vitae*. On this particular issue, see

Monica Migliorino Miller, *Sexuality and Authority in the Catholic Church* (Scranton, PA: University of Scranton Press, 1995). One of the theologians most prominent in the debate was Charles Curran. On him, see William W. May, ed., *Vatican Authority and American Catholic Dissent: The Curran Case and Its Consequences* (New York: Crossroad, 1987). Additionally, see George A. Kelly, *The Crisis of Authority: John Paul II and the American Bishops* (Chicago: Regnery Gateway, 1982).

14. Other "minor" Latin patriarchates, including those of Aquilea, the West Indies, and the East Indies (Goa), are no longer filled.

15. In time, the bestowal of the cardinalatial dignity, as I note below, came to be thought to outrank all other titles, including that of "patriarch."

16. See the website of the Czechoslovak Hussite Church at www.ccsh.cz (in Czech).

17. See F. W. Fuller, "The Canterbury Patriarchate," in *Essays and Letters on Orders and Jurisdiction* (London: Longmans, 1925).

18. On this issue, the work of Brian Tierney and Francis Oakley has been invaluable, especially in demonstrating that the "extreme" view was only one, and a minority view at that, and that the more widely held variant of "conciliarism" sought a sensible balance between the pope and councils. For Tierney, see *Foundations of Conciliar Theory: The Contribution of the Medieval Canonists from Gratian to the Great Schism* (Cambridge: Cambridge University Press, 1955). Oakley's thought is scattered throughout numerous essays and books, as Constantin Fasolt suggests in "Voluntarism and Conciliarism in the Work of Francis Oakley," *History of Political Thought* 22 (2001): 41–52. Chief among the works of Oakley is his book *Council over Pope? Towards a Provisional Ecclesiology* (New York: Herder and Herder, 1969), and then especially his recent book, *The Conciliarist Tradition: Constitutionalism in the Catholic Church 1300–1870* (Oxford: Oxford University Press, 2004). Also important are the articles he authored in the volume he edited along with Bruce Russett, *Governance, Accountability, and the Future of the Catholic Church* (New York and London: Continuum, 2004). Finally, see Oakley, "The 'New Conciliarism' and Its Implications: A Problem in History and Hermeneutics," *Journal of Ecumenical Studies* 8 (1971): 815–40.

19. It is not simply that the current Roman structures lack any serious expressions of synodality, but that they are fundamentally ecclesiologically incoherent when, e.g., they introduce the role of the nuncio into the process of episcopal appointment. The nuncio has no ecclesiastical standing per se and is not part of the structure of the Church. He is, rather, simply and only a diplomat of one *state* to another.

20. Aidan Nichols, *Christendom Awake: On Reenergizing the Church in Culture* (Grand Rapids, MI: Eerdmans, 1999), 186. Significantly, Nichols immediately continues by saying that "this crisis touches many aspects of Church life but notably theology and catechesis, liturgy and spirituality, religious life and Christian ethics at large. *Orthodoxy is well placed to stabilise Catholicism in most if not all these areas*" (my emphasis).

21. Meyendorff, "Rome and Orthodoxy," especially 144–45.

22. Reardon, "One, Holy, Catholic and Apostolic Church."

23. I have in mind here especially self-identified "apologists" for a strong papacy who even today continue to rehash their anachronistic and unconvincing arguments in such tracts as John Salza, *The Biblical Basis for the Papacy* (Huntington, IN: Our Sunday Visitor, 2007) or the several works of James Likoudis, including his most recent *Eastern Orthodoxy and the See of Peter: A Journey towards Full Communion* (Waite Park, MN: Park Press, 2006).

24. Numerous recent works have convincingly demonstrated the profound changes in the papacy with the loss of the Papal States. See Owen Chadwick, *A History of the Popes 1830–1914* (Oxford: Clarendon Press, 1998); Duffy, *Saints and Sinners;* and John Pollard, *Money and the Rise of the Modern Papacy: Financing the Vatican 1850–1950* (Cambridge: Cambridge University Press, 2005).

25. It is not for nothing that Eamon Duffy's magisterial papal history is entitled *Saints and Sinners.* Nowhere in Duffy's treatment—that is, nowhere in papal history—do we see any significant deviations from, still less destruction of, doctrinal orthodoxy (as expressed in, e.g., the Niceno-Constantinopolitan symbol of faith) when the papacy is occupied by those much more "sinful" than "saintly."

26. On which see Leon Podles' study, *Sacrilege: Sexual Abuse in the Catholic Church* (Baltimore: Crossland, 2007).

27. Alasdair MacIntyre, a moral philosopher, examining several new works in theological ethics by Catholics, opened his review with the memorable line that "If I were God, I do not think that I would want to be studied by most contemporary theologians." That is "because the general intellectual level of theological argument is perhaps lower than at any time since the tenth century." MacIntyre says most modern theology has made Christianity "banal, uninteresting, and vacuous" while "modern Roman Catholic theologians have been to an alarming degree narcissistic," giving the "impression of being only mildly interested in either God or the world; what they are passionately interested in are other Roman Catholic theologians" ("Theology, Ethics, and the

Ethics of Medicine and Health Care: Comments on Papers by Novak, Mouw, Roach, Cahill, and Hartt," *Journal of Medicine and Philosophy* 4 [1979]: 435–43).

28. Who appointed these bishops who failed to supervise their predatory priests or to discipline the theologians under their jurisdiction? It is no stretch of the imagination to lay the blame in very substantial measure at the feet of super-centralized Rome, which enjoys a monopoly on *episcopabili* and so appoints these men and then refuses generally to discipline them, even when they themselves commit horrific crimes or cover up those who do. All bishops prior to appointment are said to undergo serious scrutiny, a risible claim I dispute in "Look to Tradition: The Case for Electing Bishops," 15–18. Nothing in this argument provides support for the idea that bishops who are elected are always better, as anyone familiar with the fifteen-year-long scandal in the Orthodox Church of America realizes painfully too well. There several bishops, all elected, engaged in various forms of abuse, fraud, and cover-up. See http://www.ocanews.org/chronology.html for the details.

29. Congar, *Eglise et Papauté*, 29.

30. Magee, *Patriarchal Institution in the Church*, 194. For more on the "particularity" of the Latin Church, see the extremely illuminating article of Faris, "The Latin Church *Sui Iuris*," 280–93.

31. Michael Magee has suggested that it is "baffling that so many proponents of the Patriarchal institution should set about the important task of affirming the very existence of a 'Patriarchate of the West,' and begin immediately to cloud the same issue on the basis of an apparent presupposition that this Patriarchate is too large or too diverse." Magee questions the notions of largeness and diversity before going on to stress that it is at least theoretically possible "to hold that the Pope's universal ministry and his Patriarchal role are to be distinguished *without* conceding at the same time that his Patriarchate should be divided." Moreover, Magee argues "it seems necessary to insist . . . that the two questions *must* be treated in distinction from one another—indeed, quite separately" (*Patriarchal Institution in the Church*, 413). Magee is right that it is *theoretically* possible to be in favour of the differentiation of roles without also proposing the division of the Latin Church into additional patriarchates, but this chapter is not interested in mere theoretical possibilities: it seeks to suggest more detailed practical applications. I am not sure why Magee finds such proposals "baffling" nor am I at all convinced by his "insisting" that these questions be treated "quite separately," for reasons he does not supply.

32. If these proposals seem asymmetrical—that is, if it seems I have far more to say about the patriarchal than papal roles, about the "internal" life of

the Latin Church and only secondarily about the life of the universal Church through the papal office—that is inevitable and understandable if one realizes that the overwhelming majority of functions currently conceived of today as "papal" are in fact patriarchal—as many of the commentators, including especially Yves Congar and Joseph Ratzinger, recognized. Only a very small number of those things the pope does pertain to his role as universal pastor responsible for supervision of the whole Church. (An even smaller number of roles exercised currently by the pope are not ecclesiastical at all, but pertain to his role as sovereign of Vatican City-State, about which a few brief comments later.)

33. Much nonsense is usually talked by those invoking the ill-defined phrase of *canonical territory*. The best discussion of it to date that I have seen is Johannes Oeldemann, "The Concept of Canonical Territory in the Russian Orthodox Church," in *Religion and the Conceptual Boundary in Central and Eastern Europe*, ed. Thomas Bremer (London: Palgrave Macmillan, 2008), 229–36. The author demolishes the assertions of the Russian Orthodox Church when it invokes this phrase. The very term *universal jurisdiction* is unclear at even a theoretical level as Giuseppe Alberigo argues in "Juridiction: remarques sur un terme ambigu," *Irénikon* 49 (1976): 167–80.

34. In *The Bishop of Rome* (trans. John de Satgé [Wilmington, DE: Michael Glazier, 1983]), Tillard notes that Vatican I gives it pride of place without defining it while Vatican II uses it extremely rarely, again without defining it. The term is also used rarely in *Ut Unum Sint*.

35. See ibid., where Tillard calls *Pastor Aeternus* "a subtle document interpreted by an ultramontane outlook" (25–34); Alberigo, "Juridiction: remarques sur un terme ambigu"; and Pottmeyer, *Towards a Papacy in Communion*. Pottmeyer flatly says that "Vatican centralization cannot appeal to Vatican I for its theological justification" (74). A little later he elaborates: "the maximalist interpretation of the dogma . . . persists even today. . . .What is meant is the tendency to attach to the doctrinal utterances of the pope or the Roman Curia an extraordinarily far-reaching claim to authority and obedience" (77). Pottmeyer goes on to note that these tendencies are not only ecumenically objectionable, but in fact self-destructive of the Church and her central authority, which continue to be more and more ignored by otherwise faithful Catholics.

36. The lack of careful delineation in theological and canonical terms as to what "universal jurisdiction" means is highly troubling, and without some theological precision to it, and likely limits upon it, the Orthodox will rightly continue to be very wary of it.

37. J.-M. R. Tillard, "The Jurisdiction of the Bishop of Rome," *Theological Studies* 48 (1979): 3. Tillard quotes Bulgakov's remark that the definition of

papal infallibility at Vatican I would be "almost inoffensive" were it not attached to the claims about universal jurisdiction.

38. The phrase "canonical territory" was invoked regularly by the Russian Orthodox Church following the collapse of the Soviet Union, but it is not at all clear that even the Russians themselves know what this means or that the phrase has any significant *theological* meaning at all. Some think that it is a pseudo-theological phrase tendentiously used to smuggle in nationalistic claims. On this point, with reference to the Russian example in particular, see the interview with a Russian Orthodox bishop who denounces the phrase "canonical territory": "Russian Orthodoxy in Search of Unity" at http://www .synod.com/01newstucture/pagesen/english/pages/news/invvlmark.html. For a longer, more comprehensive and vastly more critical attempt at analysis, see the recent essay of the Canadian-Ukrainian Orthodox priest Father J. Buciora, "Canonical Territory of the Moscow Patriarchate: An Analysis of Contemporary Russian Orthodox Thought," *The Messenger: Journal of the Episcopal Vicariate of Great Britain and Ireland* 2 (May 2007): 25–54. This is an important essay whose wider usefulness is limited given the author's inclination toward a sort of "nationalist tendentiousness": his real (and quite understandable) goal seems to be to pry Ukraine away from the "neo-imperial" claims and pretences of the Russian Church. On this neo-imperialism, see Andriy Chirovsky, "Letter from Ukraine," *First Things* (October 2001), where he notes that "there is one remaining institution of the old Tsarist empire of the Romanovs: the Patriarchate of Moscow."

39. E.g., I Nicaea 15, 16; I Constantinople 2; Chalcedon 5, 6, 12, 17; and 14, 15, 34, and 35 of the so-called Apostolic Canons. It is not at all clear how the "cities" referred to in these canons ought to be interpreted today when the size and nature of today's cities are so vastly different from those in the fourth and subsequent centuries.

40. To such an extent now, in the case of the Eastern Catholic Churches in the Middle East, that the overwhelming majority of their faithful are living outside their traditional homelands. I owe this point to John Faris. See his "At Home Everywhere—A Reconsideration of the *Territorium Proprium* of the Patriarchal Churches," *Jurist* 69 (2009): 5–30.

41. The phrase "principle of accommodation" is most commonly used by Francis Dvornik. See the first chapter of his *Byzantium and the Roman Primacy*. But cf. C. Raymond Beazley, "Early Christian Geography," *Transactions of the Royal Historical Society* 10 (1896): 85–109; and Robert M. Grant, "Early Christian Geography," *Vigiliae Christianae* 46 (1992): 105–11.

42. One initial attempt, in broad terms, to trace out shifting geographic and demographic patterns among Christians is Todd M. Johnson and Sun

Young Chung, "Tracking Global Christianity's Statistical Centre of Gravity, AD 33–AD 2100," *International Review of Mission*'93 (2004): 166–81. This article is an attempt to give some statistical substance to the claim increasingly advanced in the last decade or so that Christianity is shifting from being a "Eurocentric" religion to being a religion of the "global south." This thesis has been advanced and examined by several people, including especially Philip Jenkins in his *The Next Christendom: The Coming of Global Christianity* (Oxford: Oxford University Press, 2002) and his more recent *The New Faces of Christianity: Believing the Bible in the Global South* (Oxford: Oxford University Press, 2006). A précis of his thesis about the rise of the global south may be found in his "The Next Christianity," *Atlantic Monthly* (October 2002).

43. Majdansky, "Response to 'Pope and Patriarch'," in *We Are All Brothers,* 133.

44. This is an entirely implausible suggestion for anyone to make if they know the slightest bit of history about such matters. The Patriarchate of the West, at one point, had in its territory and under its jurisdiction not just parts of North Africa now claimed by the various Orthodox patriarchates of Alexandria but also the entire Balkan region and the landmass of the country known to us today as modern Greece! (See the very illuminating map of patriarchal boundaries on p. 33 of the first edition of Duffy, *Saints and Sinners.* Cf. the map in Anton Freitag et al., *The Twentieth Century Atlas of the Christian World: The Expansion of Christianity through the Centuries* [New York: Hawthorn Books, 1963), map 4 of ch. 1.)

45. Hervé Legrand attempts to begin grappling with these questions in his "Un seul évêque par ville: Pourquoi et comment redevenir fidèle au 8e canon de Nicée? Un enjeu pour la catholicité de l'Église," *Irénikon* 77 (2004): 5–43.

46. There have been plenty of *un*serious arguments put forward, including the incredible assertions of such an otherwise astute and important theologian as the Russian Orthodox Bishop Hilarion Alfeyev in "One City, One Bishop, One Church" and "The Canonical Territories of the Local Orthodox Churches" both posted at http://www.orthodoxytoday.org/articles6/HilarionOneBishop .php; and http://www.orthodoxytoday.org/articles6/HilarionOneBishop2.php. In addition, see his "The Practical Application of the Principle of Canonical Territory" at http://orthodoxeurope.org/page/14/87.aspx#5. In this latter essay, Alfeyev expresses his "hope that the principle of 'canonical territory' will be strictly and systematically observed in inter-Orthodox and Catholic-Orthodox relations in the 21st century." Hope, like charity, one may be permitted to suggest to the bishop, ought to begin at home, and without concrete "works" to manifest it, is a rather useless and clanging cymbal. If the Russian Church is

serious about this principle, then Hilarion should be the first to demonstrate it by resigning his see in Vienna, which has only ever been a Roman Catholic "territory."

47. Cf. Ivan Ivekovic, "Nationalism and the Political Use and Abuse of Religion: The Politicization of Orthodoxy, Catholicism, and Islam in Yugoslav Successor States," *Social Compass* 49 (2002): 523–36.

48. Archbishop Vsevolod Majdansky calls for a new continental pentarchy in his "One, Holy, Catholic and Apostolic Church." On this issue see, by way of brief background, Austin Queenan, "The Pentarchy: Its Origin and Initial Development," *Diakonia* 2 (1967): 338–51.

49. See Zizioulas, "Primacy in the Church: An Orthodox Approach." Meyendorff speaks disparagingly of "the mythical system of 'pentarchy'" whose "ecclesiological meaning is impossible to define and . . . importance is limited to being a sort of symbolic model of universal conciliarity" ("The Ecumenical Patriarchate Yesterday and Today," 243).

50. Josiah Trenham upbraids the apathetic on this question and laments the fact that most people do not care enough about unity. See "Orthodox Reunion: Overcoming the Curse of Jurisdictionalism in America," *St. Vladimir's Theological Quarterly* 50 (2006): 277–303.

51. See Faris, "The Latin Church *Sui Iuris.*"

52. Interestingly, another set of suggestions, also temporary pending a genuine ecumenical council, has recently been made by the Orthodox Churches themselves in June 2009 at Chambésy. Recognizing their own jurisdictional and geographical problems, the hierarchs proposed a series of "episcopal assemblies" to co-ordinate Orthodox activity and press for greater intra-Orthodox unity. These assemblies are to be created for twelve different regions of the world: (i) North America and Central America; (ii) South America; (iii) Australia, New Zealand, and Oceania; (iv) Great Britain and Ireland; (v) France; (vi) Belgium, Holland, and Luxembourg; (vii) Austria; (viii) Italy and Malta; (ix) Switzerland and Lichtenstein; (x) Germany; (xi) Scandinavian countries (except Finland); (xii) Spain and Portugal. (See "Decision," section 3: http://www.goarch.org/archdiocese/documents/chambesy/decision.) This statement provides no clues at all about why these regions were chosen, why fully two continents—Africa and Asia—were ignored, on what basis these regions were chosen, or whether this ordering of them here is in any way significant. One can, however, speculate that the fact North America is listed first *is* significant given the nearly forty years of extensive debates about the jurisdictional chaos on that continent. One can further speculate that the list seems to move in order of regions with the largest and most ecclesially Orthodox populations to those regions with the smallest. Whether these

assemblies are ever set up, and whether they achieve what they are supposed to do, remains to be seen.

53. As Louis Bouyer has observed, "it is radically unsatisfactory" in establishing ecclesiastical structures to have a "church of a clan, race, nationality, or class" (*Church of God,* 455).

54. On nationalism and phyletism in the Eastern Catholic Churches, see the extremely important article of Peter Galadza, "The Structure of the Eastern Churches: Bonded with Human Blood or Baptismal Water?" *Pro Ecclesia* 17 (2008): 317–36. On Orthodox Churches, see, inter alia, Stephen Bigham, "Le concile de Constantinople de 1872 et le phylétisme," *Le Messager orthodoxe* 135 (2000): 30–36.

55. To paraphrase Neville Chamberlain's infamous dismissal of Czechoslovakia, to whose dismemberment and then total destruction by Hitler the British prime minister gave his misguidedly pacific consent in 1938.

56. Dvornik, *Byzantium and the Roman Primacy.*

57. A very helpful discussion of these original imperial circumscriptions and language is found in Peter Norton, *Episcopal Elections 250–600: Hierarchy and Popular Will in Late Antiquity* (Oxford: Oxford University Press, 2007), 118–76.

58. The question arises as to what to do with "possessions" of one country in the continental sphere of another—e.g., the Falkland Islands, which are part of South America but actually British territory. For sake of simplicity, and in keeping with our determination not to allow nationalist considerations to enter in here but to allow these questions to be determined only by the "impartial" nature of geography, I would propose in such instances as the Falklands that they belong to the jurisdiction of the continent in which they happen to be located. This principle would apply to outlying island countries not contiguous with continental landmasses. Such countries—e.g., Fiji—would belong to the continental patriarchate to which they were geographically closest.

59. See Wijlens, "Cooperation of Bishops on a Supranational or Continental Level," 37.

60. Pope John Paul II, *Ecclesia in America,* no. 37, available at the Vatican website http://www.vatican.va by title.

61. Wijlens, "Cooperation of Bishops on a Supranational or Continental Level," 35.

62. For more on this, see Paul Pallath, *Local Episcopal Bodies in East and West* (Kerala, India: Oriental Institute of Religious Studies, India, 1997), especially chapter 11, "Assemblies of Hierarchs of Several Churches *Sui Iuris*," 455–83.

63. Wijlens, "Cooperation of Bishops on a Supranational or Continental Level," 35.

64. Whether they would delegate some diocesan or patriarchal functions to a "vicar" of some sort—as the pope of Rome does currently with his diocese, and as several patriarchs also do—would be entirely up to an individual patriarch to decide.

65. Though it is not explicitly named as an example, I take Nicholas Afanasiev to caution against too rigid an application of such principles as that of accommodation, arguing that "external, empirical factors are thus 'ecclesialized' and the empirical principles that are their foundation come to play the role of ecclesiological principles. Thus they lose all contact with the empirical reality which was their source" (*The Church of the Holy Spirit,* ed. Michael Plekon, trans. Vitaly Permiakov [Notre Dame, IN: University of Notre Dame Press, 2007], 256).

66. In recognizing this status on the part of Alexandria, care would need to be taken to emphasize that this was a *temporary* measure, undertaken by the Catholic Church solely for her own internal structural needs and pending full unity with the Orthodox Church, when all these questions would again be revisited.

67. See William F. Macomber, "The Authority of the Catholicos Patriarch of Seleucia-Ctesiphon," in *I Patriarcati Orientali nel Primo Millennio* (Rome: PIO, 1968), 179–200 (= *Orientalia Christiana Analecta,* 181). Macomber's article demonstrates striking similarities—in both "rhetoric" and practice—between this catholicos-patriarch's claims to authority and those of the pope of Rome.

68. Peter Galadza has also lately come to this conclusion about Jerusalem. See his "Elements of a Vision for the Effective Synthesis of Universal Primacy and Conciliarity," *Logos: A Journal of Eastern Christian Studies* 50 (2009): 413–18.

69. Cf. Francis Dvornik, *The Idea of Apostolicity in Byzantium and the Legend of the Apostle Andrew* (Cambridge, MA: Harvard University Press, 1958). Additionally, Jerusalem remains a thriving city today in ways that could not be so clearly said of Antioch, Constantinople, or postwar Baghdad.

70. For the data on these three, see www.catholic-hierarchy.org, which draws on authoritative sources such as the *Annuario Pontificio.*

71. The Latin Church as a whole could also, if necessary, have a "full synod," that is, a meeting of all her bishops from all six patriarchates if this were thought necessary, but given the number of Latin bishops in the world today, such a gathering would necessarily be extremely rare if only because of the practical difficulties and costs of assembling such a large group.

72. As we have seen in chapter four, hierarchs are chosen in several ways in the Orthodox patriarchates, but many of them are elected not just by other bishops, but also by the "lower" clergy and by the lay people. It seems important that these possibilities of priestly and lay franchise be kept in mind, not least because of their venerable historical precedents.

73. Cf. Michael Fahey, "Eastern Synodal Traditions: Pertinence for Western Collegial Institutions," in *Episcopal Conferences: Historical, Canonical & Theological Studies,* ed. Thomas J. Reese (Washington, DC: Georgetown University Press, 1989). More recently, see the large and important collection of essays on synodality edited by Alberto Melloni and Silvia Scatena, *Synod and Synodality: Theology, History, Canon Law and Ecumenism in a New Context* (Münster: Lit Verlag, 2005).

74. The literature and debate on collegiality is very considerable and cannot be dealt with here. For an overview, see Patrick Granfield, "The Experience of Collegiality," in his *The Limits of the Papacy: Authority and Autonomy in the Church* (New York: Crossroad, 1987), 77–106, and for a more recent treatment his "The Collegiality Debate," in *Church and Theology: Essays in Memory of Carl J. Peter,* ed. Peter C. Phan (Washington, DC: Catholic University of America Press, 1995), 88–110. See also Clarence Gallagher, "Collegiality in the East and the West in the First Millennium: A Study Based on the Canonical Collections," *Jurist* 64 (2004): 64–81. For further canonical reflections, see Susan Wood, "The Theological Foundations of Episcopal Conferences and Collegiality," *Studia Canonica* 22 (1988): 327–38.

75. Magee, *Patriarchal Institution in the Church,* 519.

76. See John Quinn, "A Permanent Synod? Reflections on Collegiality," *Origins* 31 (2002): 730–36. Maximos first spoke of the necessity of a real synod of bishops having decisive authority over the Curia in a famous speech in French at the Second Vatican Council. For the text, see *Acta Synodalia Sacrosancti Concilii Oecumenici Vaticani Secundi* (Vatican City: Vatican Polyglot Press, 1971), 516–19. For commentary on his proposal, see Quinn, "A Permanent Synod?" and see also Ludwig Kaufmann, "Synod of Bishops: Neither *Concilium* nor *Synodus,*" *Concilium* 209 (1990): 67–78. In Robert Taft's celebrated interview with John Allen in February 2004, he argues that "the Catholic church has become so big that we need some kind of a synodal structure in the West the same way you have in the East. The United States Conference of Catholic Bishops ought to be a kind of synod of Catholic bishops in the United States." The text of the interview is available at http://nationalcatholicreporter .org/word/word020604.htm. Maxim Hermaniuk archly dismissed the current Roman synod of bishops—in several of whose sessions he participated—as "international study days of the Catholic bishops," arguing that unless the

synod had legislative rather than merely consultative powers it was a rather useless body, especially relative to the power the Curia still maintains. Hermaniuk is quoted in Granfield, *The Limits of the Papacy,* 95. Further thoughts of Hermaniuk are recorded by Andriy Chirovsky in his "Editorial," *Logos: A Journal of Eastern Christian Studies* 46 (2005): 289–300. For a broader view of Hermaniuk's role at Vatican II and in the years that followed, see Jan Grootaers, "La genèse du projet 'Hermaniuk'—une esquisse," *Logos: A Journal of Eastern Christian Studies* 51 (2010).

77. See Fahey, "Eastern Synodal Traditions," and Gregorios III, "Patriarches d'Orient et d'Occident: similarités et différences."

78. According to Brian Daley, "at least five synods are attested for Rome and eight for the province of Africa between 250 and 260" alone, and more than "four hundred synods and meetings of bishops, Eastern and Western, [are] known to have been held between the mid-second century and the pontificate of Gregory the Great" ("Structures of Charity: Bishops' Gatherings and the See of Rome in the Early Church," in *Episcopal Conferences: Historical, Canonical, and Theological Studies,* ed. Thomas J. Reese [Washington, DC: Georgetown University Press, 1989]). There were later synods as well: see Luitpold Wallach, "The Roman Synod of December 800 and the Alleged Trial of Leo III: A Theory and the Historical Facts," *Harvard Theological Review* 49 (1956): 123–42; Thomas F. X. Noble, "The Place in Papal History of the Roman Synod of 826," *Church History* 45 (1976): 434–54. There is also ample evidence of synods held elsewhere in the territory of the Western patriarchate, including frequently in France, Spain, and Britain, as well as other parts of Italy (e.g., Pope Leo I directed a "provincial synod" to be held in Aquileia in the mid-fifth century to resolve conflicts there).

79. Duffy, *Saints and Sinners,* 129. For Gregory VII, see A. J. Macdonald, *Hildebrand: A Life of Gregory VII* (London: Meuthen, 1932), 193–210; for some of Gregory's own thoughts around various synods, see Ephraim Emerton, trans., *The Correspondence of Pope Gregory VII: Selected Letters from the Registrum* (New York: Columbia University Press, 1990 [1932]). Gregory's changes included cleaning up genuinely scandalous conduct on the part of clergy— simony, fornication, greed, and graft—and on the part of the "laity," at least the princely ones who were heavily involved in the Investiture Crisis and not inclined to give up their power over parochial, abbatial, and especially episcopal appointments. The literature on this crisis is very considerable.

80. Kathleen Cushing, *Reform and the Papacy in the Eleventh Century: Spirituality and Social Change* (Manchester: Manchester University Press, 2005), 83.

81. Ibid., 84.

82. I. S. Robinson, *The Papacy 1073–1198: Continuity and Innovation* (Cambridge: Cambridge University Press, 1990). According to Robinson, "at no other period in the history of the Church did popes preside so frequently over councils of bishops from all the provinces of the Latin Church as in the later eleventh century and the twelfth century" (121).

83. As Michael Fahey among others has observed, "It is notable that only in the twelfth century was the institution of a permanent synod in the church of Rome replaced by the consistory of cardinals" ("Eastern Synodal Traditions").

84. On the sidelining of synods and their replacement with cardinals and later still curial officials, see Robinson, *The Papacy 1073–1198*, 129–33. See also Colin Morris, *The Papal Monarchy: The Western Church from 1050–1250* (Oxford: Clarendon Press, 1989), 165–73 especially.

85. Paul Pallath has argued in detail that "the bishops conference can be seen as a spontaneous attempt of the bishops of the Latin Church to re-establish the lost synodal element in the Church" (*Local Episcopal Bodies in East and West*, 453).

86. I say "in the main" because it is possible that the composition of the permanent synod may suffer from a lack of expertise in a given area—e.g., finances—and so the synod may need to have an additional member or two with the appropriate expertise.

87. Permanent synods, like all such institutions, had a less attractive side from time to time and in place to place, as John Meyendorff has noted: the permanent synod (particularly, he notes, in Constantinople and Moscow) has sometimes "ceased to promote conciliarity and has become an organ of bureaucratic administration exercising power *over* other bishops" ("The Ecumenical Patriarchate Yesterday and Today," 242). Perhaps the easiest way of ensuring that the permanent synod did not turn into another bureaucracy with its own agenda would be to require the "full" synod to return to the Nicaea-mandated pattern of meeting twice a year in the spring and autumn.

88. It would be important to have at least the occasional meeting in person. As helpful and sophisticated as today's technology is, there are still certain things that can only be accomplished by in-person gatherings, as the memoirs of so many bishops at the Second Vatican Council make clear. Technology can be an enormous help, but we are still embodied creatures of an incarnate God.

89. Every year the pope issues a "Message for World Communications Day." In his 1990 "Message for World Communications Day XXIV," Pope John Paul II said that "it is clear that the Church must also avail herself of the new resources provided by human exploration in computer and satellite

technology." See the Vatican website http://www.vatican.va under 1990 world communication day. In the 1971 pastoral instruction, *Communio et Progressio*, we are told, "The Church looks for ways of multiplying and strengthening the bonds of union between her members. For this reason, communication and dialogue among Catholics are indispensable" (§114). A little later on, it is noted that "the normal flow of life and the smooth functioning of government within the Church require a steady two-way flow of information between the ecclesiastical authorities at all levels and the faithful as individuals and as organized groups" (§120). This document is available at the Vatican website under pastoral instruction Communio et Progressio.

90. Pierre Duprey (citing Joseph Hajjar, about whom see the next note) reports that a meeting of a synod in Constantinople in September 394 is considered the first meeting of a *synodos endemousa* properly so called. See Duprey, "The Synodical Structure of the Church in Eastern Theology," *One in Christ* 7 (1971): 160. Cf. Claudia Rapp, who states that "the *synodos endemousa* is firmly attested for the first time in 448 . . . but its origins may well reach back to the fourth century." She also notes that the existence of this body provided a convenient excuse for bishops to escape their hinterland dioceses and come into the imperial capital "on official or concocted business." In the latter case, some bishops were seeking after "worldly glories and business," especially at the imperial court, which gave rise to "episcopal absenteeism—a common occurrence that the councils, east and west, tried to curb" ("The Elite Status of Bishops in Late Antiquity in Ecclesiastical, Spiritual, and Social Contexts," *Arethusa* 33 [2000]: 379–99; citation at 396). How "permanent" these synods were, then, and how often their membership was genuinely constituted by bishops legitimately in the city are thus matters of dispute. Duprey, in "Synodical Structure," exactingly argues that most of today's "permanent synods" are not always entirely the equivalent of the original *synodos endemousa* insofar as the modern versions tend to have a revolving membership of bishops who often live far afield and cycle into and out of the synod regularly rather than being permanent members by virtue of living *permanently* in or near the see-city as was the case with the original *synodos endemousa*.

91. The classic work on the *synodos endemousa* remains Joseph Hajjar, *Le Synode Permanent (Synodos endemousa) dans l'Eglise Byzantine des origines au XIe siècle* (Rome: Orientalia Christiana Analecta, 1962). Hajjar sums up some of his points in a very short treatment, "The Synod in the Eastern Church," *Concilium* 8 (1965): 55–64.

92. The origins of these sees and their precise geographical circumscriptions, as well as relations to Rome, are debated and have changed over time. Most seem to think that the suburbicarian sees as understood today date to

the papacy of Stephen III (768–72). See Patrick Saint-Roch, "Dioceses, Suburbicarian," in *The Papacy: An Encyclopedia,* ed. Philippe Levillain (New York: Routledge, 2002), 1:501. Even today, the incumbent cardinals of these suburbicarian sees are accounted the most senior members of the college, acting as its dean, vice-dean, etc. The classical treatment of the question of papal "zones" of authority and relations with neighbouring sees in the early Church remains Batiffol, *Cathedra Petri,* especially 42–79.

93. Cf. Louis Bouyer: "Consideration of 'councils' in the Church must evoke a form which, in the West, over the last centuries, has had particular importance: the congregation of cardinals" (*Church of God,* 448).

94. James H. Provost, "*Pastor Bonus:* Reflections on the Reorganization of the Roman Curia," *Jurist* 48 (1988): 499 (my emphasis).

95. One of the most important studies attempting to sort through the terminological and other issues remains Stephan Kuttner, "Cardinals: The History of a Canonical Concept," *Traditio* 3 (1945): 129–214. More generally, see M. Andrieu, "L'origine du titre de cardinal dans l'Eglise romaine," *Miscellanea Giovanni Mercati* 5 (1946): 113–44; and C. Lefebvre, "Les origines et le rôle du cardinalat au moyen âge," *Apollinaris* 41 (1968): 59–70. It is evident that some clergy were designated "cardinals" as early as the fifth century: François Jankowiak, "Cardinal," in *The Papacy: An Encyclopedia,* ed. Phillippe Levillain (New York: Routledge, 2002), 1:239–44. A major study of great depth and importance is Robinson, *The Papacy 1073–1198,* especially 33–120. The author's preface says the book is "as much a study of the cardinals as of the popes" because "it is impossible to write a history of the papacy in this period without investigating the college of cardinals and its factions" (xii). On the college, see John Broderick: "despite the importance of the Sacred College, an adequate, modern, scholarly synthesis of its history remains a desideratum" ("The Sacred College of Cardinals: Size and Geographical Composition [1099–1986]," *Archivum Historiae Pontificiae* 25 [1987]: 7). For historical disputes, see, e.g., R. N. Swanson, "The Problem of the Cardinalate in the Great Schism," in *Authority and Power: Studies on Medieval Law and Government Presented to Walter Ullmann on His Seventieth Birthday,* ed. Brian Tierney and Peter Linehan (Cambridge: Cambridge University Press, 1980), 225–35. Cardinals fit very uneasily into Catholic ecclesiology especially since the Second Vatican Council. If all bishops are sacramentally equal with the bishop of Rome and all bishops are bound together in one apostolic college through ties of collegiality, why are some bishops—based purely on papal preference rather than, say, something like election by their peers, personal seniority, or historical priority of their see—specially selected to belong to a "special" college?

96. The literature on this period, predictably, is massive. Three of the best overviews—in addition to Robinson's *The Papacy 1073–1198*—include Walter

Ullmann, *A Short History of the Papacy in the Middle Ages* (New York and London: Methuen, 1972); Kenneth Pennington, *Pope and Bishop: The Papal Monarchy in the Twelfth and Thirteenth Centuries* (Philadelphia: University of Pennsylvania Press, 1984); and Colin Morris, *The Papal Monarchy*.

97. I rely heavily here on Robinson, *The Papacy 1073–1198*. For his discussion of legates, see pp. 146–78.

98. The phrase *plenitudo potestatis* finds its origins in this period and comes from Bernard of Clairvaux writing to Pope Innocent II, who picks up the phrase and introduces it into common papal usage. On this, see J. W. Gray, "The Problem of Papal Power in the Ecclesiology of St. Bernard," *Transactions of the Royal Historical Society* 24 (1974): 1–17. More generally, see R. Benson, "*Plenitudo potestatis:* Evolution of a Formula from Gregory IV to Gratian," Collectanea Stephan Kuttner 4, *Studia Gratiana* 14 (1968): 193–217; William McCready, "Papal Plenitudo Potestatis and the Source of Temporal Authority in Late Medieval Papal Hierocratic Theory," *Speculum* 48 (1973): 654–74.

99. Ratzinger, "Primacy and Episcopacy," 204. Canon 239, §21 of the 1917 *Code of Canon Law* claimed that cardinals take precedence over everyone—patriarchs, bishops in their own dioceses, etc.

100. The text is available in a variety of places. See "Medieval Sourcebook: Decree of 1059: On Papal Elections" at http://www.fordham.edu/halsall/source/papal-elect1059.html.

101. Robinson, *The Papacy 1073–1198*, 38–41.

102. Ibid., 39; see also p. 90.

103. For more on synodality and conciliarity in the latter half of the second millennium, see Pallath, *Local Episcopal Bodies in East and West*, 309–42.

104. I. S. Robinson, *The Papacy 1073–1198*, 99–100.

105. J. A. Watt, "Hostiensis on *Per Venerabilem:* The Role of the College of Cardinals," in *Authority and Power: Studies on Medieval Law and Government Presented to Walter Ullmann on His Seventieth Birthday*, ed. Brian Tierney and Peter Linehan (Cambridge: Cambridge University Press, 1980), 105.

106. See Pierre Jugie, "Cardinal: Up to the Council of Trent," in *The Papacy: An Encyclopedia*, ed. Philippe Levillain (New York: Routledge, 2002), 1:239–43. See also John Broderick, "The Sacred College of Cardinals."

107. "Curia," in *The Papacy: An Encyclopedia*, 1:465

108. After Sixtus V, notable major reconfigurations were undertaken by Pope Pius X in 1908 (apostolic constitution *Sapienti Consilio, AAS* 1 [1909]: 7–19); and then in the apostolic constitution *Pastor Bonus* promulgated 28 June 1998 by Pope John Paul II and available at the Vatican website http://www.vatican.va by title.

109. The authoritative history of the Curia remains Niccolo del Re, *La Curia Romana. Lineamenti storico-giuridici,* 3rd ed. (Rome: Edizioni di Storia e Letteratura, 1947). See also Giuseppe Alberigo, "Serving the Communion of Churches," in *The Roman Curia and the Communion of Churches,* ed. Peter Huizing and Knut Walf (New York: Seabury Press, 1979), 12–33 (= *Concilium* 127 [1979]); Thomas Reese, *Inside the Vatican: The Politics and Organization of the Catholic Church* (Cambridge, MA: Harvard University Press, 1998), 106–39; Ignazio Gordon, "Curia: Historical Evolution," in *Sacramentum Mundi: An Encyclopedia of Theology* (New York: Herder & Herder, 1978–80), 2:49–52; and the numerous and lengthy entries, covering all major periods, in "Curia," *The Papacy: An Encyclopedia,* 1:444–74.

110. I follow Owen Chadwick and others in thinking that the "modern papacy" has roots in the loss of the Papal States and the promulgation of *Pastor Aeternus* of Vatican I, but really begins with Pope Leo XIII (1878–1903). See Chadwick's superlative study *A History of the Popes 1830–1914.* On the "modernity" of Leo XIII, see Raymond de Souza's interesting little study, "Two Popes," *First Things* 136 (October 2003): 18–24.

111. On the changes to the college, see the outstanding survey of John Broderick, "The Sacred College of Cardinals," 7–71. He makes it plain that "internationalization" of the college is not some trendy modern idea of recent provenance but in fact was an animating principle going back almost to the beginning of the college as such. Three significant changes were made to the college around the time of the Second Vatican Council. The first, by Pope John XXIII in April 1962 in his *motu proprio Cum Gravissima,* required that all cardinals be bishops. The other two changes were ushered in by Pope Paul VI. First, in 1968, in his *motu proprio Ad Purpuratorum Patrum Collegium,* he brought Eastern Catholic patriarchs into the college, allowing them to hold their patriarchal sees as "titles" rather than being appointed to a titular or "diaconal" church in Rome. (For the text of the *motu proprio,* see http://www .vatican.va/holy_father/paul_vi/motu_proprio/documents/hf_p-vi_19650211 _ad-purpuratorum_lt.html.) This decision was not without controversy among the Eastern Catholics (especially the Melkite Patriarch Maximos IV) and the Orthodox, and regardless of its merits the inclusion of Eastern Catholic patriarchs has fundamentally changed the nature of the college as an exclusively Roman institution for the governance of the Church of Rome. The next change came in another *motu proprio* issued in November 1970, *Ingravescentem Aetatem* (http://www.vatican.va/holy_father/paul_vi/motu _proprio/documents/hf_p-vi_motu-proprio_19701120_ingravescentem_it .html) restricted the right to vote in a conclave to cardinals under the age of

eighty and required that cardinals submit their resignation to the pope at the age of seventy-five; they could be allowed to stay on until eighty, but at that point automatically lost all voting rights and were retired from all official curial and diocesan positions.

112. The code later seems to recognize the ecclesiological anomaly of the cardinalate in saying that "in those matters which pertain to their own person, cardinals living outside Rome and outside their own diocese are exempt from the power of governance of the bishop of the diocese in which they are residing" (c. 357, §2). Cardinals thus enjoy special privileges, which are discussed in disturbing detail by Alan McCormack, "The Privileges of Cardinals," *Studia Canonica* 37 (2003): 125–62. McCormack notes that on the eve of the promulgation of the new *Code of Canon Law,* ten cardinals asked why the proposed new code eliminated the 1917 canons on cardinalatial privileges. The commission for the code answered that because all cardinals were now required to be bishops, and bishops are all equal, there were no such privileges still extant; the commission therefore once more ruled against including a canon on privileges in the new code. In March 1999, however, Angelo Cardinal Sodano, as papal secretary of state, smuggled many of these privileges back in by means of a document "entitled *Elenchus privilegiorum et facultatum S.R.E. Cardinalium in re liturgica et canonica . . .* in which a significant number of the suppressed privileges were revived and granted once more to all cardinals" (McCormack, 126). These include allowing "pontifical" (that is, hierarchical) insignia—liturgical and otherwise—to be worn by non-episcopal cardinals (e.g., the pectoral cross), who also have rights to bless and dedicate churches and altars as well as other furnishings and persons (e.g., abbots) that would otherwise be restricted to bishops. Moreover, they can preach everywhere, erect a private chapel in their residence, and confer certain ministries and "indulgences."

113. All except those Eastern Catholic patriarchs who accept membership in the College, taking as their "title" that of their patriarchal see and having no Roman church to "patronize" and thereby not becoming a member of the Roman clergy. This was a point of some contention when Pope Paul VI proposed patriarchal membership in the college in 1965. Maximos IV Saigh, the Melkite patriarch of Antioch, was eventually persuaded to accept membership, detailing his reasons in a short allocution published in *Documentation Catholique* 62 (1965): 1293–98. The same volume contains an article immediately preceding Maximos's: Elias Zoghby, "Patriarchat et cardinalat," denounces his patriarch's decision and Zoghby ended up resigning as patriarchal vicar in protest.

114. It is also conceivable that these new forms of patriarchal ministry could be erected or embodied in creative ways that would also, in time, be

useful to the Eastern Churches as well, showing them different ways of living this ministry, perhaps in a more organized fashion than has sometimes been the case among some Orthodox patriarchates.

Chapter Six.   Papal Structures and Responsibilities

1. Those who might cavil at the continued use of the title "supreme pontiff" should recall that it is a title one finds from time to time in Orthodox literature with reference to their own patriarchs and catholicos. Some object that this title is of secular or "pagan" origins, but I see no reason to accept this line of argumentation given that most ecclesiastical offices—e.g., diocese, metropolitan, exarch, eparch—as well as the structures (dioceses, provinces, patriarchates) of the Church do not have "sacred origins" (*hieros-archos*) but are themselves creations of the "secular" or "pagan" structures of the Roman Empire. Put positively, I think "supreme pontiff" (or, better, "Roman pontiff") is a perfectly acceptable title for those who know its Latin origins: a pontiff is simply a bridge-builder, one who seeks to overcome divides and to bring together that which is separated. This, it seems to me, is especially fitting imagery for the papal office.

2. Clément, *You Are Peter,* 93–94.

3. This emphasis on the papacy as serving unity is directly affirmed at length in *Lumen Gentium* 23, where the papacy is described as the Church's "principal and foundation of unity."

4. The numeration is mine, and so is the breakdown that follows. The encyclical simply lumps them all together.

5. My emphasis. (The internal references are to *Lumen Gentium* 27.)

6. Recall in particular the Romanian Orthodox theologian Dumitru Popescu, who argued that "during the first Christian millennium, the papal primacy was exercised within an ecclesiology of communion." If today the "experience of the papacy can be of great importance for Christian unity" it will be so when "exercised in the context of an ecclesiology which situates communion both at the visible level and at the invisible level of the Church" ("Papal Primacy in Eastern and Western Patristic Theology," 111 and 113).

7. Zizioulas, "Primacy in the Church: An Orthodox Approach," 118–21.

8. Zizioulas, "Recent Discussions on Primacy," 243.

9. Ibid., 246. For more on this, see John Zizioulas, "The Father as Cause: Personhood Generating Otherness," in his *Communion and Otherness: Further Studies in Personhood and the Church,* ed. Paul McPartlan (London: T&T Clark, 2006), esp. 145–49. But cf. Nicholas Loudovikos's critical discussion of

Zizioulas on this point in "Christian Life and Institutional Church," in *The Theology of John Zizioulas: Personhood and the Church,* ed. Douglas H. Knight (Burlington, VT: Ashgate, 2007), 125–32, esp. 129. See also Constantine Scouteris, "The Church: Filled with the Holy Trinity," in *Ecclesial Being: Contributions to Theological Dialogue,* ed. Christopher Veniamin (South Canaan, PA: Mount Thabor Publishing, 2006), 28–43.

10. See Pennington, *Pope and Bishop.*

11. "It behooves the Bishops of every nation to know the one among them who is the premier or chief, and to recognize him as their head, and to refrain from doing anything superfluous without his advice and approval: but, instead, each of them should do only whatever is necessitated by his own parish and by the territories under him. But let not even such a one do anything without the advice and consent and approval of all. For thus will there be concord, and God will be glorified through the Lord in Holy Spirit—the Father, the Son, and the Holy Spirit."

12. Hopko cited in Andriy Chirovsky, "Inspiration Rather than Imitation: Seeing the Papacy of the Third Millennium through the Eyes of the First," *Logos: A Journal of Eastern Christian Studies* 46 (2005): 300.

13. My emphasis.

14. For more on this, see Hervé Legrand, "Un seul évêque par ville: Pourquoi et comment redevenir fidèle au 8e canon de Nicée?"

15. There is nothing in *Pastor Aeternus* preventing papal consultation before a binding declaration, and, indeed, much commending such consultation (see ch. 4, §5). Indeed, in the only instance in which the doctrine of papal infallibility has been used, the 1950 definition by Pope Pius XII of the bodily Assumption into heaven of the Mother of God, it is explicitly noted at some length in the apostolic constitution, *Munificentissimus Deus,* that the pope only proceeded after very prolonged and extensive consultation with "all our venerable brethren in the episcopate" who were requested "directly and authoritatively that each of them should make known to us his mind in a formal statement. Hence, on May 1, 1946, we gave them our letter 'Deiparae Virginis Mariae,' a letter in which these words are contained: 'Do you, venerable brethren, in your outstanding wisdom and prudence, judge that the bodily Assumption of the Blessed Virgin can be proposed and defined as a dogma of faith? Do you, with your clergy and people, desire it?'" (no. 11). Only once he had secured the "universal agreement of the Church's ordinary teaching authority" in and with the bishops did he proceed to the declaration (no. 12). The apostolic constitution is available at the Vatican website http://www.vatican.va by title.

16. *Pastor Aeternus* 4, §5.

17. *Pastor Aeternus* 4, §9 (my emphasis). In proceeding in this manner, the resultant declaration would arguably be far less controversial, and the matter to be decided much more firmly persuasive of the faithful, given that it was not the decision of one man acting in isolation, but a concerted effort to discern the will of the Holy Spirit, and a united decision to proceed with the matter. Such a manner of proceeding would, moreover, more clearly manifest the infallibility *of the Church,* as the conciliar decree itself puts it. Yves Congar, among others, has argued that "the fundamental locus of ecclesiastical authority in the Church is not the papacy but the episcopal college. Papal authority is always a collegial act" (cited in Richard Gaillardetz, *Witnesses to the Faith: Community, Infallibility, and the Ordinary Magisterium of Bishops* [New York: Paulist Press, 1992], 108). Even more directly, Congar elsewhere argued during the course of the Second Vatican Council that "[r]ight up to the time when a juridical and unilateral theory, dominated by the idea of the pontifical monarchy, was victorious, Catholic tradition preserved the idea that the real subject of infallibility is the *Ecclesia universalis*" ("Remarks on the Council as an Assembly and on the Church's Fundamentally Conciliar Nature" cited in Margaret O'Gara, *Triumph in Defeat: Infallibility, Vatican I, and the French Minority Bishops* [Washington, DC: Catholic University of America Press, 1988], 170). In addition to O'Gara's landmark work, further reflections attempting to understand infallibility not in exclusively papal but wider episcopal and ecclesial terms may be found in Francis A. Sullivan, *Magisterium: Teaching Authority in the Catholic Church* (Mahwah, NJ: Paulist Press, 1983), esp. 4–23. Additionally, see Peter Chirico, "The Bishops as Bearers of Infallibility," in his *Infallibility: The Crossroads of Doctrine* (Wilmington, DE: Michael Glazier, 1983), 245–69.

18. Lay people and parish clergy have a long and rich history of involvement in episcopal elections in Rome and elsewhere. See two new books in this regard: Joseph F. O'Callaghan, *Electing Our Bishops* and, especially rich in its historical accounts, Norton, *Episcopal Elections 250–600.*

19. I am aware that the Church of Rome is represented in conclave by each cardinal—save those Eastern patriarchs who lack such "titles"—having a link to a church of the Diocese of Rome, to which he holds the "title," but this practice cannot be seriously said to result in a substantial relationship and consequent form of local representation.

20. The patriarchs and other bishops could also immediately ordain the pope-elect if he were not already a bishop.

21. His ability to do this would depend on maintaining good relations with the other patriarchs, and, in kenotic fashion, allowing them to sometimes occupy "centre stage" when circumstances warrant. Equally, however, they, too,

would have to be willing to live kenotically and modify any passions of envy if much or most of the attention focused on the pope much or most of the time.

22. As A. Pearce Higgins ("The Papacy and International Law," *Journal of the Society of Comparative Legislation* 9 [1908]: 252–64) points out, "When he ceased to be a temporal sovereign, the tradition which had so long attached to his dual position was not easily disregarded" (252). On this point—viz., the transformation of the papacy into global teacher and universal spokesman— recent scholarship is very clear that the transformation is dependent on in- creasing centralization in the Church following Vatican I and the loss of the Papal States. See Pollard, *Money and the Rise of the Modern Papacy;* Chadwick, *A History of the Popes, 1830–1914;* and Duffy, *Saints and Sinners.*

23. Higgins forcefully notes that "it may well be contended that the Papacy, by becoming a purely spiritual institution, free to devote itself to the further- ance of religion, has increased in authority since the Pope ceased to be the temporal sovereign of a petty Italian State" ("The Papacy and International Law," 260).

24. William R. Farmer and Roch Kereszty, *Peter and Paul in the Church of Rome: The Ecumenical Potential of a Forgotten Perspective* (New York: Paulist Press, 1990), 11.

25. For some of the historical and contextual background to the status of the Vatican and the Church prior to 1929, see Higgins, "The Papacy and Inter- national Law"; and Luigi Sturzo and Angeline Helen Lograsso, "The Roman Question before and after Fascism," *Review of Politics* 5 (1943): 488–508. For more general context, see the outstanding work of Owen Chadwick, *A History of the Popes, 1830–1914.* See also the important and influential scholarship of John Pollard: *The Vatican and Italian Fascism, 1929–32: A Study in Conflict* (Cambridge: Cambridge University Press, 1985) and *Money and the Rise of the Modern Papacy.*

26. For details see Umberto Toschi, "The Vatican City State: From the Standpoint of Political Geography," *Geographical Review* 21 (1931): 529–38. For a more recent overview, see the CIA *World Factbook* entry, "Holy See (Vatican City)" at https://www.cia.gov/library/publications/the-world-factbook/geos/ vt.html. For even more statistics, charts, and maps, see Joël-Benoît d'Onorio, "Vatican City State," in *The Papacy: An Encyclopedia,* ed. Philippe Levillain (New York and London: Routledge, 2002), 3:1590.

27. For overviews that raise some theological issues, see Isidoro Martin, "The Church's Relations with Foreign Governments," *Concilium* 8 (1970): 94–103; and Pio Ciprotti, "The Holy See: Its Function, Form, and Status in International Law," *Concilium* 8 (1970): 63–73. See, from a "secular" perspec- tive, D. A. Binchy, "The Vatican and International Diplomacy," *International*

Affairs 22 (1946): 47–56. Since Binchy's article was published, the Vatican has of course gone on to establish diplomatic relations with many more countries. For a comprehensive accounting of those relations by a papal diplomat—who, as such, offers a less than fully critical treatment—see Hyginus Eugene Cardinale, *The Holy See and the International Order* (Toronto: Macmillan, 1976). The text of the Treaty, which is comprised of three parts—the Treaty of Conciliation, comprising twenty-seven articles, the Financial Convention annexed to the treaty and composed of three articles, and the Concordat of forty-five articles regulating Church-state relations in Italy—is available at http://www .aloha.net/~mikesch/treaty.htm. It makes for instructive reading, not least in the constant use of terms like "sovereignty" and its cognates. The Treaty also, in article 8, considers attacks on the pope as a form of regicide punishable by the same penalties as attacks on the king of Italy. The treaty, predictably, has generated comment and scholarship over the years. For a very good early overview, especially of the practical manifestations of the Vatican's statehood, see Gordon Ireland, "The State of the City of the Vatican," *American Journal of International Law* 27 (1933): 271–89. For another overview, see Francesco Margiotta Broglio, "Lateran Pacts," in *The Papacy: An Encyclopedia,* ed. Philippe Levillain (New York: Routledge, 2002), 2:901–5. For an attempt to see how well the Treaty's provisions stood up in the Second World War, see Herbert Wright, "The Status of the Vatican City," *American Journal of International Law* 38 (1944): 452–57. On the updating of the Treaty, see Maruo Giovannelli, "The 1984 Covenant between the Republic of Italy and the Vatican: A Retrospective Analysis after Fifteen Years," *Journal of Church and State* 42 (2000): 529–38.

28. As an example of the more skeptical, see Josef L. Kunz, "The Status of the Holy See in International Law," *American Journal of International Law* 46 (1952): 308–14. Consider Olivier Clément's rather insouciant and thoroughly unconvincing comment that "it is in no way essential that his [the pope's] administrative headquarters should be a sovereign territory and that he should be a head of state" (*You Are Peter,* 94). In a footnote, Clément continues: "That the existence of the Vatican State guarantees the independence of the papacy is a myth. . . . Today everything depends on the political and ideological situation of Italy and western Europe" (ibid., 95 n2). As I have argued elsewhere, one must be extremely cautious in dismissing the Vatican's hard-won freedom, and not indulge in romantic fatuities by thinking that it is necessarily morally better to be divested of the status and apparatus of a state so as to live some supposedly simpler life. The dangers with this line of argumentation are painfully evident when one considers, e.g., the severely harassed Ecumenical Patriarchate in Istanbul, whose every word is scrutinized by the

Turkish government, which does not think twice about rebuking the patriarch if he dares voice even modest criticisms of how the tiny handful of Orthodox Christians not yet driven from the country are treated. See, e.g., the patriarch's December 2009 interview with *60 Minutes,* in which he spoke of being "crucified" by the Turkish government: http://www.cbsnews.com/stories/2009/12/17/ 60minutes/main5990390.shtml?tag=currentVideoInfo;segmentUtilities. The Turkish government reacted strongly, and the patriarch was forced to issue a "clarification" to calm the waters: see http://www.alarabiya.net/articles/2009/ 12/19/94668.pdf for the government's condemnation, and here for the "clarification": http://www.armtown.com/news/en/pan/20091225/41227/. To cite but a few examples of criticisms being ignored, see Yasmin Abdullah, "The Holy See at United Nations Conferences: State or Church?" *Columbia Law Review* 96 (1996): 1835–75. Lukas Vischer, in his "The Holy See, the Vatican State, and the Churches' Common Witness: A Neglected Ecumenical Problem," *Journal of Ecumenical Studies* 11 (1974): 617–36, suggested that the status of the Holy See/Vatican was an ecumenical problem in need of study, but this suggestion seems to have been ignored in the more than three decades since he wrote.

29. D'Onorio, "Vatican City State," 3:1590. This claim is also detailed and examined in Francis X. Murphy, "Vatican Politics: Structure and Function," *World Politics* 26 (1974): 542–59. It is given sympathetic understanding in Higgins, "The Papacy and International Law," where the author argues that "it is important to understand why the Pope attaches so much importance to the possession of temporal sovereignty . . . [which exists] for the purpose of assuring his independence in the exercise of his spiritual functions" (255).

Afterword

1. I am at work on this topic currently and hope to publish an article about it soon.

2. Zizioulas, "Primacy in the Church: An Orthodox Approach," 123.

3. On this see the very apt reflections of the Orthodox theologian John Jillions: "In the Shadow of Pseudo-Dionysius," at http://www.ocanews.org/ JillionsDionysius.html.

4. For a more general treatment of a Trinitarian ecclesiology relevant here, see the statement of the JIC, "The Mystery of the Church and of the Eucharist in the Light of the Mystery of the Holy Trinity."

5. Scouteris, *Ecclesial Being,* 36.

6. Cited in ibid., 29.

7. *Theosis* has come in for extensive recent scholarly reconsideration. See, e.g., Michael J. Christensen and Jeffery A. Wittung, eds., *Partakers of the Divine Nature: The History and Development of Deification in the Christian Traditions* (Grand Rapids, MI: Baker Academic, 2008); Stephen Thomas, *Deification in the Eastern Orthodox Tradition: A Biblical Perspective* (Piscataway, NJ: Gorgias Press, 2007); Daniel Keating, *Deification and Grace* (Naples, FL: Sapientia Press, 2007). The first is an ecumenical collection of articles; the second obviously an Orthodox treatment; the third is a self-consciously Roman Catholic consideration of the concept.

8. 1 John 4:16.

9. Cited in Nicholas Afanasiev, *The Church of the Holy Spirit,* 265.

10. Ibid., 272.

11. Cf. Phil. 2:6–10.

12. Afanasiev, *The Church of the Holy Spirit,* 272–73. Cf., in speaking of Catholic-Orthodox unity on the question of the pope, Afanasiev notes that "to attain this the effort in Love is necessary, a great sacrifice, an element of self-renunciation. To restrict the doctrine of the power of the pope within the limits of the catholic church would be, for the church of Rome, the result of a great sacrificial spirit toward the goal of re-establishing the union-of-the-churches-joined-in-Love" ("Una Sancta," in *Tradition Alive: On the Church and the Christian Life in Our Time—Readings from the Eastern Church,* ed. Michael Plekon (New York: Rowman and Littlefield, 2003), 26.

13. Afanasiev, *The Church of the Holy Spirit,* 275. Cf. Pope Benedict XVI's first encyclical letter, *Deus Caritas Est,* especially the second part available on the Vatican website http://www.vatican.va by title.

BIBLIOGRAPHY

Abdullah, Yasmin. "The Holy See at United Nations Conferences: State or Church?" *Columbia Law Review* 96 (1996): 1835–75.

Adams, Michael. *Vatican II on Ecumenism*. Dublin and Chicago: Scepter Books, 1966.

Afanasiev, Nicholas. "Canons and Canonical Consciousness." *Put'* (1933) (in Russian). http://www.orthodoxresearchinstitute.org/articles/canon_law/afanasiev_canonical_consciousness.htm (in English).

———. *The Church of the Holy Spirit*. Translated by Vitaly Permiakov. Edited by Michael Plekon. Notre Dame, IN: University of Notre Dame Press, 2007.

———. "The Church Which Presides in Love." In *The Primacy of Peter*, edited by John Meyendorff, 91–143. Crestwood, NY: St. Vladimir's Seminary Press, 1992.

———. "Una Sancta." In *Tradition Alive: On the Church and the Christian Life in Our Time—Readings from the Eastern Church*, edited by Michael Plekon. New York: Rowman and Littlefield, 2003.

Afonsky, Gregory. "The Canonical Status of the Patriarch of Constantinople in the Orthodox Church." http://www.holy-trinity.org/ecclesiology/afonsky-constantinople.html.

Alappatt, Paul. *The Election of the Patriarch in the Eastern Catholic Canonical Tradition: A Historical-Juridical Study*. Rome: PIO, 1997.

Alberigo, Giuseppe. "Juridiction: remarques sur un terme ambigu." *Irénikon* 49 (1976): 167–80.

———. "Serving the Communion of Churches." In *The Roman Curia and the Communion of Churches*, edited by Peter Huizing and Knut Walf, 12–33. New York: Seabury Press, 1979. (= *Concilium* 127 [1979])

Alberigo, Giuseppe, and Joseph Komonchak, eds. *History of Vatican II*. Vol. 1, *Announcing and Preparing Vatican Council II*. Maryknoll, NY and Louvain: Orbis and Peeters, 1995.

Alberigo, Giuseppe, et al., eds. *History of Vatican II*. Vol. 3, *The Mature Council*. Maryknoll, NY and Louvain: Orbis and Peeters, 2000.

Alexander, Edward. "The Armenian Church in Soviet Policy." *Russian Review* 14 (1955): 357–62.

Alexi. "Statement Reacts to Vatican Establishment of Four Russian Dioceses." *Origins* 31 (2002): 618–20.

Alfeyev, Hilarion. "The Canonical Territories of the Local Orthodox Churches." http://www.orthodoxytoday.org/articles6/HilarionOneBishop2.php.

———. "One City, One Bishop, One Church." http://www.orthodoxytoday.org/articles6/HilarionOneBishop.php.

———. *Orthodox Witness Today.* Geneva: WCC Press, 2006.

———. "The Practical Application of the Principle of Canonical Territory." http://orthodoxeurope.org/page/14/87.aspx#5.

Allen, John. "Interview with Robert Taft," 2004. http://ncronline.org/mainpage/specialdocuments/taft.htm.

———. "Mourning Bells to Chime for Pope's Visit," *National Catholic Reporter,* 5 May 2001.

———. "Orthodox Christians Wary of Papal Visits." *National Catholic Reporter,* 13 April 2001.

Aloor, Francis. "The Territoriality of 'Ecclesia Sui Iuris': A Historical, Ecclesiological and Juridical Study." Doctoral dissertation, Pontificia Universitas Sanctae Crucis, Rome, 2007.

Amadouni, Garabed. "L'autocéphalie du Katholikat arménien." In *I Patriarcati Orientali Nel Primo Millennio,* 137–78. Rome: PIO, 1968. (= *Orientalia Christiana Analecta* 181)

Anastos, Milton. *Aspects of the Mind of Byzantium: Political Theory, Theology, and Ecclesiastical Relations with the See of Rome.* London: Ashgate, 2001.

Anderson, Kjartan. "Pilgrims, Property, and Politics: The Russian Orthodox Church in Jerusalem." In *Eastern Christianity: Studies in Modern History, Religion and Politics,* edited by Anthony O'Mahony, 388–430. London: Melisende, 2004.

Andrieu, M. "L'origine du titre de cardinal dans l'Eglise romaine." *Miscellanea Giovanni Mercati* 5 (1946): 113–44.

Aram I. "The Armenian Church Beyond Its 1700th Anniversary." *Ecumenical Review* 54 (2002): 88.

Armes, Keith. "Chekists in Cassocks: The Orthodox Church and the KGB." *Demokratizatsiya: The Journal of Post-Soviet Democratization* 1 (1994): 72–83.

Azkoul, Michael. "What Are the Differences between Orthodoxy and Roman Catholicism?" http://www.ocf.org/OrthodoxPage/reading/ortho_cath.htm.

Bartholomew. "A Common Code for the Orthodox Churches." *Kanon* 1 (1973): 45–53.

Batiffol, Pierre. *Cathedra Petri: Etudes d'Histoire ancienne de l'Eglise.* Paris: Cerf, 1938.

Baum, Gregory. *The Quest for Christian Unity.* London and New York: Sheed and Ward, 1963.

———. *That They May be One: A Study of Papal Doctrine (Leo XIII–Pius XII).* London: Bloomsbury, 1958.

Baumgartner, Frederic J. *Behind Locked Doors: A History of the Papal Elections.* New York: Palgrave Macmillan, 2003.

Bavoillot-Laussade, Richard. "Tiara." In *The Papacy: An Encyclopedia,* edited by Philippe Levillain. 3 vols. London: Routledge, 2002. 3:1488–92.

Baynes, N. H. *Byzantine Studies and Other Essays.* London: Greenwood Press, 1955.

Bea, Augustin. *Ecumenism in Focus.* London: Geoffrey Chapman, 1969.

Beazley, C. Raymond. "Early Christian Geography." *Transactions of the Royal Historical Society* 10 (1896): 85–109.

Benjamin, Daniel D. *The Patriarchs of the Church of the East: Dinkha III not IV.* Translated by Youel A. Baaba. Piscataway, NJ: Gorgias Press, 2006.

Benson, R. "*Plenitudo potestatis:* Evolution of a Formula from Gregory IV to Gratian." Collectanea Stephan Kuttner 4. *Studia Gratiana* 14 (1968): 193–217.

Bestawros, Adel Azer. "The Concept of the Protos 'Patriarch' in the Coptic Orthodox Church." *Kanon* 3 (1975): 135–41.

Bigham, Stephen. "Le concile de Constantinople de 1872 et le phylétisme." *Le Messager orthodoxe* 135 (2000): 30–36.

Bilas, Ivan. "The Moscow Patriarchate, the Penal Organs of the USSR, and the Attempted Destruction of the Ukrainian Greco-Catholic Church during the 1940s." *Logos: A Journal of Eastern Christian Studies* 38 (1997): 41–92.

Binchy, D. A. "The Vatican and International Diplomacy." *International Affairs* 22 (1946): 47–56.

Binns, John. *An Introduction to the Christian Orthodox Churches.* Cambridge: Cambridge University Press, 2002.

Bliss, Frederick. *Catholic and Ecumenical: History and Hope.* Franklin, WI: Sheed and Ward, 1999.

Blumenthal, U. R. *The Investiture Controversy: Church and Monarchy from the Ninth to the Twelfth Century.* Philadelphia: University of Pennsylvania Press, 1988.

Bociurkiw, B. R. *The Ukrainian Greek Catholic Church and the Soviet State (1939–1950).* Edmonton and Toronto: Canadian Institute of Ukrainian Studies Press, 1996.

Bogolepov, Alexander. "The Statutes of the Russian Orthodox Church of 1945." *St. Vladimir's Seminary Quarterly* 2 (1958): 23–39.

————. *Toward an American Orthodox Church: The Establishment of an Auto-cephalous Orthodox Church*. Crestwood, NY: St. Vladimir's Seminary Press, 2001 (1963).

Bourdeaux, Michael, and Alexandru Popescu. "The Orthodox Church and Communism." In *The Cambridge History of Eastern Christianity*, edited by Michael Angold, 558–75. Cambridge: Cambridge University Press, 2006.

Bouyer, Louis. *The Church of God*. Translated by C. U. Quinn. Chicago: Franciscan Herald Press, 1982.

Boyle, John P. *Church Teaching Authority: Historical and Theological Studies*. Notre Dame, IN: University of Notre Dame Press, 1995.

Braaten, Carl E., and Robert W. Jenson, eds. *Church Unity and the Papal Office: An Ecumenical Dialogue on John Paul II's Encyclical* Ut Unum Sint. Grand Rapids, MI: Eerdmans, 2001.

Bremer, Thomas, ed. *Religion and the Conceptual Boundary in Central and Eastern Europe*. London: Palgrave Macmillan, 2008.

————. "Rome and Moscow: A Step Further." *Religion in Eastern Europe* 23 (2003).

Broderick, John F. "The Sacred College of Cardinals: Size and Geographical Composition (1099–1986)." *Archivum Historiae Pontificiae* 25 (1987): 7–71.

Broglio, Francesco Margiotta. "Lateran Pacts." In *The Papacy: An Encyclopedia*, edited by Philippe Levillain. 3 vols. New York and London: Routledge, 2002. 2:901–5.

Broun, Janice. "The Bulgarian Orthodox Church: The Continuing Schism and the Religious, Social and Political Environment." *Religion, State & Society* 32 (2004): 209–45.

————. "The Schism in the Bulgarian Orthodox Church." *Religion, State & Society* 21 (1993): 207–20.

————. "The Schism in the Bulgarian Orthodox Church, Part 2: Under the Socialist Government." *Religion, State & Society* 28 (2000): 263–89.

————. "The Schism in the Bulgarian Orthodox Church, Part 3." *Religion, State & Society* 30 (2002): 365–94.

Brown, Raymond, et al., eds. *Peter in the New Testament: A Collaborative Assessment by Protestant and Roman Catholic Scholars*. Minneapolis: Augsburg, 1973.

Bryner, Erich. "Stumbling-Blocks to Ecumenism." *Religion, State & Society* 26 (1998): 83–88.

Buciora, J. "Canonical Territory of the Moscow Patriarchate: An Analysis of Contemporary Russian Orthodox Thought." *Messenger: Journal of the Episcopal Vicariate of Great Britain and Ireland* 2 (May 2007): 25–54.

Bundy, David. "Armenian Relations with the Papacy after the Mongol Invasions." *Patristic and Byzantine Review* 5 (1986): 19–32.

Burgess, Michael. *The Eastern Orthodox Churches: Concise Histories with Chronological Checklists of Their Primates.* London and Jefferson, NC: McFarland, 2005.

Burke, Cormac. *Authority and Freedom in the Church.* Dublin: Four Courts Press, 1988.

Burkle-Young, Francis A. *Passing the Keys: Modern Cardinals, Conclaves, and the Election of the Next Pope.* New York: Madison Books, 2001.

Canon Law Society of America. *Code of Canon Law.* Washington, DC: Canon Law Society of America, 1983.

———. *Code of Canons of the Eastern Churches.* Washington, DC: Canon Law Society of America, 1990.

Cardinale, Hyginus Eugene. *The Holy See and the International Order.* Toronto: Macmillan, 1976.

Cassidy, Edward Idris. *Ecumenism and Interreligious Dialogue.* New York: Paulist Press, 2005.

———. "Vatican II and Catholic Principles on Ecumenism." *Centro Pro Unione Bulletin* 50 (1996): 3–10.

Chadwick, Owen. *From Bossuet to Newman: The Idea of Doctrinal Development.* Cambridge: Cambridge University Press, 1957.

———. *A History of the Popes, 1830–1914.* Oxford: Clarendon Press, 1998.

Chirico, Peter. *Infallibility: The Crossroads of Doctrine.* Wilmington, DE: Michael Glazier, 1983.

Chirovsky, Andriy. "Editorial." *Logos: A Journal of Eastern Christian Studies* 46 (2005): 289–300.

———. "Inspiration Rather than Imitation: Seeing the Papacy of the Third Millennium through the Eyes of the First." *Logos: A Journal of Eastern Christian Studies* 46 (2005): 289–300.

———. "Letter from Ukraine." *First Things* 116 (October 2001): 15–18.

Christensen, Michael J., and Jeffery A. Wittung, eds. *Partakers of the Divine Nature: The History and Development of Deification in the Christian Traditions.* Grand Rapids, MI: Baker Academic, 2008.

Ciprotti, Pio. "The Holy See: Its Function, Form, and Status in International Law." *Concilium* 8 (1970): 63–73.

Clapsis, Emmanuel. "The Papal Primacy." *Greek Orthodox Theological Review* 32 (1987): 115–30.

Clément, Olivier. *Conversations with Ecumenical Patriarch Bartholomew I.* Translated by Paul Meyendorff. Crestwood, NY: St. Vladimir's Seminary Press, 1997.

———. "The Pope, the Council and the Emperor during the Period of the Seven Ecumenical Councils." *Sourozh: A Journal of Orthodox Life and Thought* 42 (November 1990): 1–15.

———. *Rome autrement: Un orthodoxe face à la papauté.* Paris: Desclée de Brouwer, 1997. In English as *You Are Peter: An Orthodox Theologian's Reflection on the Exercise of Papal Primacy.* Translated by M. S. Laird. New York: New City Press, 2003.

Clifford, Catherine. "The Joint Declaration, Method, and the Hermeneutics of Ecumenical Consensus." *Journal of Ecumenical Studies* 38 (2001): 79–91.

———. "Lonergan's Contribution to Ecumenism." *Theological Studies* 63 (2002): 521–38.

Congar, Yves. *Eglise et Papauté.* Paris: Cerf, 1994.

———. "Titre donnés au Pape." *Concilium* 108 (1975): 56–67.

———. *Vraie et Fausse Réforme dans l'Eglise.* Paris: Cerf, 1950.

Cooke, Peter M. "The Armenian Church—A Guiding Light on the Ecumenical Highway?" *One in Christ* 37 (2002): 75–88.

Cowdrey, H. E. J. *Pope Gregory VII 1073–1085.* Oxford: Oxford University Press, 1998.

Cracraft, James. *The Church Reform of Peter the Great.* Stanford, CA: Stanford University Press, 1971.

Cummings, D., trans. *The Rudder (Pedalion) of the Metaphorical Ship of the One Holy Catholic and Apostolic Church of the Orthodox Christians, or, All the Sacred and Divine Canons . . . as Embodied in the Original Greek Text . . . and Explained by Apapius and Nicodemus.* Chicago: Orthodox Christian Educational Society, 1957.

Cushing, Kathleen. *Reform and the Papacy in the Eleventh Century: Spirituality and Social Change.* Manchester: Manchester University Press, 2005.

Daley, Brian E., S.J. "Headship and Communion: American Orthodox-Catholic Dialogue on Synodality and Primacy in the Church." *Pro Ecclesia* 5 (1996): 55–72.

———. "Position and Patronage in the Early Church: The Original Meaning of 'Primacy of Honour.'" *Journal of Theological Studies* 44 (1993): 529–53.

———. "Structures of Charity: Bishops' Gatherings and the See of Rome in the Early Church." In *Episcopal Conferences: Historical, Canonical, and Theological Studies,* edited by Thomas J. Reese. Washington, DC: Georgetown University Press, 1989.

Damaskinos. "Un pas courageux et essential de l'Eglise catholique." *La Croix,* 1 June 1995, 9.

Daneels, Godfried. "On Papal Primacy and Decentralization." *Origins* (30 October 1997): 339–41.

Davey, Colin. "'Clearing a Path through a Minefield:' Orthodox-RC Dialogue 1983–90." *One in Christ* 26 (1990): 285–307.

———. "Statements on Primacy and Universal Primacy by Representatives of the Orthodox Churches." *One in Christ* 35 (1999): 378–82.

Davis, Leo Donald. *The First Seven Ecumenical Councils (325–787): Their History and Theology.* Collegeville, MN: Liturgical Press, 1983.

Davis, Stephen J. *The Early Coptic Papacy: The Egyptian Church and Its Leadership in Late Antiquity.* Cairo and New York: American University of Cairo Press, 2004.

de Halleux, André. Review of *"Papa Patriarca D'Occidente? Studio Storico-dottrinale." Revue Theologique de Louvain* 23 (1992): 208–11.

de Souza, Raymond. "Two Popes." *First Things* 136 (October 2003): 18–24.

Destivelle, Hyacinthe. *Le Concile de Moscou (1917–1918): La création des institutions conciliaires de l'Église orthodoxe russe.* Paris: Cerf, 2005.

DeVille, Adam A. J. "The Development of the Doctrine of 'Structural Sin' and a 'Culture of Death' in the Thought of Pope John Paul II." *Eglise et Theologie* 30 (1999): 307–25.

———. "A Diversity of Polities: Patriarchal Leadership of the Orthodox Churches." *Jurist* 68 (2008): 460–96.

———. "*Kenosis* vs. *La Bella Figura*." *Canadian Journal of Orthodox Christianity* 2 (Fall 2007): 94–106.

———. "Letter from the East: Olivier Clément's *You Are Peter: An Orthodox Theologian's Reflection on the Exercise of Papal Primacy*." *First Things* 147 (November 2004): 46–50.

———. "Look to Tradition: The Case for Electing Bishops." *Commonweal* 134 (23 March 2007): 15–18.

———. "On the Patriarchate of the West." *Ecumenical Trends* 35 (June 2006): 1–7.

———. "Orthodoxy, Catholicism, and Primacy: A Plea for a New Common Approach." *Ecumenical Trends* 37 (April 2008): 5–8.

———. "Primacy Time." *Touchstone* 18 (June 2005): 44–45.

———. "Ravenna and Beyond: The Question of the Roman Papacy and the Orthodox Churches in the Literature 1962–2006." *One in Christ* 41 (2008): 99–138.

———. "Review Essay: The Vatican's Ecumenists." *Pro Ecclesia* 117 (2008): 112–22.

———. Review of *Electing Our Bishops: How the Catholic Church Should Choose Its Leaders* by Joseph F. O'Callaghan. *Anglican Theological Review* 89 (2007): 677–79.

———. Review of *Heirs of the Fisherman* by John-Peter Pham. *Studia Canonica* 39 (2005): 389–91.

———. Review of *Popes and Patriarchs* by Michael Whelton. *Canadian Journal of Orthodox Christianity* 2, no. 1 (2007).

Dick, Ignace. *What Is the Christian Orient?* Translated by C. Gerard Guertin. Westminster, MD: Newman Press, 1967.

Dimitrov, Ivan Zhelev. "Bulgarian Christianity." In *The Blackwell Companion to Eastern Christianity,* edited by Ken Parry, 47–72. Oxford: Blackwell, 2007.

Diocese of the Armenian Church of America. *The Armenian Church: A Brief Outline.* New York, 1973.

D'Onorio, Joël-Benoît. "Vatican City State." In *The Papacy: An Encyclopedia,* edited by Philippe Levillain. 3 vols. New York and London: Routledge, 2002.

Downey, Glanville. "The Claim of Antioch to Ecclesiastical Jurisdiction over Cyprus." *Proceedings of the American Philosophical Society* 102 (1958): 224–28.

Duffy, Eamon. *Saints and Sinners: A History of the Popes.* New Haven, CT: Yale University Press, 1997.

Dulles, Avery Cardinal. "Review Essay: A New Orthodox View of the Papacy." *Pro Ecclesia* 12 (Summer 2003): 345–58.

Dulles, Avery, and Patrick Granfield. *The Church: A Bibliography.* Wilmington, DE: Michael Glazier, 1985.

Dunn, Dennis J. *The Catholic Church and Russia: Popes, Patriarchs, Tsars and Commissars.* Aldershot: Ashgate, 2004.

Duprey, Pierre. "The Synodical Structure of the Church in Eastern Theology." *One in Christ* 7 (1971): 152–82.

Durā, V. Nicolae. "The 'Petrine Primacy': The Role of the Bishop of Rome according to the Canonical Legislation of the Ecumenical Councils of the First Millennium—An Ecclesiological-Canonical Evaluation." In *The Petrine Ministry: Catholics and Orthodox in Dialogue,* edited by Walter Kasper. New York: Newman Press, 2006. 159–87.

———. "The Protos in the Romanian Orthodox Church According to Its Modern Legislation." *Kanon* 3 (1975): 144.

Dvornik, Francis. *Byzantium and the Roman Primacy.* New York: Fordham University Press, 1966.

———. *General Councils of the Church.* London: Burns & Oates, 1961.

———. *The Idea of Apostolicity in Byzantium and the Legend of the Apostle Andrew.* Cambridge, MA: Harvard University Press, 1958.

Dymyd, Michel. "Les enjeux de l'abandon du titre de 'patriarch d'Occident.'" *Istina* 51 (2006): 30–32.

Emerton, Ephraim, trans. *The Correspondence of Pope Gregory VII: Selected Letters from the Registrum.* New York: Columbia University Press, 1990 (1932).

Erickson, John H. "The 'Autocephalous Church.'" In *The Challenge of Our Past: Studies in Orthodox Canon Law and Church History,* 91–113. Crestwood, NY: St. Vladimir's Seminary Press, 1991.

———. "Autocephaly in Orthodox Canonical Literature to the Thirteenth Century." *St. Vladimir's Theological Quarterly* 15 (1971): 28–41.

———. "First among Equals: Papal Primacy in an Orthodox Perspective." *Ecumenical Trends* 27, no. 2 (February 1998): 1–9.

———. "A New Crisis in Catholic-Orthodox Dialogue." *Ecumenism* 107 (1992): 22–24.

———. "A Retreat from Ecumenism in Post-Communist Russia and Eastern Europe?" *Ecumenical Trends* 30 (2001): 129–38.

Erickson, John, and John Borelli, eds. *The Quest for Unity: Orthodox and Catholics in Dialogue.* Crestwood, NY: St. Vladimir's Seminary Press, 1996.

Evans, Andrew. "Forced Miracles: The Russian Orthodox Church and Postsoviet International Relations." *Religion, State & Society* 30 (2002): 33–43.

Evans, G. R. *Method in Ecumenical Theology: The Lessons So Far.* Cambridge: Cambridge University Press, 1996.

Evdokimov, Paul. "Can a Petrine Office Be Meaningful in the Church? A Russian Orthodox Reply." In *Papal Ministry in the Church,* edited by Hans Küng, 122–26. New York: Herder and Herder, 1971.

Evtuhov, Catherine. "The Church in the Russian Revolution: Arguments for and against Restoring the Patriarchate at the Church Council of 1917–1918." *Slavic Review* 50 (1991): 497–511.

Fagan, Geraldine, and Aleksandr Shchipkov. "'Rome Is Not Our Father But Neither Is Moscow Our Mother:' Will There Be a Local Ukrainian Orthodox Church?" *Religion, State & Society* 29 (2001): 197–205.

Fahey, Michael. "Eastern Synodal Traditions: Pertinence for Western Collegial Institutions." In *Episcopal Conferences: Historical, Canonical & Theological Studies,* edited by Thomas J. Reese. Washington, DC: Georgetown University Press, 1989.

———. "A Note on the 'Code of Canons of the Eastern Churches' and Orthodox/Catholic Reunion." *Jurist* 56 (1996): 456–64.

Faris, John D. "At Home Everywhere—A Reconsideration of the *Territorium Proprium* of the Patriarchal Churches." *Jurist* 69 (2009): 5–30.

———. *Eastern Catholic Churches: Constitution and Governance.* Brooklyn: St. Maron Publications, 1992.

———. "The Latin Church *Sui Iuris.*" *Jurist* 62 (2002): 280–93.

Farmer, William R., and Roch Kereszty. *Peter and Paul in the Church of Rome: The Ecumenical Potential of a Forgotten Perspective*. New York: Paulist Press, 1990.

Fasolt, Constantin. "Voluntarism and Conciliarism in the Work of Francis Oakley." *History of Political Thought* 22 (2001): 41–52.

Fedorov, Vladimir. "Barriers to Ecumenism: An Orthodox View from Russia." *Religion, State & Society* 26 (1998): 129–43.

Fejsak, Josef. "The Orthodox Church in Czechoslovakia: The Path to Autocephaly." *Journal of the Moscow Patriarchate* 12 (1981): 46–49.

Ferencz, Nicholas. *American Orthodoxy and Parish Congregationalism*. Piscataway, NJ: Gorgias Press, 2006.

Filatov, Sergei, and Lyudmila Vorontsova. "Catholic and Anti-Catholic Traditions in Russia." *Religion, State & Society* 28 (2000): 69–84.

Fitzgerald, Thomas. "Conciliarity, Primacy and the Episcopacy." *St. Vladimir's Theological Quarterly* 38 (1994): 17–43.

Flora, Gavril, Gerogina Szilagyi, and Victor Roudometof. "Religion and National Identity in Post-Communist Romania." *Journal of Southern Europe & the Balkans* 7 (2005): 35–55.

Fortescue, Adrian. "Introduction." In *The Patriarchs of Constantinople*, edited by Claude Delaval Cobham. Cambridge: Cambridge University Press, 1911.

Frazee, Charles A. "The Christian Church in Cilician Armenia: Its Relations with Rome and Constantinople to 1198." *Church History* 45 (1976): 166–84.

Freeze, Gregory. "Handmaiden of the State? The Church in Imperial Russia Reconsidered." *Journal of Ecclesiastical History* 36 (1985): 82–102.

Freitag, Anton, et al., eds. *The Twentieth Century Atlas of the Christian World: The Expansion of Christianity through the Centuries*. New York: Hawthorn Books, 1963.

Fuller, F. W. "The Canterbury Patriarchate." In *Essays and Letters on Orders and Jurisdiction*. London: Longmans, 1925.

Gaillardetz, Richard. *Teaching with Authority: A Theology of the Magisterium in the Church*. Collegeville, MN: Liturgical Press, 1997.

———. *Witnesses to the Faith: Community, Infallibility, and the Ordinary Magisterium of Bishops*. New York: Paulist Press, 1992.

Galadza, Peter. "Liturgical Latinization and Kievan Ecumenism: Losing the Koinê of Koinonia." *Logos: A Journal of Eastern Christian Studies* 35 (1994): 173–94.

Gallagher, Clarence, S.J. "Collegiality in the East and the West in the First Millennium: A Study Based on the Canonical Collections." *Jurist* 64 (2004): 64–81.

———. "Roman Papal Primacy: Obstacle or Bridge to Unity?" *Logos: A Journal of Eastern Christian Studies* 37 (1996): 206–17.

Garuti, Adriano. "Ancora a Proposito del Papa Patriarca d'Occidente." *Antonianum* 70 (1995): 31–45.

———. *Papa Patriarca D'Occidente? Studio Storico-dottrinale*. Bologna: Edizioni Francescane, 1990.

———. *Primacy of the Bishop of Rome and the Ecumenical Dialogue*. Translated by Michael J. Miller. San Francisco: Ignatius Press, 2004.

Geanakoplos, Deno J. *A Short History of the Ecumenical Patriarchate of Constantinople (330–1990)*. Brookline, MA: Holy Cross Orthodox Press, 1990.

Giannakakis, Basil. *International Status of the Ecumenical Patriarchate*. Cambridge, MA: n.p., 1959.

Giovannelli, Maruo. "The 1984 Covenant between the Republic of Italy and the Vatican: A Retrospective Analysis after Fifteen Years." *Journal of Church and State* 42 (2000): 529–38.

Gleeson, Brian. "Power Sharing in the Catholic Church Today: Making Collegiality Really Happen." *Australian E-Journal of Theology* 1 (2003). http://dlibrary.acu.edu.au/research/theology/ejournal/aet_1/BGleeson.htm.

Gnilka, Joachim. "The Ministry of Peter—New Testament Foundations." In *The Petrine Ministry: Catholics and Orthodox in Dialogue,* edited by Walter Kasper, 24–36. New York: Newman Press, 2006.

Gooley, Anthony. "Has the Catholic Church Lost Its Way with the Revival of Genuine Episcopal Collegiality?" *Australian E-Journal of Theology* 1 (2003). http://dlibrary.acu.edu.au/research/theology/ejournal/aet_1/Gooley.htm.

Gordon, Ignazio. "Curia: Historical Evolution." In *Sacramentum Mundi: An Encyclopedia of Theology,* 2:49–52. New York: Herder & Herder, 1978–80.

Granfield, Patrick. "The Collegiality Debate." In *Church and Theology: Essays in Memory of Carl J. Peter,* edited by Peter C. Phan, 88–110. Washington, DC: Catholic University of America Press, 1995.

———. *The Limits of the Papacy: Authority and Autonomy in the Church*. New York: Crossroad, 1987.

———. *The Papacy in Transition*. Dublin: Gill and Macmillan, 1980.

Grant, Robert M. "Early Christian Geography." *Vigiliae Christianae* 46 (1992): 105–11.

Gray, J. W. "The Problem of Papal Power in the Ecclesiology of St. Bernard." *Transactions of the Royal Historical Society* 24 (1974): 1–17.

Green, Thomas. "Reflections on the Eastern Code Revision Process." *Jurist* 51 (1991): 18–37.

Gregorios III. "Patriarches d'Orient et d'Occident: similarités et différences. Comment Rome pourrait fonctionner comme l'un d'entre eux?" *Logos: A Journal of Eastern Christian Studies* 46 (2005): 13–34.

Grossi, Vittorino. "Patristic Testimonies on Peter, Bishop of the Church of Rome: Aspects of a Historical-Theological Reading." In *The Petrine Ministry: Catholics and Orthodox in Dialogue,* edited by Walter Kasper, 83–122. New York: Newman Press, 2006.

Groupe des Dombes. *Pour la communion des Eglises: L'apport du Groupe des Dombes 1937–1987.* Paris: Le Centurion, 1988.

Gudziak, Boris. "The Creation of the Moscow Patriarchate." *Logos: A Journal of Eastern Christian Studies* 37 (1996): 219–71.

Gulesserian, Papken. *The Armenian Church.* Translated by Terenig Vartabed Poladian. New York: AMS Press, 1970 (1939).

Guroian, Vigen. "A Communion of Love and the Primacy of Peter: Reflections from the Armenian Church." In *Ecumenism Today,* edited by Francesca Murphy et al., 139–50. Burlington, VT: Ashgate, 2008.

———. "The Crisis of Orthodox Ecclesiology." In *The Ecumenical Future,* edited by Carl E. Braaten and Robert W. Jenson, 162–75. Grand Rapids, MI: Eerdmans, 2004.

———. *Rallying the Really Human Things: The Moral Imagination in Politics, Literature, and Everyday Life.* Wilmington, DE: ISI Books, 2005.

———. "Religion and Armenian National Identity: Nationalism Old and New." *Religion in Eastern Europe* (1994).

Hackel, Sergei. "Managerial Patterns in a Patriarchal Church." *Sobornost* 23 (2001): 7–22.

Hagopian, Harry. "The Armenian Church in the Holy Land." In *Eastern Christianity: Studies in Modern History, Religion and Politics,* edited by Anthony O'Mahony, 215–68. London: Melisende, 2004.

Hajjar, Joseph. "The Synod in the Eastern Church." *Concilium* 8 (1965): 55–64.

———. *Le Synode Permanent (Synodos endemousa) dans l'Eglise Byzantine des origins au XIe siècle.* Rome: Orientalia Christiana Analecta, 1962.

Harkianakis, Stylianos. "Can a Petrine Office Be Meaningful in the Church? A Greek Orthodox Reply." In *Papal Ministry in the Church,* edited by Hans Küng. New York: Herder and Herder, 1971.

Hart, David. "The Future of the Papacy: A Symposium." *First Things* 111 (March 2001).

Hawley, Earl. *An Historic Pilgrimage: Photo Story of Pope Paul VI and His Historic Trek to the Holy Land.* Los Angeles: Matthews Press, 1964.

Hayda, Roma, ed. *Orientale Lumen VII Conference 2003 Proceedings.* Fairfax, VA: Eastern Christian Publications, 2004.

Herder and Herder. *Pope Paul VI in the Holy Land.* New York: Herder and Herder, 1964.

Higgins, A. Pearce. "The Papacy and International Law." *Journal of the Society of Comparative Legislation* 9 (1908): 252–64.

Holmes, James Derek. *The Papacy in the Modern World, 1914–1978.* London: Burns & Oates, 1981.

Hopko, Thomas. "Roman Presidency and Christian Unity in Our Time." http:// www.svots.edu/Faculty/Thomas-Hopko/Articles/Roman-Presidency-and -Christian-Unity.html.

Hotchkin, John Francis, and John Basil Sheerin. *Addresses and Homilies on Ecumenism, 1978–1980.* Washington, DC: United States Catholic Conference, 1981.

Hryniewicz, Waclaw. "The Cost of Unity: The Papal Primacy in Recent Orthodox Reflection." *Journal of Eastern Christian Studies* 55 (2003): 1–27.

Huizing, Peter, and Knut Walf, eds. *The Roman Curia and the Communion of Churches.* New York: Seabury Press, 1979. (= *Concilium* 127 [1979])

Hussey, J. M. *The Orthodox Church in the Byzantine Empire.* Oxford: Clarendon Press, 1986.

Ireland, Gordon. "The State of the City of the Vatican." *American Journal of International Law* 27 (1933): 271–89.

Istavridis, Vasil. "The Authority of the Ecumenical Patriarch in the Life of the Orthodox Church." *Greek Orthodox Theological Review* 35 (1990): 5–20.

Ivekovic, Ivan. "Nationalism and the Political Use and Abuse of Religion: The Politicization of Orthodoxy, Catholicism, and Islam in Yugoslav Successor States." *Social Compass* 49 (2002): 523–36.

Jaeger, Lorenz. *A Stand on Ecumenism: The Council's Decree.* Translated by Hilda Graef. London: Geoffrey Chapman, 1965.

Jankowiak, François. "Cardinal." In *The Papacy: An Encyclopedia,* edited by Philippe Levillain. 3 vols. New York: Routledge, 2002. 1:239–44.

Jenkins, Philip. *The New Faces of Christianity: Believing the Bible in the Global South.* Oxford: Oxford University Press, 2006.

———. *The Next Christendom: The Coming of Global Christianity.* Oxford: Oxford University Press, 2002.

———. "The Next Christianity." *The Atlantic Monthly* (October 2002).

Johnson, Todd M., and Sun Young Chung. "Tracking Global Christianity's Statistical Centre of Gravity, AD 33–AD 2100." *International Review of Mission* 93 (2004): 166–81.

Jugie, Pierre. "Cardinal: Up to the Council of Trent." In *The Papacy: An Encyclopedia,* edited by Philippe Levillain. 3 vols. New York: Routledge, 2002. 1:239–243.

Kanev, Peter. "Religion in Bulgaria after 1989: Historical and Socio-Cultural Aspects." *South-East Europe Review* 1 (2002): 75–96.

Karekin I. "Ecumenical Trends in the Armenian Church." *Ecumenical Review* 51 (1999): 31–39.

Karmiris, John. "The Schism of the Roman Church." http://www.myriobiblos .gr/texts/english/roman_church.htm.

Kasper, Walter. "Ce qui demeure et ce qui change dans le ministère de Pierre." *Concilium* 108 (1975): 29–41.

———. "Lasting Significance and Urgency of *Unitatis Redintegratio.*" http:// www.vatican.va/roman_curia/pontifical_councils/chrstuni/card-kasper -docs/rc_pc_chrstuni_doc_20041111_kasper-ecumenism_en.html.

———. "Petrine Ministry and Synodality." *Jurist* 66 (2006): 298–309.

———, ed. *The Petrine Ministry: Catholics and Orthodox in Dialogue.* New York: Newman Press, 2006.

———. *That They May All Be One: The Call to Unity Today.* London: Burnes & Oates, 2004.

Kaufmann, Ludwig. "Synod of Bishops: Neither *Concilium* nor *Synodus.*" *Concilium* 209 (1990): 67–78.

Keating, Daniel. *Deification and Grace.* Naples, FL: Sapientia Press, 2007.

Keleher, Serge. "Orthodox Rivalry in the Twentieth Century: Moscow versus Constantinople." *Religion, State & Society* 25 (1997): 125–37.

———. *Passion and Resurrection: The Greek Catholic Church in Soviet Ukraine 1939–1989.* Lviv: Stauropegion, 1993.

Kelly, George A. *The Crisis of Authority: John Paul II and the American Bishops.* Chicago: Regnery Gateway, 1982.

Ker, Ian. *John Henry Newman: A Biography.* Oxford: Clarendon Press, 1988.

Kesich, Veselin. "Peter's Primacy in the New Testament and the Early Tradition." In *The Primacy of Peter: Essays in Ecclesiology and the Early Church,* edited by John Meyendorff. Crestwood, NY: St. Vladimir's Seminary Press, 1992.

Kireopoulos, Antonios. "Papal Authority and the Ministry of Primacy." *Greek Orthodox Theological Review* 42 (1997): 45–62.

Knight, Douglas H., ed. *The Theology of John Zizioulas: Personhood and the Church.* Burlington, VT: Ashgate, 2007.

Knox, Zoe. "Postsoviet Challenges to the Moscow Patriarchate, 1991–2001." *Religion, State & Society* 32 (2004): 87–113.

———. "Russian Orthodoxy, Russian Nationalism and Patriarch Aleksii II." *Nationalities Papers* 33 (2005): 533–45.

———. "The Symphonic Ideal: The Moscow Patriarchate's Post-Soviet Leadership." *Europe-Asia Studies* 55 (2003): 575–96.

Komonchak, Joseph. "The Secretariat for Promoting Christian Unity and the Preparation of Vatican II." *Centro Pro Unione Bulletin* 50 (1996): 11–17.

Korz, Geoffrey. "Papal Hopes and Orthodox Popes: Did the Turks Get Something Right?" *Orthodox Canada: A Journal of Orthodox Christianity on the 'Net* 2 (2007). http://www.orthodoxcanada.com/journal/2007-04-09.html.

Koulomzine, Nicholas. "Peter's Place in the Primitive Church." In *The Primacy of Peter: Essays in Ecclesiology and the Early Church,* edited by John Meyendorff, 11–34. Crestwood, NY: St. Vladimir's Seminary Press, 1992.

Krikorian, Mesrob K. "Conflict of Laws and Respective Rules within the Community of the Oriental Churches." *Kanon* 3 (1975).

———. "The Primacy of the Successor of the Apostle St. Peter from the Point of View of the Oriental Orthodox Churches." In *Petrine Ministry and the Unity of the Church: "Toward a Patient and Fraternal Dialogue",* edited by James F. Puglisi. Collegeville, MN: Liturgical Press, 1999.

Krindatch, Alexei D. "Religion in Postsoviet Ukraine as a Factor in Regional, Ethno-Cultural and Political Diversity." *Religion, State & Society* 31 (2003): 37–73.

Küng, Hans, ed. *Papal Ministry in the Church.* New York: Herder and Herder, 1971.

Kunz, Josef L. "The Status of the Holy See in International Law." *American Journal of International Law* 46 (1952): 308–14.

Kutash, Ihor. "Response to Fr. Andrew Onuferko, 'The New Code of Canons of the Eastern Churches.'" *Logos: A Journal of Eastern Christian Studies* 35 (1994): 169–72.

Kuttner, Stephan. "Cardinals: The History of a Canonical Concept." *Traditio* 3 (1945): 129–214.

Lanne, Emmanuel. "Eastern Catholics: Religious Freedom and Ecumenism." *One in Christ* 26 (1990): 308–27.

———. "To What Extent Is Roman Primacy Unacceptable to the Eastern Churches?" In *Papal Ministry in the Church,* edited by Hans Küng. New York: Herder and Herder, 1971.

Lanne, Emmanuel, and M. van Parys. "Le dialogue catholique-orthodoxe à Baltimore-Emmitsburg." *Irénikon* 3–4 (2000): 405–18.

Larchet, Jean-Claude. "The Question of the Roman Primacy in the Thought of Saint Maximus the Confessor." In *The Petrine Ministry: Catholics and*

Orthodox in Dialogue, edited by Walter Kasper, 188–209. New York: New-man Press, 2006.

Leeming, Bernard. *The Vatican Council and Christian Unity.* London: Darton, Longman, and Todd, 1966.

Lefebvre, C. "Les origines et le rôle du cardinalat au moyen âge." *Apollinaris* 41 (1968): 59–70.

Legrand, Hervé. "Il Papa Patriarca in Occidente: Attualità di un Titolo Inat-tuale." *Nicolaus: Rivista di Teologia ecumenico-patristica* 34 (2007): 19–42.

———. "Un seul évêque par ville: Pourquoi et comment redevenir fidèle au 8e canon de Nicée? Un enjeu pour la catholicité de l'Église." *Irénikon* 77 (2004): 5–43.

Lévy, Antoine. "Au service de l'évêque de Rome: Collège patriarchal et unité de l'Eglise." *Istina* 51 (2006): 33–51.

L'Huillier, Peter. "Accession to Autocephaly." *St. Vladimir's Theological Quarterly* 37 (1993): 267–304.

———. "The Origins, Development and Significance of the Administrative Institutions of the Orthodox Church: Patriarchates, Autonomous Churches and Autocephalous Churches." In *The Splendour of Orthodoxy: 2000 Years of History, Monuments, Art.* Vol. 2, *Patriarchates and Autocephalous Churches,* edited by Kostas E. Tsiropoulos. Athens: Ekdotike Athenon, 2000.

———. "Problems Concerning Autocephaly." *Greek Orthodox Theological Review* 24 (1979): 165–91.

Likoudis, James. *Eastern Orthodoxy and the See of Peter: A Journey towards Full Communion.* Waite Park, MN: Park Press, 2006.

Lombardi, A. Raphael. *The Restoration of the Role of the Patriarch of the West.* Fairfax, VA: Eastern Christian Publications, 2006.

Lossky, Nicholas. "Conciliarity-Primacy in a Russian Orthodox Perspective." In *Petrine Ministry and the Unity of the Church: "Toward a Patient and Fraternal Dialogue",* edited by James Puglisi, 27–35. Collegeville, MN: Liturgical Press, 1999.

Losten, Basil. "Pope and Patriarch: Different Levels of Roman Authority." *Logos: A Journal of Eastern Christian Studies* 35 (1994): 201–38.

Loudovikos, Nicholas. "Christian Life and Institutional Church." In *The Theology of John Zizioulas: Personhood and the Church,* edited by Douglas H. Knight, 125–32. Burlington, VT: Ashgate, 2007.

Lourié, Basil. "Russian Christianity." In *The Blackwell Companion to Eastern Christianity,* edited by Ken Parry, 207–30. Oxford: Blackwell, 2007.

Loya, Joseph. "Interchurch Relations in Post-Perestroika Eastern Europe: A Short History of an Ecumenical Meltdown." *Religion in Eastern Europe* 25 (2005).

Luxmore, Jonathan. "Why the Pope's 'Deep Regret' Didn't Win over the Greeks." *Our Sunday Visitor* 86 (27 May 2001): 2.

Macdonald, A. J. *Hildebrand: A Life of Gregory VII*. London: Meuthen, 1932.

Mack, John. "Peter the Great and the Ecclesiastical Regulation: Secularization or Reformation?" *St. Vladimir's Theological Quarterly* 49 (2005): 243–69.

MacIntyre, Alasdair. "Poetry as Political Philosophy: Notes on Burke and Yeats." In *On Modern Poetry: Essays Presented to Donald Davie,* edited by Verene Bell and Laurence Lerner. Nashville: Vanderbilt University Press, 1988.

———. "Theology, Ethics, and the Ethics of Medicine and Health Care: Comments on Papers by Novak, Mouw, Roach, Cahill, and Hartt." *Journal of Medicine and Philosophy* 4 (1979): 435–43.

Macomber, William F. "The Authority of the Catholicos Patriarch of Seleucia-Ctesiphon." In *I Patriarcati Orientali nel Primo Millennio,* 179–200. Rome: PIO, 1968. (= *Orientalia Christiana Analecta* 181)

Magee, Michael. *The Patriarchal Institution in the Church: Ecclesiological Perspectives in the Light of the Second Vatican Council*. Rome: Herder, 2006.

Majdansky, Vsevolod. "One, Holy, Catholic and Apostolic Church." In *Orientale Lumen VII Conference 2003 Proceedings,* 83–89. Fairfax, VA: Eastern Christian Publications, 2004.

———. "Response to Bishop Basil (Losten): 'Patriarch and Pope: Different Levels of Roman Authority.'" *Logos: A Journal of Eastern Christian Studies* 35 (1994): 239–55.

———. *We Are All Brothers*. Fairfax, VA: Eastern Christian Publications, 1999.

Maksoudian, Krikor. *Chosen of God: The Election of the Catholicos of All Armenians*. New York: St. Vartan Press, 1995.

Maloney, George A. "Papal Primacy and Reunion." *Diakonia* 14 (1979): 185–88.

Mannion, Gerard, et al. eds. *Readings in Church Authority: Gifts and Challenges for Contemporary Catholicism*. Aldershot, Hants, England; Burlington, VT: Ashgate, 2003.

Marini, Francis J. *The Catholic View of Patriarchal Jurisdiction and Its Relation to Future Church Unity*. Fairfax, VA: Eastern Christian Publications, 2003.

———. *The Power of the Patriarch—Patriarchal Jurisdiction on the Verge of the Third Millennium*. Brooklyn: St. Maron Publications, 1998.

Martin, Isidoro. "The Church's Relations with Foreign Governments." *Concilium* 8 (1970): 94–103.

Mason, Whit. "Constantinople's Last Hurrah: Turkey and the Ecumenical Patriarchate." *World Policy Journal* 18 (2001): 55–64.

Mates, Michael. "Politics, Property Restitution, and Ecumenism in the Romanian Orthodox Church." *Logos: A Journal of Eastern Christian Studies* 46 (2005): 73–94.

Maximos IV (Saigh). "Allocution." *Documentation Catholique* 62 (1965): 1293–98.

Maximos of Sardes. *The Oecumenical Patriarchate in the Orthodox Church.* Thessaloniki: Patriarchal Institute for Patristic Studies, 1976.

May, William W., ed. *Vatican Authority and American Catholic Dissent: The Curran Case and Its Consequences.* New York: Crossroad, 1987.

McAreavey, John. "The Primacy of the Bishop of Rome: A Canonical Reflection in Response to *Ut Unum Sint.*" *Studia Canonica* 34 (2000): 119–54.

McCord, Peter J., ed. *A Pope for All Christians? An Inquiry into the Role of Peter in the Modern Church.* New York: Paulist Press, 1976.

McCormack, Alan R. A. "The Privileges of Cardinals." *Studia Canonica* 37 (2003): 125–61.

McCready, William. "Papal Plenitudo Potestatis and the Source of Temporal Authority in Late Medieval Papal Hierocratic Theory." *Speculum* 48 (1973): 654–74.

McManus, Eamon. "Primacy in the Thought of Two Orthodox Theologians." *One in Christ* 36 (2000): 234–50.

McManus, Frederick. "The Code of Canons of the Eastern Catholic Churches." *Jurist* 53 (1993): 22–61.

McMylor, Peter, and Maria Vorozhishcheva. "Sociology and Eastern Orthodoxy." In *The Blackwell Companion to Eastern Christianity,* edited by Ken Parry. Oxford: Blackwell, 2007.

Meyendorff, John. *The Byzantine Legacy in the Orthodox Church.* Crestwood, NY: St. Vladimir's Seminary Press, 1982.

———. *Catholicity and the Church.* Crestwood, NY: St. Vladimir's Seminary Press, 1983.

———. "Ecclesiastical Organization in the History of Orthodoxy." *St. Vladimir's Seminary Quarterly* 4 (1960): 2–22.

———. "Ecclesiastical Regionalism: Structures of Communion or Cover for Separatism? Issues of Dialogue with Roman Catholicism." *St. Vladimir's Theological Quarterly* 24 (1980): 155–80.

———. "The Ecumenical Patriarch, Seen in the Light of Orthodox Ecclesiology and History." *Greek Orthodox Theological Review* 24 (1979): 227–44.

———. "The Ecumenical Patriarchate Yesterday and Today," In *The Byzantine Legacy in the Orthodox Church.* Crestwood, NY: St. Vladimir's Seminary Press, 1982.

———. *Imperial Unity and Christian Divisions: The Church 450–680 A.D.* Crestwood, NY: St. Vladimir's Seminary Press, 1989.

———. *The Primacy of Peter: Essays in Ecclesiology and the Early Church.* Crestwood, NY: St. Vladimir's Seminary Press, 1992.

———. "Rome and Orthodoxy: Authority or Truth." In *A Pope for All Christians: An Inquiry into the Role of Peter in the Modern Church,* edited by Peter J. McCord. New York: Paulist Press, 1976.

———. *Rome, Constantinople, Moscow: Historical and Theological Studies.* Crestwood, NY: St. Vladimir's Seminary Press, 1996.

———. "Vatican II: Definitions or Search for Unity?" *St. Vladimir's Seminary Quarterly* 7 (1963): 164–68.

Miller, J. Michael. *The Divine Right of the Papacy in Recent Ecumenical Theology.* Rome: Gregorian University Press, 1980.

———. *The Shepherd and the Rock: Origins, Development, and Mission of the Papacy.* Huntington, IN: Our Sunday Visitor, 1995.

Miller, Monica Migliorino. *Sexuality and Authority in the Catholic Church.* Scranton, PA: University of Scranton Press, 1995.

Misner, Paul. *Papacy and Development: Newman and the Primacy of the Pope.* Leiden: E. J. Brill, 1976.

Mitrokhin, Nikolai. "Aspects of the Religious Situation in Ukraine." *Religion, State & Society* 29 (2001): 173–96.

Morris, Colin. *The Papal Monarchy: The Western Church from 1050 to 1250.* Oxford: Clarendon Press, 1989.

Murphy, Francis X. "Vatican Politics: Structure and Function." *World Politics* 26 (1974): 542–59.

Murre–van den Berg, Heleen. "Syriac Christianity." In *The Blackwell Companion to Eastern Christianity,* edited by Ken Parry, 249–68. Oxford: Blackwell, 2007.

Murvar, Vatro. "Russian Religious Structures: A Study in Persistent Church Subservience." *Journal for the Scientific Study of Religion* 7 (1968): 1–22.

Neale, John Mason. *The Patriarchate of Alexandria.* London: J. Masters, 1847.

Nedungatt, George. "Patriarchal Ministry in the Church of the Third Millennium." *Jurist* 61 (2001): 1–89.

Nersessian, Vrej Nerses. "Armenian Christianity." In *The Blackwell Companion to Eastern Christianity,* edited by Ken Parry, 23–46. Oxford: Blackwell, 2007.

Nersoyan, Tiran. "The Administration and Governing of the Armenian Church." In *Armenian Church Historical Studies,* edited by Nerses Vrej. New York: St. Vartan Press, 1996.

———. "Laity in the Administration of the Armenian Church." *Kanon* 3 (1975): 96–119.

Neuhaus, Richard John. "A Prospect Postponed." *First Things* 81 (1998): 69–71.

Newsome, David. *The Parting of Friends: The Wilberforces and Henry Manning.* Grand Rapids, MI: Eerdmans, 1993 (1966).

Nichols, Aidan. *Christendom Awake: On Reenergizing the Church in Culture.* Grand Rapids, MI: Eerdmans, 1999.

Nicol, Donald M. "The Byzantine View of Papal Sovereignty." In *The Church and Sovereignty c. 590–1918: Essays in Honour of Michael Wilks,* edited by Diana Wood. Oxford: Blackwell, 1991.

Nissiotis, Nikos A. "Orthodox Reflections on the Decree on Ecumenism." *Journal of Ecumenical Studies* 3 (1966): 329–42.

Noble, Thomas F. X. "The Place in Papal History of the Roman Synod of 826." *Church History* 45 (1976): 434–54.

Norris, Thomas. "The Development of Doctrine: 'A Remarkable Philosophical Phenomenon.'" *Communio* 22 (1995): 483–507.

Norton, Peter. *Episcopal Elections 250–600: Hierarchy and Popular Will in Late Antiquity.* Oxford: Oxford University Press, 2007.

Oakley, Francis. *The Conciliarist Tradition: Constitutionalism in the Catholic Church 1300–1870.* Oxford: Oxford University Press, 2004.

———. *Council over Pope? Towards a Provisional Ecclesiology.* New York: Herder and Herder, 1969.

———. "The 'New Conciliarism' and Its Implications: A Problem in History and Hermeneutics." *Journal of Ecumenical Studies* 8 (1971): 815–40.

Oakley, Francis, and Bruce Russett, eds. *Governance, Accountability, and the Future of the Catholic Church.* New York and London: Continuum, 2004.

O'Brien, John A. "Reform of the Roman Curia." *Christian Century* (25 June 1969): 869–71.

O'Callaghan, Joseph F. *Electing Our Bishops: How the Catholic Church Should Choose Its Leaders.* Lanham, MD: Rowman and Littlefield, 2007.

O'Donnell, Christopher. "Patriarchs." In *Ecclesia: A Theological Encyclopedia of the Church.* Collegeville, MN: Liturgical Press, 1996.

O'Gara, Margaret. *Triumph in Defeat: Infallibility, Vatican I, and the French Minority Bishops.* Washington, DC: Catholic University of America Press, 1988.

Onuferko, Andrew. "The New Code of Canons of the Eastern Churches: Ecclesiological Presuppositions." *Logos: A Journal of Eastern Christian Studies* 35 (1994): 133–72.

Ormanian, Malachia. *The Church of Armenia: Her History, Doctrine, Rule, Discipline, Liturgy, Literature, and Existing Condition.* Edited by Terenig Poladian. Translated by G. M. Gregory. London: A. R. Mowbray, 1912.

Pacurariu, Mircea. "The Patriarchate of Rumania: History and Spiritual Tradition." In *The Splendour of Orthodoxy: 2000 Years of History, Monuments, Art.* Vol. 2, *Patriarchates and Autocephalous Churches,* edited by Kostas E. Tsiropoulos, 298–321. Athens: Ekdotike Athenon, 2000.

———. "Romanian Christianity." In *The Blackwell Companion to Eastern Christianity,* edited by Ken Parry, 186–206. Oxford: Blackwell, 2007.

Pallath, Paul. *Local Episcopal Bodies in East and West.* Kerala, India: Oriental Institute of Religious Studies, India, 1997.

Panagopoulos, John. "*Ut Unum Sint:* Remarks on the New Papal Encyclical from an Orthodox Perspective." In *Ecology and Poverty,* edited by Leonardo Boff and Virgil Elizondo, 137–40. London: SCM Press, 1995.

Papadakis, Aristeides, and John Meyendorff. *The Christian East and the Rise of the Papacy: The Church 1071–1453 A.D.* Crestwood, NY: St. Vladimir's Seminary Press, 1994.

Papadopoulos, Theodore. *The History of the Greek Church and People under Turkish Domination.* New York: AMS Press, 1973.

Park, Chris. "Religion and Geography." In *Routledge Companion to the Study of Religion,* edited by John Hinnells, 439–55. London: Routledge, 2005.

Patelos, Constantin G. *The Orthodox Church in the Ecumenical Movement: Documents and Statements 1902–1975.* Geneva: WCC Press, 1978.

Patsavos, Lewis J. *Primacy and Conciliarity: Studies in the Primacy of the See of Constantinople and the Synodal Structure of the Orthodox Church.* Brookline, MA: Holy Cross Orthodox Press, 1995.

———. "The Synodal Structure of the Orthodox Church." *St. Vladimir's Theological Quarterly* 39 (1995): 71–98.

Paul VI. "Address to the Secretariat for Promoting Christian Unity." In *Doing the Truth in Charity: Statements of Pope Paul VI, Popes John Paul I, John Paul II, and the Secretariat for Promoting Christian Unity 1964–1980,* edited by Thomas F. Stransky and John B. Sheerin. New York: Paulist Press, 1982. (French original: *AAS* 59 [1967]: 493–98.)

Pavlowitch, Stevan K. "The Church of Macedonia: 'Limited Autocephaly' or Schism?" *Sobornost* 9 (1987): 42–59.

Payne, Daniel. "Nationalism and the Local Church: The Source of Ecclesiastical Conflict in the Orthodox Commonwealth." *Nationalities Papers* 35 (2007): 831–52.

Pennington, Kenneth. "The Canonists and Pluralism in the Thirteenth Century." *Speculum* 51 (1976): 35–48.

———. *Pope and Bishop: The Papal Monarchy in the Twelfth and Thirteenth Centuries.* Philadelphia: University of Pennsylvania Press, 1984.

Peri, Vittorio. "The Role of the Bishop of Rome in the Ecumenical Councils." In *The Petrine Ministry: Catholics and Orthodox in Dialogue*, edited by Walter Kasper. New York: Newman Press, 2006.

Petrossian, Yeznik. "The Development of the Law of the Armenian Apostolic Church during the 19th and 20th Century." *Kanon* 18 (1991): 45–55.

Pham, John-Peter. *Heirs of the Fisherman: Behind the Scenes of Papal Death and Succession*. Oxford and New York: Oxford University Press, 2004.

Pheidas, Vlasios. "Papal Primacy and Patriarchal Pentarchy in the Orthodox Tradition." In *The Petrine Ministry: Catholics and Orthodox in Dialogue*, edited by Walter Kasper, 65–82. New York: Newman Press, 2006.

Plekon, Michael, ed. *Tradition Alive: On the Church and the Christian Life in Our Time—Readings from the Eastern Church*. New York: Rowman and Littlefield, 2003.

Plokhy, Serhii, and Frank E. Sysyn. *Religion and Nation in Modern Ukraine*. Edmonton and Toronto: Canadian Institute of Ukrainian Studies, 2003.

Podles, Leon. *Sacrilege: Sexual Abuse in the Catholic Church*. Baltimore: Crossland, 2007.

Pollard, John. *Money and the Rise of the Modern Papacy: Financing the Vatican 1850–1950*. Cambridge: Cambridge University Press, 2005.

———. *The Vatican and Italian Fascism, 1929–32: A Study in Conflict*. Cambridge: Cambridge University Press, 1985.

Pontifical Council for Promoting Christian Unity (PCPCU). "Petrine Ministry." *Information Service* 1–2, no. 109 (2002).

———. "Statement on the Suppression of the Papal Title 'Patriarch of the West.'" *Origins* 36 (2006): 94–95.

Popescu, Dumitru. "Papal Primacy in Eastern and Western Patristic Theology: Its Interpretation in the Light of Contemporary Culture." In *Petrine Ministry and the Unity of the Church: "Toward a Patient and Fraternal Dialogue"*, edited by James F. Puglisi. Collegeville, MN: Liturgical Press, 1999.

Pospielovsky, Dimitry. *The Orthodox Church in the History of Russia*. Crestwood, NY: St. Vladimir's Seminary Press, 1998.

———. *The Russian Church under the Soviet Regime 1917–1982*. Crestwood, NY: St. Vladimir's Seminary Press, 1984.

Pospishill, Victor. "The Constitutional Development of the Eastern Catholic Churches in the Light of the Re-Codification of Their Canon Law." *Kanon* 5 (1978): 36–71.

Pottmeyer, Hermann. *Towards a Papacy in Communion: Perspectives from Vatican Councils I & II*. New York: Crossroad, 1998.

Provost, James H. "*Pastor Bonus*: Reflections on the Reorganization of the Roman Curia." *Jurist* 48 (1988): 499–535.

Puglisi, James F., ed. *Petrine Ministry and the Unity of the Church: "Toward a Patient and Fraternal Dialogue"*. Collegeville, MN: Liturgical Press, 1999.

Queenan, Austin. "The Pentarchy: Its Origin and Initial Development." *Diakonia* 2 (1967): 338–51.

Quinn, John. "The Exercise of the Primacy and the Costly Call to Unity." In *The Exercise of the Primacy: Continuing the Dialogue,* edited by Phyllis Zagano and Terrence W. Tilley, 7–12. New York: Crossroad, 1998.

———. "A Permanent Synod? Reflections on Collegiality." *Origins* 31 (2002): 730–36.

———. *The Reform of the Papacy: The Costly Call to Christian Unity.* 2nd ed. New York: Crossroad, 2007 (1999).

Rapp, Claudia. "The Elite Status of Bishops in Late Antiquity in Ecclesiastical, Spiritual, and Social Contexts." *Arethusa* 33 (2000): 379–99.

Ratzinger, Joseph. *Called to Communion: Understanding the Church Today.* Translated by Adrian Walker. San Francisco: Ignatius Press, 1996.

———. *God and the World: A Conversation with Peter Seewald.* San Francisco: Ignatius Press, 2002.

———. "Primacy and Episcopacy." *Theology Digest* 26 (1971): 201–17.

———. "Primato ed Episcopato." In *Il Nuovo Popolo di Dio: Questioni Ecclesiologiche.* Brescia: Queriniana, 1992 [1969].

Rausch, Thomas P. *Authority and Leadership in the Church: Past Directions and Future Possibilities.* Wilmington, DE: Michael Glazier, 1988.

Re, Niccolo del. *La Curia Romana. Lineamenti storico-giuridici.* 3rd ed. Rome: Edizioni di Storia e Letteratura, 1970.

Reardon, Patrick. "One, Holy, Catholic and Apostolic Church." http://www.beliefnet.com/story/44/story_4478.html.

Rinne, John. "The Role of the Laity in the Administration of the Orthodox Patriarchates of Serbia, Rumania, and Bulgaria." *Kanon* 3 (1975): 143–55.

Roberson, Ron. *The Eastern Christian Churches: A Brief Survey.* 6th ed. Rome: PIO, 1999.

Robinson, I. S. *The Papacy 1073–1198: Continuity and Innovation.* Cambridge: Cambridge University Press, 1990.

———. *The Papal Reform of the Eleventh Century: Lives of Pope Leo IX and Pope Gregory VII.* Manchester: Manchester University Press, 2004.

———. "Pope Gregory VII: Bibliographical Survey." *Journal of Ecclesiastical History* 36 (1985): 439–83.

Rodopoulos, Panteleimon. "Autocephaly in the Orthodox Church and the Manner in Which It Is Declared: The Orthodox Church in Montenegro." *Greek Orthodox Theological Review* 42 (1997): 213–21.

Romanides, John. *An Outline of Orthodox Patristic Dogmatics.* Edited and translated by George Dion Dragas. Rollinsford, NH: Orthodox Research Institute, 2004.

Roudometof, Victor, Alexander Agadjanian, and Jerry Pankhurst, eds. *Eastern Orthodoxy in a Global Age: Tradition Faces the Twenty-First Century.* New York: Rowman and Littlefield, 2005.

Roussos, Sotiris. "Patriarchs, Notables and Diplomats: The Greek Orthodox Patriarchate of Jerusalem in the Modern Period." In *Eastern Christianity: Studies in Modern History, Religion and Politics,* edited by Anthony O'Mahony, 372–87. London: Melisende, 2004.

Saad, S. M., and N. M. Saad. "Electing Coptic Patriarchs: A Diversity of Traditions." *Bulletin of Saint Shenouda the Archimandrite Coptic Society* 6 (2001): 20–32.

Sabev, Todor. "The Patriarchate of Bulgaria." In *The Splendour of Orthodoxy: 2000 Years of History, Monuments, Art.* Vol. 2, *Patriarchates and Autocephalous Churches,* edited by Kostas E. Tsiropoulos, 324–25. Athens: Ekdotike Athenon, 2000.

Saint-Roch, Patrick. "Dioceses, Suburbicarian." In *The Papacy: An Encyclopedia,* edited by Philippe Levillain. 3 vols. London: Routledge, 2002. 1:501.

Salachas, Dimitri. "The Local Church in the Universal Communion of Churches According to the Ancient Canonical Legislation." *Ephrem's Theological Journal* 5 (2001): 137–63.

Salza, John. *The Biblical Basis for the Papacy.* Huntington, IN: Our Sunday Visitor, 2007.

Schatz, Klaus, S.J., *Papal Primacy: From Its Origins to the Present.* Translated by John Otto and Linda Maloney. Collegeville, MN: Liturgical Press, 1996.

Schlafly, Daniel. "Roman Catholicism in Post-Soviet Russia: Searching for Acceptance." *Religion in Eastern Europe* 21 (2001).

———. "Roman Catholicism in Today's Russia: The Troubled Heritage." *Journal of Church and State* 39 (1997): 681–96.

Schmemann, Alexander. "The Idea of Primacy in Orthodox Ecclesiology." In *The Primacy of Peter: Essays in Ecclesiology and the Early Church,* edited by John Meyendorff. Crestwood, NY: St. Vladimir's Seminary Press, 1992.

———. "A Response." In *The Documents of Vatican II: Introductions and Commentaries by Catholic Bishops and Experts; Responses by Protestant and Orthodox Scholars,* edited by Walter Abbott, translated by Joseph Gallagher, 387–88. New York: New Century, 1966.

Scouteris, Constantine. *Ecclesial Being: Contributions to Theological Dialogue.* Edited by Christopher Veniamin. South Canaan, PA: Mount Thabor Publishing, 2006.

Secretariat for Promoting Christian Unity. *Directory for the Application of Principles and Norms on Ecumenism.* http://www.vatican.va/roman_curia/ pontifical_councils/chrstuni/general-docs/rc_pc_chrstuni_doc_19930325 _directory_en.html.

———. *Ecumenical Directory, Ad Totam Ecclesiam. AAS* 1967: 574–92.

Smith, Terrence V. *Petrine Controversies in Early Christianity: Attitudes towards Peter in Christian Writings of the First Two Centuries.* Tübingen: J. C. B. Mohr, 1985.

Soloviev, Vladimir. *Russia and the Universal Church.* Translated by Herbert Rees. London: Geoffrey Bles, 1948.

———. *La Russie et l'église universelle.* Paris: A. Savine, 1889.

Stan, Lavina, and Lucian Turcescu. *Religion and Politics in Post-Communist Romania.* Oxford: Oxford University Press, 2007.

———. "The Romanian Orthodox Church and Post-communist Democratisation." *Europe-Asia Studies* 52 (2000): 1467–88.

Staniloae, Dumitru. "The Orthodox Conception of Tradition and the Development of Doctrine." *Sobornost* 5 (1969): 652–62.

———. *Theology and the Church.* Translated by Robert Barringer. Crestwood, NY: St. Vladimir's Seminary Press, 1980.

Stavrides, Vasil. "A Concise History of the Ecumenical Patriarchate." *Greek Orthodox Theological Review* 45 (2000): 57–153.

Stephanopulos, Robert. "Christian Unity and the Petrine Ministry: Remarks of an Orthodox Christian." *Journal of Ecumenical Studies* 11 (1974): 309–14.

Stewart, Richard J. "I Want to Serve Unity: Pope John Paul II and Ecumenism." *One in Christ* 17 (1981): 271–90.

Stormon, E. J., ed. *Towards the Healing of Schism: The Sees of Rome and Constantinople: Public Statements and Correspondence between the Holy See and the Ecumenical Patriarchate, 1958–84.* New York: Paulist Press, 1987.

Stramara, Daniel. "'Patriarch of the West' and the Importance of the Title *Patriarch.*" *Ecumenical Trends* 35 (November 2006): 7–10.

Stransky, Thomas F., and John B. Sheerin, eds. *Doing the Truth in Charity: Statements of Pope Paul VI, Popes John Paul I, John Paul II, and the Secretariat for Promoting Christian Unity 1964–1980.* New York: Paulist Press, 1982.

Stricker, Gerd. "Fear of Proselytism: The Russian Orthodox Church Sets Itself against Catholicism." *Religion, State & Society* 26 (1998): 155–65.

Stroyen, William. *Communist Russia and the Russian Orthodox Church 1943–1962.* Washington, DC: Catholic University of America Press, 1967.

Sturzo, Luigi, and Angeline Helen Lograsso. "The Roman Question before and after Fascism." *Review of Politics* 5 (1943): 488–508.

Stylianopoulos, Theodore. "Concerning the Biblical Foundation of Primacy." In *The Petrine Ministry: Catholics and Orthodox in Dialogue,* edited by Walter Kasper. New York: Newman Press, 2006.

Sullivan, Francis A. *Magisterium: Teaching Authority in the Catholic Church.* Mahwah, NJ: Paulist Press, 1983.

Suttner, Ernst. *Church Unity: Union or Uniatism? Catholic-Orthodox Ecumenical Perspectives.* Rome: Centre for Indian and Inter-religious Studies, 1991.

Swanson, R. N. "The Problem of the Cardinalate in the Great Schism." In *Authority and Power: Studies on Medieval Law and Government Presented to Walter Ullmann on His Seventieth Birthday,* edited by Brian Tierney and Peter Linehan, 225–35. Cambridge: Cambridge University Press, 1980.

Taft, Robert F. "Eastern Presuppositions and Western Liturgical Renewal." *Antiphon* 5 (2000): 10–22.

———. "The Problem of 'Uniatism' and the 'Healing of Memories': Anamnesis, Not Amnesia." *Logos: A Journal of Eastern Christian Studies* 41–42 (2000–01): 155–96.

———. "Reflections on 'Uniatism' in the Light of Some Recent Books." *Orientalia Christiana Periodica* 65 (1999): 153–84.

Tanner, Norman P., ed. *Decrees of the Ecumenical Councils.* 2 vols. London: Sheed & Ward; Washington, DC: Georgetown University Press, 1990.

Tarchnisvili, Michael. "The Origin and Development of the Ecclesiastical Autocephaly of Georgia." *Greek Orthodox Theological Review* 46 (2001): 89–111.

Tavard, George. *Two Centuries of Ecumenism.* Translated by Royce W. Hughes. Notre Dame, IN: Fides, 1960.

Tchilingirian, Hratch. "The Armenian Apostolic Orthodox Church." http://hyeforum.com/index.php?showtopic=5432.

———. "The Catholicos and the Hierarchical Sees of the Armenian Church." In *Eastern Christianity: Studies in Modern History, Religion and Politics,* edited by Anthony O'Mahoney. London: Melisende, 2004.

Tellenbach, Gerd. *Church, State and Christian Society at the Time of the Investiture Contest.* Translated by R. F. Bennett. Oxford: Blackwell, 1940.

Thomas, Stephen. *Deification in the Eastern Orthodox Tradition: A Biblical Perspective.* Piscataway, NJ: Gorgias Press, 2007.

Tierney, Brian. *The Crisis of Church and State 1050–1300.* Englewood Cliffs, NJ: Prentice-Hall, 1964.

———. *Foundations of Conciliar Theory: The Contribution of the Medieval Canonists from Gratian to the Great Schism.* Cambridge: Cambridge University Press, 1955.

Tillard, J.-M. R. *The Bishop of Rome*. Translated by John de Satgé. Wilmington, DE: Michael Glazier, 1983.

———. *Church of Churches: The Ecclesiology of Communion*. Translated by R. C. De Peaux. Collegeville, MN: Liturgical Press, 1992.

———. "The Jurisdiction of the Bishop of Rome." *Theological Studies* 48 (1979): 3–22.

Timbie, Janet. "Coptic Christianity." In *The Blackwell Companion to Eastern Christianity*, edited by Ken Parry, 94–116. Oxford: Blackwell, 2007.

Timiadis, Emilianos. "'Tu Es Petrus': An Orthodox Approach." *Patristic and Byzantine Review* 2 (1983): 5–26.

Tomkins, Oliver Stratford. "The Roman Catholic Church and the Ecumenical Movement, 1910–1948." In *A History of the Ecumenical Movement 1517–1948*, edited by Ruth Rouse and Stephen Charles Neill, 677–93. London: SPCK, 1954.

Toschi, Umberto. "The Vatican City State: From the Standpoint of Political Geography." *Geographical Review* 21 (1931): 529–38.

Trembelas, Panagiotis. *The Autocephaly of the Metropolia in America*. Translated by Robert Stephanopoulos. Brookline, MA: Holy Cross Orthodox Press, 1973.

Trenham, Josiah. "Orthodox Reunion: Overcoming the Curse of Jurisdictionalism in America." *St. Vladimir's Theological Quarterly* 50 (2006): 277–303.

Tsiropoulos, Kostas E., ed. *The Splendour of Orthodoxy: 2000 Years of History, Monuments, Art*. Vol. 2, *Patriarchates and Autocephalous Churches*. Athens: Ekdotike Athenon, 2000.

Ugolnik, Anthony. "The Art of Belonging." *Religion and the Intellectual Life* 1 (1984): 113–27.

———. "Tradition as Freedom from the Past: Eastern Orthodoxy and the Western Mind." *Journal of Ecumenical Studies* 21 (1984): 278–94.

Ullmann, Walter. *A Short History of the Papacy in the Middle Ages*. New York and London: Methuen, 1972.

Vatican. *Annuario Pontificio, 2004*. Vatican City: Vatican Polyglot Press, 2004.

Verghese, Paul. "Aggiornamento and the Unity of All: An Eastern Orthodox View of the Vatican Council." *Ecumenical Review* 15 (1963): 377–84.

Verkhovsky, Aleksandr. "The Role of the Russian Orthodox Church in Nationalist, Xenophobic and Antiwestern Tendencies in Russia Today: Not Nationalism, But Fundamentalism." *Religion, State & Society* 30 (2002): 333–45.

Vischer, Lukas. "The Holy See, the Vatican State, and the Churches' Common Witness: A Neglected Ecumenical Problem." *Journal of Ecumenical Studies* 11 (1974): 617–36.

Viscuso, Patrick. "Orthodox-Catholic Unity and the Revised Code of Eastern Canon Law." *Journal of Ecumenical Studies* 27 (1990): 108–15.

Vorgrimler, Herbert, ed. *Commentary on the Documents of Vatican II.* Vol. 2. Montreal: Palm; Freiburg: Herder, 1967–69.

Wallach, Luitpold. "The Roman Synod of December 800 and the Alleged Trial of Leo III: A Theory and the Historical Facts." *Harvard Theological Review* 49 (1956): 123–42.

Walters, Philip. "Notes on Autocephaly and Phyletism." *Religion, State & Society* 30 (2002): 357–64.

Ware, Timothy (Kallistos). "Autocephaly Crisis: Deadlock between Constantinople and Moscow." *Eastern Churches Journal* 3 (1971): 311–15.

———. *Eustratios Argenti: A Study of the Greek Church under Turkish Rule.* Oxford: Oxford University Press, 1964.

———. *The Orthodox Church.* London: Penguin Books, 1993.

———. "Primacy, Collegiality and the People of God." In *Orthodoxy: Life and Freedom,* edited by A. J. Philippou. Oxford: Oxford University Press, 1973.

Watt, J. A. "Hostiensis on *Per Venerabilem:* The Role of the College of Cardinals." In *Authority and Power: Studies on Medieval Law and Government Presented to Walter Ullmann on His Seventieth Birthday,* edited by Brian Tierney and Peter Linehan. Cambridge: Cambridge University Press, 1980.

Weakland, Rembert. "Inside the Orthodox Psyche." *Tablet* 254 (28 October 2001): 1446–47.

Webster, Alexander F. C. "Split Decision: The Orthodox Clash over Estonia." *Christian Century* 113 (5 June 1996): 614–21.

Weigel, George. "The Church's Teaching Authority and the Call for Democracy in North Atlantic Catholicism." In *Church Unity and the Papal Office: An Ecumenical Dialogue on John Paul II's Encyclical* Ut Unum Sint, edited by Carl E. Braaten and Robert W. Jenson. Grand Rapids, MI: Eerdmans, 2001.

———. "Papacy and Power." *First Things* 110 (February 2001): 18–25.

———. *Witness to Hope: The Biography of Pope John Paul II.* New York: HarperCollins, 1999.

Werth, Paul. "Georgian Autocephaly and the Ethnic Fragmentation of Orthodoxy." *Acta Slavica Iaponica* 23 (2006): 74–100.

Wessel, Susan. *Leo the Great and the Spiritual Rebuilding of a Universal Rome.* Leiden: Brill, 2008.

Whelton, Michael. *Popes and Patriarchs: An Orthodox Perspective on Roman Catholic Claims.* Ben Lomond, CA: Conciliar Press, 2006.

———. *Two Paths: Papal Monarchy—Collegial Tradition: Rome's Claims of Papal Supremacy in the Light of the Orthodox Church.* Salisbury, MA: Regina Orthodox Press, 2001.

Wijlens, Myriam. "Cooperation of Bishops on a Supranational or Continental Level: A New Institution on the Intermediate Level?" In *Synod and Synodality: Theology, History, Canon Law and Ecumenism in New Contact,* edited by Alberto Melloni and Silvia Scatena, 33–60. Münster: Lit Verlag, 2005.

———. "The Intermediate Level in the Roman Catholic Church: An Organizational or Ecclesiological Category?" In *Of All Times and All Places: Protestants and Catholics on the Church Local and Universal,* edited by Leo J. Koffman and Henk Witte, 95–130. Meinema, Netherlands: Zoetermeer, 2001.

Wilken, R. L. "Gregory VII and the Politics of the Spirit." *First Things* 89 (1999): 26–32.

Williams, George Huntston. "The Ecumenical Intentions of Pope John Paul II." *Harvard Theological Review* 75 (1982): 141–76.

Winter, Michael. *Saint Peter and the Popes.* Baltimore: Helicon Press, 1960.

Wood, Susan. "The Theological Foundations of Episcopal Conferences and Collegiality." *Studia Canonica* 22 (1988): 327–38.

Wright, Herbert. "The Status of the Vatican City." *American Journal of International Law* 38 (1944): 452–57.

Yurash, Andrij. "Orthodox-Greek Catholic Relations in Galicia and Their Influence on the Religious Situation in Ukraine." *Religion, State & Society* 33 (2005): 185–205.

Zizioulas, John. *Being as Communion: Studies in Personhood and the Church.* Crestwood, NY: St. Vladimir's Seminary Press, 1985.

———. "The Father as Cause: Personhood Generating Otherness." In *Communion and Otherness: Further Studies in Personhood and the Church,* edited by Paul McPartlan. London: T&T Clark, 2006.

———. "Primacy in the Church: An Orthodox Approach." In *Petrine Ministry and the Unity of the Church: "Toward a Patient and Fraternal Dialogue",* edited by James F. Puglisi. Collegeville, MN: Liturgical Press, 1999.

Zoghby, Elias. "Patriarchat et cardinalat." *Documentation Catholique* 62 (1965): 1291–93.

Žužek, Ivan. "The Patriarchal Structure According to the Oriental Code." In *The Code of Canons of the Oriental Churches: An Introduction,* edited by Clarence Gallagher, 38–50. Rome: Mar Thoma Yogam—St. Thomas Christian Fellowship, 1991.

Zyablitsev, Gregory. "The Ecumenical Problem in the Russian Orthodox Church in Relation to the 1994 Synod." *Concilium* 32 (1996): 101–9.

INDEX

Afanasiev, Nicholas, 19, 20, 46, 163,
189n75, 220n65, 235n12
Alfeyev, Hilarion, 3, 43, 49, 165n14,
166nn15–18, 217n46
views concerning traditional
papal titles, 49
Annuario Pontificio, 7, 47, 180n5

Bartholomew, Ecumenical Patriarch,
4, 80, 86–87, 123
definition of his responsibilities,
86
Benedict XVI. *See* Ratzinger, Joseph
Bliss, Frederick, 58
differentiation of papal and
patriarchal roles, 58

Catholicosate, Armenian. *See* Patriarchates, Armenian
Christodoulos of Athens, 50
views concerning traditional
papal titles, 50
Clément, Olivier, 2, 12, 34, 120, 147,
233n28
concerning *Ut Unum Sint,* 12
Congar, Yves, 6, 55, 118, 121, 125,
184n31, 215n32, 231n17
views concerning Roman patriarchate, 55, 125, 184n31, 215n32,
231n17
views concerning Tradition, 6, 121

Duffy, Eamon, 138, 191n8, 213nn24–25
Dymyd, Michel, 62–63

Eastern ethos, 8, 30, 70, 78, 80
and diversity of patriarchal
polities, 8, 30, 70, 78–116
and reformed papacy, 47, 57, 60,
62–63, 80, 114, 118, 124
ecclesiology
and geography, 51, 182n17, 219n58
of *koinonia,* 36, 52
Erickson, John, 15, 17, 33, 36–37, 44, 79
Evdokimov, Paul, 24

Ferencz, Nicholas, 79, 84
and Ecumenical Patriarchate, 84

Gregorios III, Patriarch, 61, 137
confusion of patriarchal and
papal roles, 61
gradual development of patriarchal practices, 79
"patriarchal principle," 61
Greshake, Gisbert, 64
agreement with Ratzinger, 64
loss of patriarchal structures
within the Latin Church, 64
solution to East-West problems,
64
triadic structure of the ideal
Church, 64

ADAM A. J. DEVILLE

is assistant professor of theology
at the University of Saint Francis, Fort Wayne, Indiana.